Jeremy Black is one of the UK's most respected and prolific historians. He is Emeritus Professor of History at the University of Exeter and a renowned expert on the history of war. He is a Senior Fellow at both Policy Exchange and the Foreign Policy Research Institute. His recent books include *Military Strategy: A Global History*, *A History of the Second World War in 100 Maps*, *Tank Warfare* and *The World of James Bond*. He appears regularly on TV and radio.

A BRIEF HISTORY OF

Germany

JEREMY BLACK

ROBINSON

ROBINSON

First published in Great Britain in 2022 by Robinson

1 3 5 7 9 10 8 6 4 2

Copyright © Jeremy Black, 2022
Map copyright © iStock

The moral right of the author has been asserted.

A CIP catalogue record for this book
is available from the British Library.

ISBN: 978-1-47214-593-2

Typeset in Scala by Hewer Text UK Ltd, Edinburgh
Printed and bound in Great Britain by Clays Ltd, Elcograf S.p.A.

Papers used by Robinson are from well-managed
forests and other responsible sources.

Robinson
An imprint of
Little, Brown Book Group
Carmelite House
50 Victoria Embankment
London EC4Y 0DZ

An Hachette UK Company
www.hachette.co.uk

www.littlebrown.co.uk

For Graham Stewart

'The Germans in general are a good-natured people, hospitable and generous, lovers of pomp and magnificence. I would not look for French vivacity, Italian cunning or English good sense amongst them. Take them as you find them and a traveller may pass his time very well amongst them.'

William Lee, 1753

Contents

···············

Preface

....

> 'The word Germany is as uncertain in its derivation, as it is often vague and indefinite in its application ... the extent of country comprised under the term Germany has varied in every century since it first became known to the Romans.'
>
> > John Ramsay McCulloch, *A Dictionary,*
> > *Geographical, Statistical and Historical*
> > (1841, 2nd ed., 1849)

Several tasks, none of them easy, but each exciting. The key clarity in offering an account of German history is one of accepting its complexity and seeking to work with it rather than treat it as an impediment. This includes the topic of Germany in the world and, notably, how best to engage with its recent or, indeed, earlier, history. Simplicity will not work with presenting either the differing strands of Germany's account of itself or those of others' views of Germany, both country and nation. Nor indeed with the traveller's experience, which is part of my subject.

There are many Germanys that can be proffered and, therefore, differing chronologies, narratives, causations and epiphanies. Is it appropriate to project some sort of German identity far back into the past and, if so, does it have some kind of timeless space and character? Is Germany the modern state and, if not, what geography is our subject? The Germany of the Empire, later Holy Roman Empire, variously included Bohemia, the Low Countries and northern Italy. It was swept aside by Napoleon, to be replaced in 1806 by the Confederation of the Rhine, but that, in turn, was overthrown by his enemies, and a new, and very different, federation was created in 1814, only in 1866 to be replaced by a Prussian-dominated Germany. That fell foul of a war it caused and was replaced by a more geographically circum-scribed republic in 1919, a state that – under Adolf Hitler as Chancellor from 1933 – first expanded and was then conquered. In turn, this was partitioned and two Germanies were created from much of the rubble. That situation ended in 1990 when, depending on the narrative, Germany was united or reunited. Maps have long provided differing criteria, notably of the Empire or of Germans but also using other definitions, for example by the drainage basin of German rivers, as in Philipp Heinrich Zollmann's 1712 map.

And so also with 'Germans'. Is language the key element and, if so, what is to be made of the very different dialects, which for many were incomprehensible? Does, for recent and earlier times, the category 'German' include all who spoke German or might consider themselves ethnically German? In which case, our history is also that of Austria and much of Switzerland. Or is it essentially a matter of the inhabitants of what is today Germany? T. S. Eliot captured this uncertainty in *The Waste Land* (1922): '*Bin gar keine Russin, stamm'aus Litauen, echt deutsch.*' ('I am not Russian at all, I come from Lithuania, I am a real German'), a remark allegedly heard in Munich.

As in Britain, history records different legal classifications. Thus, in 1913, the *Reichstag*, in which the Social Democrats were more powerful after the 1912 election, decided that citizenship did not any longer require residence in Germany, instead granting citizenship to six million Germans who lived outside Germany. This was a basis for the treatment of refugees after the two world wars. So, very differently, with the subsequent treatment of Turkish 'guest workers' and the eventual 2000 German Nationality Act which granted citizenship to all born in Germany, regardless of their heritage.

As also with the values and collective identity (ies) that are supposed to characterise or even define Germanness, and the degree to which they were/are to be associated with particular parts of Germany and aspects of its politics and society. Were and/or are Bavaria or Prussia more 'German' and, if so, how, when and for whom? There is also always a tension between big-picture and small-picture approaches: between *Reich*/Germany, *volk*/nation, and the regions. Terminology, however, was, for a long time, less clear-cut than that might suggest; in particular, the term 'Germans', for example, used also to describe those who lived in Swabia.

The process by which regions were created that were to be sustained to the present is complex. Ethnicity played a role, and DNA analysis can be helpful in this context, but far more was involved in the process. The topography of particular areas was linked to agricultural possibilities and to the related agrarian regime and social geography, notably in the nature of settlement. Yet, alongside this continuity, there was the more diffuse one of whatever could or can be put in the box of specific area and the resulting role and range of possibilities, as with the 'stem' or tribal duchies of the tenth to twelfth centuries, which created a sense of identity. The role of possibilities provides a very different causation to that of allegedly deterministic patterns. Furthermore, the role of politics in the modern world in affecting the character of regions was amply demonstrated in 1944–90, as large numbers of people moved to avoid the Soviet advance and later in response to the history and legacy of East Germany.

Given this lesson from the recent past, it is probable that there should also be an emphasis for the distant past on a moulding by events. This is an important qualification to the facile habit of tracing long-term causes back to some supposed distant foundational period, as in the observation that modern areas of far-right support are focused on the trans-Elbian regions and definitely not on those that had been under Roman control. Such links may be suggestive, but much work is required to move from the coincidental to the causative.

Linked to the question of regional significance and identity comes that of the images of Germany. The ruralism that is so important to the notion of local identity – *Heimat* – is replicated at the national level, notably with the theme of forests, but that is scarcely a pertinent image across the entire country. In 2012, forests covered 11.4 million hectares, or 32 per cent of the country. This was particularly the case in the *Länder* (states) of Hesse and Rhineland-Palatinate, each with 42.3 per cent, while the largest state, Bavaria, had the most forest. Spruce, followed by pines, beech and oak, together made up three-quarters of the forested area. Yet, the wooded hilly areas that tend to match suppositions of German forest, notably the Bavarian Forest, the Black Forest and also, for example, the Spessart, are not found across northern Germany, where forests, such as the Spreewald, Brandenburg, the Jasmund on Rügen, and the Gespensterwald near the Baltic, are all far flatter. Moreover, despite the undoubted importance of the Greens and the strong commitment they represent, it is unclear that young city-dwellers are as likely to feel as committed to a *Völkisch* ruralism (a sense of ethnic identity with the countryside) as would have been the case for many in the 1900s and 1920s.

In looking at national developments, where is the emphasis to be placed? For the late nineteenth century, what of Prussianisation, of the various strands of conservatism and of political parties, such as the National Liberals who helped give the Second Reich (1871–1918) the character of a constitutional monarchy, and also of the more left-wing Social Democratic Party, the most popular party in federal elections from 1890.

What also with reference to the place of history? Later Germans proudly proclaimed the valour of Arminius and the Teutoburg Forest battle in which the Romans were defeated in CE (AD) 9; but that is no longer a value with traction, no more than the Second Reich seeing a link with Frederick Barbarossa (r. 1155–90) in the quest to unite Germany. The current focus on the last century helps ensure that deep history, to a degree, is less a German experience today than in most other European states. That itself is a product of recent history, but not one that means that this deep history is without consequence.

Today, with many Germans unsure who Bismarck was, let alone of his significance, the emphasis is on a nationalism that turns to ethics, economics and sport, rather than military power or territorial expansion. Germany and German history, however, are still strongly overshadowed by the Nazi years (1933–45) and the Holocaust or moral politics today is a consequence of this. This perspective contrasts with the earlier situation when, after 1945, Nazism, the Second World War and the Holocaust were for a while largely ignored and even to a degree excused in large part by those who had been adults then.

Every account exploring the history of a country is individual. Mine will be an end-loaded history because there is considerable need for caution in linking aspects of the 'deep history', such as the limits of Roman rule or the partition of 843, to developments over the last two centuries of nationalism, industrialisation, urbanisation, mass literacy, participatory politics and dictatorships.

My memory of Germans comes before that of Germany, as we had a series of German au pairs when I was small, notably Babel. I first visited Germany as a child with my father. We took the overnight Harwich–Hook ferry (I remember lying awake listening to lorries straining against their chains as the ship rolled), drove through the Netherlands without stopping (which I found a surprise), paused in Germany at a service station – where, as if in a sweetshop, I was amazed at the range of food on offer – took the bends of the E5 autobahn through the wooded Spessart, and spent the night at a bed-and-breakfast in

Ochsenfurt, the guest of a policeman and his wife. They provided dinner – a carp with a little flag out of its mouth wishing us a good appetite.

The next morning, the wondrous fresco of *Apollo and the Continents* over the great staircase in the Würzburg Residenz, painted for the Prince-Bishop from 1749 to 1754, Karl Philipp von Greiffenclau, by Giambattista Tiepolo in 1750–3. This is an instance of the role of cosmopolitanism in German culture, a strand that it is all too easy to downplay when writing a national history. At the same time as this cosmopolitanism, the vaulting of the imperial hall came first, and for that, in 1752, Tiepolo produced a programme including *The Marriage of Emperor Frederick Barbarossa to Beatrice of Burgundy*, a wedding that took place at Würzburg in 1156, and *The Investiture of Herold as Duke of Franconia by Barbarossa at the Imperial Diet in Würzburg in 1168*.

Over the years, I have been very many times to Germany, whether for holiday, research, lecturing or conferences. My favourite area is Lake Constance, to which I have managed five visits; but the very variety of this large and populous country commands interest, as does its difficult history. Thus, on the last visit, I noted in a church in Lindau a notice put up to explain the inclusion of Waffen SS members on a war memorial.

It is a great pleasure to thank Peter Brown, Charles Coutinho, Steven Fischer, Lothar Höbelt, Paul Kerry, Jürgen Luh, Jeremy Noakes, Thomas Otte, Duncan Proudfoot, Alexander Querengässer, Martyn Rady, Harold Raugh, Joanne Schneider, Falko Schnicke, Alaric Searle and Ulf Sundberg for their advice on all or part of an earlier draft. Peter-Carlo Lehrell offered advice on particular points. They are in no way responsible for the comments here and the errors that survive, but I much appreciate their help. It is greatly valued for morale as well as specifics.

In guiding this work through, Duncan Proudfoot has again managed that wonderful, but difficult, combination of

PREFACE

professionalism and friendship. I have benefitted greatly indeed
from the help of Amanda Keats on the production side. The book
is dedicated to Graham Stewart, an historian and friend with
whom I have much enjoyed making a regular series of podcasts.

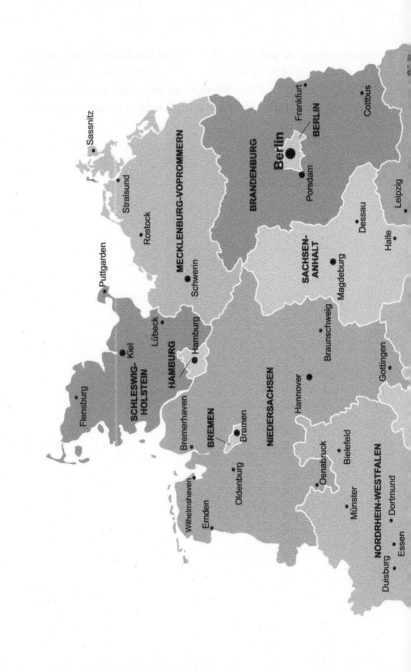

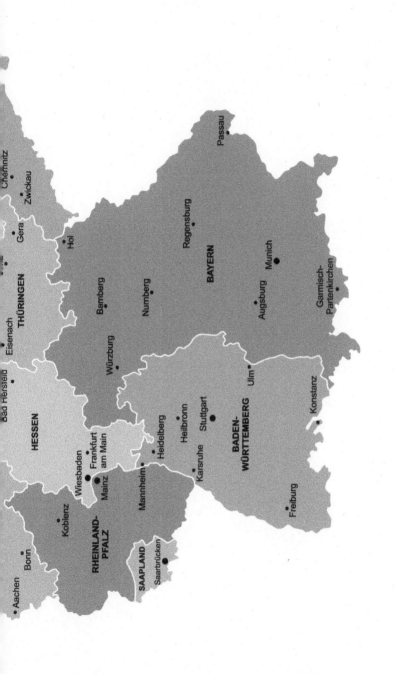

Introduction: On the Grand Tour in Germany

....

'Bad weather and impracticable roads from hence to Dresden, keep us at present.'

John Sturrock, Kassel, December 1740

'A beautiful town with a magnificent bridge over the Elbe with sentinels who make you go on one side and come back on the other, a restraint that Englishmen are very refractory about ... I never had so violent a desire to walk up and down the same side of a bridge in my life.'

Thomas Brand, Dresden, 1787

Hurtling across Germany by means of ICE (Intercity-Express) trains, on autobahns or by air, travellers today have scant sense of the experience of their predecessors. Difference, of course, can be readily within recent memory. I remember the terrible state of the street lighting, pavements and trains when researching in East Germany in 1980 and, on subsequent visits, noted change. However, a sense that distance keeps Germany apart or, at least, of sustaining difference, can more readily be grasped from the accounts of British grand tourists of the eighteenth century. Moreover, turning to those ensures that we do not take the 'primeval forests to modern society' approach, which it is all too easy to pursue.

As is still the case, Germany lacked the tourist appeal to foreigners of France and Italy but, nevertheless, the number of British tourists who visited increased during the late seventeenth and eighteenth centuries. The greater amount of time required to incorporate Germany into a British itinerary, otherwise focused on Paris and Italy, affected tourist numbers, as did accommodation and transport problems, as well as the greater historical cultural significance of Paris and Italy, notably Rome. Nevertheless, the interest of visiting German capitals increased after the accession of the Hanoverian dynasty in the person of George I (r. 1714–27) to the British throne and that of Frederick II, the Great (r. 1740–86), to the Prussian.

British tourists to Germany arrived by means of a number of routes, but, most usually, via a crossing from Harwich to Hoek van Holland ('hoek van' being the 'corner of'), and then from the Netherlands east to Hanover. From there, it was possible to travel via Berlin, Dresden, Prague and Vienna to go on to Italy. Another route was via Paris and Strasbourg.

In 1748, Robert Lowth found Berlin, the capital of Prussia:

'a very large and a very fine town: the palace is truly magnificent, the public buildings in general are handsome and in good taste; the streets spacious and well-built, especially the new town ... you would wonder how ever they are supplied with provisions, if you were to see the country round about, which is a deep sand.'

The frequently caustic Nathaniel Wraxall was less positive in 1777: 'The diversions of Berlin are mean ... I think it a magnificent, but not an agreeable city ... a kind of gloomy grandeur and sombre magnificence which strikes, but does not pleasingly affect, the mind.' In 1794, Randle Wilbraham found the Prussian court more lively and welcoming, and left for Dresden 'delighted with the civilities we had met with':

'Our route lay through a flattish, sandy country covered in a great measure with forests of fir, the blackness of which, contrasted with the snow which lay upon the ground, had a very fine effect, in one of the clearest moonlight nights I ever remember, during the whole of which we travelled.'

Travel focused on cities. Dresden, the capital of Saxony, was less forbidding than Berlin, and more cosmopolitan than Hanover. As yet, there was not much of the Sturm und Drang cult of 'sublime' landscape, nor the resulting vogue for an identity in terms that would have been familiar a century later. Instead, as the 1781 travels of the Berlin writer Christoph Friedrich Nicolai (1733–1811) indicated, there was a distaste of forests and mountains: he criticised, for example, the Black Forest. By the 1790s, the situation, as in Britain, was increasingly different, with more interest in landscape and, to a lesser extent, the common people. The Gothic came into fashion, which affected the response to the German past and to Gothic cities and buildings; for example, Nuremberg, and Cologne Cathedral. Mountains and forests were in, as was the Rhine gorge.

Social customs varied from home. In Leipzig, in August 1751, William, 2nd Earl of Dartmouth, found a dinner convention of going round the table and kissing all the women 'sad, clammy work', as well as indecent. Thomas, 7th Earl of Elgin, was more willing to engage, writing to his mother in 1787, 'I have only to show myself to excite tender passions. *Veni, vidi, vici.*' There were also unrequited passions. The young and wealthy John, 3rd Duke of Roxburghe, fell for Christiane Sophia Albertina, the eldest daughter of the Duke of Mecklenburg-Strelitz, while on a continental tour in 1761. As, however, her younger sister, Charlotte, soon became engaged to George III, whom she indeed married, it was deemed necessary to break off the match for reasons of politics and protocol. Neither Roxburghe nor Christiane ever wed.

Another to fall in love on his travels was the young William Drummond, in 1787, who dined at the Poste at Montabaur, en route between Bonn and Frankfurt:

'The man who keeps it has a beautiful daughter, who attended us at dinner. A more elegant, innocent, graceful and engaging creature I scarcely ever have met with in my travels. She charmed us so, that had we not been wiser than the companions of Ulysses, we should have remained there too long: we did leave it with regret and we shall not forget her.'

Such thoughts would have helped him cope with the roads: Germany lacked both the basis of Roman roads and coordinated governmental activity to address the situation. George, Viscount Parker, found the roads so narrow between Munich and Augsburg in 1719 that he was forced to change his coach, while – also in Bavaria – Sacheverell Stevens was obliged to walk nearly half the way between Donauwörth and Nuremberg. In 1752, David, 7th Viscount Stormont, found rain made the already bad road between Leipzig and Hanover almost impassable, while it took William, 4th Earl of Essex, four days and four nights to travel with six horses from Hanover to Utrecht.

Travel was very weather-dependent, as so many road surfaces were largely unimproved; hard frosts were welcomed for providing roads with a firm surface. The nature of the ground itself – for example, the sandy soil found between Emden in East Friesland and Hamburg – very much affected ease of movement. East Friesland is still an area visited by very few tourists, as is the northern Netherlands to the west. Poor roads from Mainz to Cologne led to Robert Arbuthnot being advised in April 1787 to sail down the Rhine (passing upriver was a very different process) and Sir John Macpherson to decide to go to Italy in 1790.

These were not the sole problems. In 1788, William Smith MP encountered difficulties after leaving Cologne:

'We had not gone far on our way to Düsseldorf when we perceived our postilion to be a very obstinate fellow who, notwithstanding all the signs we could make, would not move beyond a foot's pace, till the gentlemen got out to walk, and then he endeavoured to ride away from them. We were near four hours going ten miles to Opladen; here the master of the inn used all his eloquence to make us pass the night, but finding it was all labour lost, he was near forty minutes before he produced the horses, with a postilion as slow as the last. Threats, entreaties, signs were as ineffectual as with the other. We still moved on, [at] our accustomed funeral pace . . . between one and two the carriage stopped at the gates of Düsseldorf, having been nine hours coming twenty-one miles . . . We found, as we knew we should, the gates of the city shut and had, therefore, the pleasure of sitting in the carriage till five o'clock when they were opened.'

Used to the new turnpike roads of Britain, its travellers could be particularly critical, but in practice the situation in Germany had greatly improved, with better roads matched by improved facilities, notably post-houses. In 1500, a journey from Hamburg to Augsburg had taken a month; by 1780, it took just over a week. Carriage services became more frequent and increasingly prompt.

Contrasts: Speyer and Schwetzingen

The attractive variety of Germany, a country dense in interesting things for the visitor, is captured with the proximity of Speyer on the Upper Rhine and nearby Schwetzingen. The former contains a wonderful cathedral, as well as an attractive old town including the galleried Trinity church, while Schwetzingen, the summer residence of the Electors Palatine in the eighteenth century, includes a very attractive landscaped park with both French and English styles on display, and some fascinating buildings within the park, including a mosque-inspired structure built in 1779–91.

As elsewhere in rural Europe, the accommodation for travellers could be poor and, where bedding was available, it was not always pleasing, with straw often provided instead of beds. Of the post-house at Leese in north-west Germany, George Ogilvie recorded in 1779, 'our beds stink abominably and half the panes of glass in the windows were broken, so that we almost froze to death'. In the same area, another tourist found a one-room inn, in which the 'parlour cowhouse stable hogsty and barn' lacked a chimney and was therefore full of smoke as well as animals.

Food varied, in availability, range, and quality, William Lee finding from Magdeburg to Berlin in 1753 'little to eat but bad, sour, heavy rye bread, and salt butter'. Samuel Pratt thought the bread had a 'bitter and sour taste' and, in Potsdam, Thomas Brand 'could get little else to eat than sour-crout and sausages and my napkin had served some greasy, whiskered Hussar the day before'. However, German game – for example, wild-boar ham – was generally praised, as were Rhenish and Moselle wines.

Zweites Frühstück (Second Breakfast)

Archival research in 1980 in Münster meant strawberries in the beer and working in what was a carpenter's workshop in the local government building rather than in the archive itself; the collection I was interested in was both bulky and not in demand.

I was put in the charge of this worthy carpenter and told I had to fit in with his hours and not those of the archive. While that meant a 7.30 a.m. start, it also meant that at 9 a.m. we went to the very reasonably priced canteen where I would sit with the carpenter and his mates while they discussed football and ate a 'second breakfast'. Hard-boiled eggs were very much on the menu, as was bread. In Bavaria, the focus is on the Weisswurst (white sausage).

I also remember being puzzled on my visit to the archives in Munich by a persistent buzz, only to discover that this was my first encounter with air conditioning.

The tourists reflected on what they saw and here they join us, albeit commenting in the context of the then present, adopting a different perspective. In 1748, David Hume wrote to his brother, 'Germany is undoubtedly a very fine country, full of industrious, honest people, and were it united it would be the greatest power that ever was in the world.' This well-considered point appeared highly implausible and was not generally made. Indeed, the War of the Austrian Succession that came to an end that year had seen Germany very divided. Differently, the perceptive Elizabeth Montagu wrote from Düsseldorf, the main seat of the Elector Palatine, in 1763, 'It grieves one to see princes so magnificent and luxurious while their subjects are so poor and wretched.' Such a comment could be made across the country, except in the Imperial Free Cities.

Religious commitment was more apparent in Catholic areas, although in 1785, one tourist noted at St Goar in the Rhineland, 'The watch proclaim the hour by blowing so many times with a horn and making a little pious address to the people who are all Protestants, to thank God for giving them another hour.' Five years later, Friedrich Köhler, a theology student touring the Swabian Alps, noted the persistence of the past, in the form of Sunday regional costumes, as well as most houses still having thatched roofs.

En route to Pumpernickel [Weimar] in *Vanity Fair* (1847–8)
The novelist, William Makepeace Thackeray placed on the steamboat from London a company including:

> 'jaunty young Cambridge men travelling with their tutor, and going for a reading excursion to Nonnenwerth or Königswinter ... old Pall Mall loungers bound for Ems and Wiesbaden, and a course of waters to clear off

the dinners of the season, and a little roulette and *trente-et-quarante* to keep the excitement going: there was old [Lord] Methuselah, who had married his young wife, with Captain Papillon of the Guards holding her parasol and guide-books!'

From Rotterdam, another steamer took them on up the Rhine:

'To lay down the pen and even to think of that beautiful Rhineland makes one happy. At this time of summer evening, the cows are trooping down from the hills, lowing, and with their bells tinkling, to the old town, with its old moats, and gates, and spires, and chestnut trees, with long blue shadows stretching over the grass; the sky and the river below flame in crimson and gold; and the moon is already out, looking pale towards the sunset. The sun sinks behind the great castle-crested mountains, the night falls suddenly, the river grows darker and darker, lights quiver in it from the windows in the old ramparts, and twinkle peacefully in the villages under the hills on the opposite shore.'

With Romanticism greatly influencing travel impressions from the 1790s, the Rhineland entranced British tourists as well as German travellers. The first passenger steamer arrived in 1816 and the railway followed on both banks from 1844.

Modern tourists will not be able to recreate the experiences of their eighteenth-century predecessors. Walkers can slow the pace to less than that of a carriage, but they will be travelling now through a Germany in which material circumstances are much more homogeneous than those of the past. There are variations in beer, cuisine, housing style, religious commitment, plants and much else; but their impacts have all been lessened through the effect of the state, universal education, national broadcasting and consumer products and travel. In the past, moreover, the size of Germany posed particular problems in governing, both politically and administratively.

Now, motorways and trains smash through the terrain, with the 1960s having proved crucial for the former; notably linking Hamburg to Basle in 1962 and Frankfurt to Munich via Nuremberg. Yet, terrain still has an obvious presence for the traveller. And most clearly so in the contrast between a northern Germany that is generally flat and a southern Germany that is more mountainous, especially so as you go further north and south.

At the same time, there is no uniformity. Northern Germany includes the hills of the Harz, the Teutoburger Forest, and the Weser Mountains, while southern Germany includes not only mountains, notably the Alps, but also the hilly areas of Baden-Württemberg, the flat lands of the Swabian-Franconian Basin and the Bavarian Plateau. It is tempting to link flat lands via agricultural production, to state formation, in the shape of the above and Prussia, Hanover, Saxony, Württemburg and Bavaria. Conversely, the mountainous or hilly lands of central Germany, including the Rhineland Schist Massif west of the Rhine and the Sauerland, Taurus, Thüringer Forest, and the mountainous or hilly areas in northern Germany, were not the basis for major states. In northeast Bavaria, the Fichtel Mountains were where, in 1797, the last German bear was killed.

There are other areas of complexity. Some of the flat lands are fertile, but others, notably those scoured by the glaciers in northern Germany, are not and/or are poorly drained. This is particularly a problem in East Friesland between the Ems and the Weser and the Elbe, notably on Lüneburg Heath, and in Mecklenburg and Western Pomerania.

Climate is another factor, notably with cold easterly winds in the winter and winds from the Atlantic and the North Sea that can lash with rain. The Alps are a cause of climatic variations in southern Germany. More generally, Germany is divided as well as united by the weather.

Travellers will also find great varieties in townscapes, although their regional identity has generally been subsumed by economic development and military damage.

Know Your Sausage

A bratwurst is a sausage consisting of more than 50 per cent pork. It is grilled. However, I recommend instead a bockwurst, which generally consists of more than 50 per cent veal, simmered or steamed.

Attributed to Herta Heuwer in Berlin in 1949, drawing on ketchup and curry powder from British troops, curry-wurst is seasoned with curry powder or curry sauce and then ketchup. It is a very popular dish; a museum dedicated to it opened in 2009 in Berlin, and in 2019 the state mint issued a commemorative coin. I like German sausage, especially with *weissbier* (pale beer), but neither with curry sauce nor with cheese.

Where is Germany?

One of the oldest frontiers in Europe is that of Saxony and Bohemia along the *Erzebirge*, a frontier established through the Peace of Eger in 1459. Thereafter, the county of Schwarzenberg was divided between Bohemia and Saxony in 1546, while the frontier moved south in 1938 to include the Sudetenland, but was re-established in 1945. Other frontiers have been more varied. Indeed, the changing frontiers of Germany in the twentieth century can be readily mapped, with the successive falls of the Second and Third Reich leading to border changes with France, Denmark, Poland and Russia. That, in contrast, makes the borders with the Netherlands and Switzerland appear stable, but, in practice, that also has not been the case.

Eastward Dutch expansion into German territories led to tension from Dutch independence in the sixteenth century into the early eighteenth century. There was no obvious frontier and, instead, reasons of protection to drive the Dutch to expand, as they also did into Belgium. This led to tension along the frontier from the Lower Rhineland to the North Sea. Dutch garrisons in the Lower Rhineland, as in Wesel, were an issue in the seventeenth century. Moreover, immediately after the death of the childless William III in 1702, the Dutch seized the Orange counties of Moers and Lingen, in north-west Germany, ostensibly on behalf of a claimant, the prince of Nassau-Dietz, but in reality to prevent the claims of Frederick I of Prussia, seen as an unwelcome neighbour. Despite protests by Frederick and the Westphalian Circle and a judgement by the Imperial Court, the Dutch refused to withdraw. Meanwhile, Frederick William I was unwilling to renounce the family's claim to the Orange inheritance for nearly a decade. In the event, a compromise left the Prussians in control.

East Friesland then became the key area of dispute, but here the Prussians succeeded in 1744, and thus became a block on Dutch intervention and even expansion. To the south, the county of Bentheim was another area of competing claims, but the Dutch did not expand into that region. Moreover, the grip of outside powers in north-west Germany was lessened in 1773 when the king of Denmark exchanged his rule over the non-contiguous Duchies of Oldenburg and Delmenhorst for the continuous ducal parts of Holstein.

In south-west Germany, Rottweil, an Imperial Free City from 1268, joined the Swiss Confederacy in 1463 with, from 1519, an

'Eternal Covenant', which lasted until 1802 when the territory was allocated to Württemberg. Constance, another Imperial Free City, had tried to join the Confederacy when its hinterland, the Thurgau region, was conquered by the Swiss in the fifteenth century, but the Swiss refused and the city instead joined the Swabian League. Repeatedly, force and intimidation played roles in the fixing and refixing of German frontiers.

To focus on the history of Germany and not Germans, means not offering an account of many areas outside its current borders, not least Austria, Silesia, East Prussia and eastern Pomerania. Thus, there is inherently a process of distortion as there was nothing in the past that inevitably led to the establishment of borders there nor anything unique to its current territory. Indeed, all of those areas were in the German world for centuries, with eastern Pomerania part of Prussia from 1648 to 1945 and Silesia from 1742 to 1945. Yet, boundaries exist today, boundaries fixed in 1945 for a state unified in 1990, that are not troubled by any demand for revision and they present us with the task of providing the history of the present country rather than that of the very many Germanies of the past.

Reconciliation

A visit to St Stephan, Mainz, is one of ethereal peacefulness due to the light, the unusual blue warmth from the nine stained-glass windows that Marc Chagall, a Russian Jew, provided between 1978 and his death in 1985, for a Gothic church that had been very badly damaged in Second World War bombing. The symbolism is clear, but so is the artistic excellence. Peace comes as well from the adjoining cloister rebuilt in 1968–71.

German Recreations

1 'Without smoking and drinking the winter evenings will seem very tedious.'

> Charles Whitworth, British diplomat,
> envoy to the Imperial Diet at Regensburg, 1714

2 'Here is neither diversion nor conversation ... people's spirits are under such a perpetual constraint.'

> Whitworth, Berlin, 1721

3 From hunting whores and hunting play
and minding nothing else all day
and all the night too you will say.
To make grave legs in formal fetters
Converse with fops and write dull letters
To go to bed twixt eight and nine
And sleep away my precious time
In such an idle sneaking place
where vice and folly hide their face
And in a troublesome disguise
the wife seems modest, husband wise
for pleasure here has the same fate
which does attend affairs of state.
The plague of ceremony infects,
Even in love, the softer sex
Who an essential will neglect
rather than lose the least respect.
With regular approach we storm
and never visit but in form.
That is sending to know before
At what o'clock they'll play the whore.
The nymphs are constant, gallants private

One scarce can guess who 'tis they drive at
It seems to me a scurvy fashion
who have been bred in a free nation
with Liberty of speech & passion
Yet I cannot forbear to spark it
And make the best of a bad market
Meeting with one, by chance kindhearted
Who no preliminaries started
I enter'd beyond expectation
Into a close negotiation
Of which hereafter a relation
Humble to fortune not her slave
I still was pleased with what she gave
And with a firm & cheerfull mind
I steer my course with every wind
To all the ports she has designed.'

Sir George Etherege, envoy to the
Imperial Diet at Regensburg, 1686.

4 'As I know that both your rammer and balls are made for a German calibre, you may certainly attack with infinite success.'

Philip, 4th Earl of Chesterfield, to his fellow
diplomat James, Lord Waldegrave, 1728

Humour Issues

National styles and idioms of humour vary and do not always appeal. My father, in Frankfurt for a business fair, was kindly treated to dinner by a German company, after which the managing director insisted that everyone round the table should tell a joke in order. They were ponderous, but received with hearty laughter until my father delivered his joke. 'The masochist says to the sadist, "Whip me! Whip me!" and the sadist says, "No."' It was met by stunned silence. After a while, the MD gave a short laugh, whereupon everyone else laughed.

Which Capital City?

On 20 June 1991, the Bundestag voted for Berlin to be the seat of newly unified Germany's capital, rather than the former West Germany's Bonn; but the majority was only 338–320 (two abstained and one vote was invalid). Yet no other city had even that much traction, although Frankfurt, once the capital in 1848–9 as seat of the national assembly, was briefly mentioned.

In practice, Germany has never been short of capitals. The first Empire was polycentric, with Regensburg, Mainz, Aachen and Frankfurt all having particular significance. The individual states each had their own capital, thus helping create a basis for a range of choices in 1848, including Dresden, Nuremberg and Erfurt. Although Weimar was the place in which the constitution was written, Berlin was the capital of the 'Weimar Republic'. Thus, the role of history, and yet again of conjuncture, is seen in the location of the capital. Moreover, as with the rulers of the First Reich, who spent much time in Italy, Hitler – while happy to indulge his architectural fantasies in Berlin – preferred to spend time in Bavaria.

The choice of Bonn for capital, however, had not had any of the apparent inevitability of Berlin and the Second

Reich. Symbolic of the federal structure of West Germany, Bonn, initially a provisional capital, was the choice of Adenauer, who wanted a Rhenish and Catholic location, and was also seen as a way to anchor the Rhineland in the new state and thus thwart possible French plans for the region. Bonn was also halfway between north and south. The only skyscraper allowed was an office block for Bundestag members.

2

Differing Germanias, –1517

The Arminius Monument, south of Detmold, is a dramatic demonstration, visible from a considerable distance, of a later vision of German history. Finished in 1875, it centres on a large statue of Arminius, his sword aloft, and was a celebration of the destruction of a Roman army in the Teutoburger Forest in CE 9. The usefulness of the past owes much to its role in identity and identification and this was especially so for German commentators and leaders seeking to ground an idea of Germanness. That was made far more complex by the degree to which different Germanies were on offer and in competition. Thus, Arminius (or Hermann) was also to be deployed by critics of the Catholic Church in the early sixteenth century. Ulrich von Hutten (1488–1523), a supporter of Martin Luther, in his *Arminius* (1519), praised his hero as a defender of Germany against the tyranny of Rome: ironically *Arminius* is a Latin work. Defying Imperial Rome drew on a longstanding Christian resonance as it was Imperial Rome that had executed Jesus.

Neither issue nor symbol was lost. In the 1740s there was much interest in Arminius, and in 1769, the emperor Joseph II, the ruler of Austria and an opponent of papal power, was the dedicatee of the play *Die Hermannsschlacht (Hermann's Battle)*, a glorification of the struggle of the ancient Germans written by the poet Friedrich Klopstock (1724–1803). Klopstock spent much of his life in Hamburg and also sought, in *Oden* (1771) and other works, to replace classical myths with Germanic ones.

Arminius was also an inspiration in the struggle with Napoleon, as in Heinrich von Kleist's play *Die Hermannsschlacht* (1809) which was later much performed as a nationalist text under the Second and Third Reichs and in Caspar David Friedrich's painting *Old Heroes' Graves* (1812), in which Arminius is named. Thus, the Arminius Monument drew on a long tradition of nationalism, but one with different contexts and variable meanings.

The early history of Germany is like that of much of Europe and the wider world as a whole, with similar developments in human species, agriculture, settlement and metalworking. Neandertal, a small valley of the river Düssel, east of Düsseldorf, was the site of the industrial limestone quarrying that led to the discovery in 1856 of the bones of the Neanderthal man, which can be better understood at the modern museum at Mettmann. There are a number of other Neanderthal sites in Germany. However, as elsewhere, the separate Neanderthal strand – which it is difficult to date – was to end, possibly about 40,000 years ago. This was probably due to conquest and/or absorption by *Homo sapiens*, in a context made difficult by low population, climate change and disease. Genetic analysis certainly indicates a degree of absorption.

The ice ages – for there was no single ice age – provided a very changeable physical environment, but Germany was an area of settlement, and notably so with the Vogelherd Cave in the eastern Swabian Jura. Excavation in 1931 showed small figures of mammoth ivory from about 32,000 years ago and additional excavations in 2005–12 have yielded findings of some of the world's oldest-known works of figurative art, including sculptures of a mammoth, a cave lion and a horse, across a considerable time span. This led to the cave becoming part in 2017 of the UNESCO World Heritage site, Caves and Ice Age Art in the Swabian-Jura.

At Breitenbach in Saxony-Anhalt, a very extensive site, there were occupations between 28,800 and 24,860 BCE. Many flint and bone tools have been found there. Subsequently, following a common pattern of location reuse, a Neolithic settlement of about 5,500–3,500 BCE also occupied the same place. Flint tools at Sahlenburg, part of Cuxhaven, date from about 16,000 BCE.

The last ice age reached its peak around 18,000 BCE and then, after an ablation (recession) beginning in about 14,000 BCE, was followed by a 're-chill' that began around 10,800 BCE and ended around 9,700 BCE. During this re-chill, part of northern Germany was covered by the permanent ice cap, the Fenno-Scandinavian Ice Sheet, with much of its soil pushed south by glaciers when the ice advanced. To the south, there was tundra and permafrost, although there was also glacial advance from the Alps.

Climate warming at the end of the last ice age led to the spread of plants, animals and humans in Germany. The humans were for a long time hunter-gatherers, until they were supplemented by those who brought cultivation, notably of oats and rye, along with wild cattle, pigs and other sources of food. The plentiful timber and workable mud and wild grasses of the region ensured that buildings could be constructed. Permanent settlements followed, along with social stratification, trade and protection. Metallurgy also provided a means of increasing the effectiveness of both agriculture and warfare. Funeral rituals indicate developed belief systems as exemplified by the skulls, dated to 7,000 BCE, of the Ofnet caves near Nördlingen – arranged concentrically with their faces turned toward the setting sun and covered with a layer of red ochre.

By 5,000 BCE, Germany was very much in the developing world of cultivation, with early settlements in a number of places including Duvensee in Schleswig-Holstein. A wooden paddle has been found on the site, as well as wooden arrow and axe shafts and flint tools. The stone age was followed by the copper and then by the bronze ages, with the latter seeing barrow burials, as at Bonstorf on Lüneburg Heath. Settlement was concentrated on lightly forested and open areas, especially if the soil was loess, which was both fertile and easily worked.

Work published in 2019 on ancient DNA from skeletons of about 2,800–1,700 BCE in the Lech Valley in southern Bavaria, a longstanding farming region, has suggested, as also indicated by grave goods, social contrasts within individual households, which may indicate servants or slaves. The presence in the graves of high-status women from far away is a matter for speculation. In 1999, near Nebra, Saxony-Anhalt, a bronze-age find, probably from about 1,600 BCE, but possibly iron-age, yielded a bronze disc with gold symbols offering a depiction of the solar system. Unearthed by illegal treasure hunters, the hoard was traded privately before being seized by the police in 2002 and the disc is now held in the Saxony-Anhalt prehistory museum in Halle. The find was in an area of neolithic settlement and plentiful barrows and the sun sets each solstice behind the Brocken, the highest mountain in the Harz. The minerals in the disc reflect trade patterns, coming from Austria and Cornwall.

There are often major issues in the evaluation of findings, both in their own right and with reference to broader developments. Thus, in 1996, a perceptive amateur archaeologist discovered in the Tollense valley what was regarded as the site of one of Europe's oldest battles. Aside from human remains, including a skull with blunt-force trauma, possibly caused by a club, and an arm bone pierced by an arrowhead, weapon finds included a bronze sword, flint and bronze arrowheads, cudgels, spearheads and daggers. Initial investigations suggested that the battle, in the bronze age in about 1,200 BCE, roughly when Troy was destroyed, involved as many as 4,000 warriors, of whom possibly 1,400 died. It arose from an invasion of the north by south Germany. In contrast, more recent genetic analysis has established few ties of kinship among the dead and therefore made it improbable that the find was of a migrating group. Instead of a battle, an ambush of a trade convoy is now suggested.

Parts of Germany consisted of sections of several prehistoric cultures, including the Lusatian and Urnfield cultures, and were affected by the spread of Indo-European groups, notably the Celtic peoples who appeared in southern Germany around 800 BCE. Their sites include Heuneburg, close to the upper Danube near

Herbertingen, Württemberg, a hillfort and settlement which was an important centre in c. 700–c. 500 BCE, one involved in trade with southern Europe. As with other early settlements, the inter-pretation of this site has varied greatly, both in terms of its history and its significance. It is possible, indeed, that Heuneburg was the Celtic city called Pyrene by the Greek historian Herodotus.

Although processes are unclear, there appears to have been a Celtic-Germanic sub-language family spun off from one of the original proto-Indo-European clusters of 3,500–3,000 BCE. It seems that this family then broke up. The Germanic peoples were an Indo-European ethnolinguistic group that appears to have emerged in southern Scandinavia during the Nordic bronze age of 1,700–500 BCE. They moved south, at the expense of the Celts, and also clashed with the Romans. This was most notably in 102–101 BCE, when the Cimbri and Teutones invaded southern France and northern Italy, only to be defeated by the Romans.

From about 500 BCE, in the iron age, iron axes and ploughs made it easier to clear the woodland and to work the soil. Large parts of lowland Germany were cleared of trees, opening up what became a permanent difference between upland and lowland areas.

Rome

Germania was a term used by the Romans, notably by Caesar in his *Gallic Wars* (58–49 BCE), and by the Greek polymath Posidonius (135–51 BCE), who travelled extensively in the Roman Empire, producing a now lost geography of the Celtic lands that was referred to by other writers. Caesar invaded Germania in 53 BCE, building an impressive bridge over the Rhine, the first to span the river.

In his *Germania* (98 CE), the Roman historian Publius Cornelius Tacitus, who had never visited the region, refers to the name Germani as an '*inventus nomen*' (invented name) of recent origin. To Tacitus, the borders of Germania were the Rhine, Danube and Vistula.

Knowledge of Germania was of significance to the Romans because the Danube and Rhine frontiers of their Empire became a consistent area of confrontation, with the Romans advancing beyond both in the 10s BCE, indeed, probably to the Elbe. However, after their defeat in 9 CE in the Teutoburger Forest, the Romans pulled back to what became the Rhine frontier. *Limes*, or fortified frontiers, were then created, notably the *Limes Germanicus* between the two rivers in 83 CE.

At Saalburg, a Roman fort near Bad Homburg, there is a reconstructed fort and a museum. These fortifications consolidated Germania Superior, which was made into a province based on Mogontiacum (Mainz, founded in about 13–12 BCE), separate to Germania Inferior, based on Colonia (Cologne), the latter the basis of the excellent Romano-Germanic Museum which is designed around an impressive Dionysus mosaic of about 220 CE. Conquered in 15 BCE, the province of Raetia in modern southern Germany had its capital at Augusta Vindelicorum (Augsburg), which was founded in 15 BCE. Initially its frontier was on the Danube, before the *Limes* were constructed about a hundred miles to the north. Regensburg was the base of a legion by 179 CE.

Trier: A City of Roman Remains

Founded by the Celts and renamed by the Romans as Augusta Treverorum around 16 BCE, Trier became one of the most important Roman cities north of the Alps and was variously the capital of the province of Belgic Gaul and of the Prefecture of the Gauls, one of the four prefectures into which the Empire was divided in 337. This entailed the government of the Roman west, in the shape of Iberia, France, Belgium, Roman Britain and Roman Germany, and

---

part of Roman North Africa. It held this position until either 395 or 407 when the capital was moved to Arelate (Arles). Trier's population was about 75,000 and it was the seat of the oldest bishopric north of the Alps. The remains of the Roman period include the impressive Porta Nigra, the largest surviving Roman city gate north of the Alps, its name derived from the grey sandstone. Begun in about 170 CE, this was one of the four city gates. Other remains include those of the imperial palace, the Aula Palatina (the largest extant hall from antiquity), the amphitheatre and the bridge over the Moselle. The Roman remains form part of Trier's UNESCO World Heritage site.

The History of German Wine

In the 1880s, hundreds of cultured grape seeds dating to 1500 BCE were discovered at Hagnau on Lake Constance, then Celtic territory and today still a locale for prime wine. The Romans, therefore, most likely reintroduced rather than began winemaking. Some of the sites of production go back to the Roman period. The wine was probably produced by, and for, garrisons, with pruning knives dating from around the first century CE. The Moselle region, near the major governmental centre of Trier, became an important region of production. Decimus Ausonius (c. 310–c. 395) made reference to winemaking both in his native Bordeaux region and in his poem *Mosella* (c. 370), where he described the valley vineyards. The wild vine already grew in the Upper Rhineland, but Roman-era techniques probably reflected the practices brought by the Romans.

If the early areas of wine production were very much linked to Roman rule, the middle ages brought expansion elsewhere in Germany that was related to Christianisation and, in particular, the establishment of monasteries. There appears to have been a peak in production around the eve of the Reformation. Subsequently, it was hit by the breakup of monastic communities and the resulting loss of their skills, the spread of beer production, the climate cooling of the little ice age and its impact on northerly production areas and, in the seventeenth century, by the disruption of the Thirty Years' War (1618-48), which much increased the risks of commerce.

While there are German rosés and, far more, reds (production of the latter grew greatly from the 1980s), most German wines are white. Key white grape varieties are riesling, grauer burgunder, silvaner and Müller-Thurgau. The cost is high because the steep vineyards do not lead themselves to easy mechanisation and wages are not low. The market focuses on German consumers, and many German wines, such as the undistinguished *Sekt* – sparkling wine – are not much drunk outside Germany, except for riesling.

Apfelwein (apple wine) is cider and is generally fairly tart, due to the use of sour apples. It is particularly drunk in Hesse, where on trips to the archives in Marburg in 1980 and later, I got used to drinking it hot with cinnamon or sugar, rather like mulled wine.

Thus, much of modern southern and western Germany was under German rule, which was an aspect of an early division of the modern country, albeit without the modern counterpart of Scotland and Ireland remaining outside Roman Britain. Many of the Germanic tribes who lived to the north of the Roman Empire, and were perceived as 'barbarians' by the Romans, were partly romanised by their contact with them, which, by the later imperial period, included military service.

After the Romans

Increased pressure forced the Romans onto the defensive. Recent archaeology, for example, has established that Constance was fortified with new walls in the fourth century. However, in the early fifth century, the Germanic tribes overran the Western Roman Empire, with *Romanitas* having less of an afterlife than in the case of France, Spain and, in particular, Italy, all of which had been settled over a longer period and more intensively. In part, the decline of *Romanitas* reflected the dominance of the military in the urban life of Roman Germany and the consequent lesser possibility of a strong post-Roman identity. However, all the major Roman cities in Germany were to be significant.

There was no unity among these tribes but, instead, a shifting pattern of advantage reflecting feuds within and between ruling families and a violent practice and ethos of rulership and politics. The major tribes in Germany were the Franks, Saxons, Thuringians, Alemanni, Bavarians and Helvetii, but mapping their bounds is unwise, not least given the vagueness of contemporary ideas of overlordship.

A Forgotten Dynasty

Based in Regensburg, the Agilolfings ruled Bavaria as allies of the Merovingian rulers of the Franks from the sixth century until deposed by Charlemagne in 788. Tassilo I was appointed king by Childebert II, the Frankish king, in 591, as part of a somewhat obscure peace in which Tassilo's predecessor was removed in part to thwart his alignment with the related Lombards of northern Italy. Much of the early history of Bavaria is obscure, not least its degree of independence from the Franks and its separate alignment with Italy. The death of Duke Theodo in 716 was followed by the division of

---

the inheritance between sons probably based in Salzburg, Regensburg, Passau and Freising, leading to civil war and the death of all bar one of the sons, Grimoald. He was, in turn, killed in 725 by the invading Frankish leader Charles Martel. The Frankish attempt to extend control was resisted by Grimoald's successor, Hugbert (r. 725–36), who sought to create an independent church as a source of legitimacy. Links between ruling families and the Church were important to the position, stability and ideology of the former and helped differentiate these families from ordinary nobles. Bishoprics were established in 739 by Odilo (r. 736–48).

Bavaria was the most viable centre of a German Christian polity, one seen with the development of the Church and its close links with the dynasty, both the new bishoprics and new monasteries such as Niederaltaich (741), the abbot of which compiled the collection of Bavarian laws, and Mondsee (748). Another source of support was the nobles, some of whom rebelled against Odilo in 741, greatly limiting his freedom to engage with the Franks, who defeated him in 743 and made him accept their overlordship. The subsequent fate of the dynasty owed much to Frankish politics, with Tassilo III becoming ruler, first as a ward and in 757 as a vassal. He was deposed in 788 and made to enter a monastery. This was an important success for Charlemagne, one that was significant not only for that region, but also for wider politics in Germany, Italy and central Europe. Even today, however, the Bavarians consider themselves a people apart from the rest of the Germans.

The Franks were long the dominant group – for example, conquering the Thuringians in 531–2 – but were prone to division between royal sons – as in 511, 561 and 639. Politics was a system operating by spoils, providing, therefore, a basis for dispute.

Kings, relatives, aristocrats and clerics were all landowners and the payments, produce and services they received as a result kept the system going. The agricultural services were provided by serfs whose labour was gruelling and rewards few.

Ultimately, a new dynasty – that of the Carolingians, with its capital at Aachen, and in the person of Charlemagne (r. 771–814) – won control of France and Germany, with the eventual hard-fought conquest of the Saxons by 804 crucial to the latter. In defeating the Saxons, Charlemagne allied with the Obotrites, a confederation of west Slavic tribes in Mecklenberg, cooperating in a victory at Bornhöved in 798. As a result, the Obotrites briefly gained part of Holstein. The frontier with Denmark was fixed on the Eider River in 811. Thuringia was brought under stronger Carolingian control after a rebellion was suppressed in 786, while, in 806, the Sorbs, a Slavic group that had settled widely in Lusatia and Thuringia, were defeated near modern Weissenfels and submitted.

CHRISTIANISATION

Conquests furthered conversion to Christianity in a long-term process. The Christianisation of the parts of Germany under Roman rule was disrupted by 'barbarian invasions', not least because there were conversions to Arian Christianity rather than the orthodox Trinitarian creed of the Catholic Church. After the fall of the Western Roman Empire, notable conversions to Christianity included the ruling Frankish Merovingian dynasty in 498. However, the conversion of the Franks was a more gradual process, as it was with other groups, the Alemanni becoming Christian in the seventh century and the Saxons as a result of Charlemagne, who destroyed their sacred pillar of Irminsul in 772.

Saint Boniface (c. 675–754), an English missionary, was appointed missionary bishop for Germania and cut down the Donar Oak, a pagan sacred tree near Fritzlar, Hesse, the wood of which became the basis for a chapel dedicated to St Peter. Winning the backing of the Frankish leaders, Boniface became part of their campaign against groups including the pagan Saxons. In 732, he was given archepiscopal jurisdiction over Germany by Pope Gregory III and later became the papal legate for Germany and, in 745, archbishop of Mainz, with authority over all Germany east of the Rhine. Boniface founded the dioceses of Eichstätt, Erfurt and Würzburg and won the support of Odilo of Bavaria, only to be martyred while on missionary work near Dokkum in Frisia in 754. He became patron saint of Germania, with his remains venerated at Fulda.

The defeat of the Saxons, in turn, was followed by the foundation of new bishoprics, such as Paderborn in 799. Monasteries were a centre for Christian activity and settlement, as with Gars abbey founded by Tassilo III of Bavaria in 768 and Prüm, founded in 721 and generously supported by Charlemagne.

Counterfactuals come into play with the Saxons, in the shape of a continued German polity and culture that remained outside medieval Christendom. They might not have lasted in that way as long as Scandinavia or even Lithuania, but have remained long enough to ensure a different basis for state-building. In particular, this counterfactual might be one in which the imperial tradition, as reformed by Charlemagne, that was to be the basis for the Empire, was not to cover Germany as a whole.

Religious conviction was an aspect of a society in which there was a strong belief in the need to fight evil. This is in evidence in texts from the period, such as *Muspilli*, a poem from ninth-century Bavaria, in which the wounds Christ suffered prove to be a vital help at the Last Judgement. The life of Jesus, in the style of a German epic, was the subject of the *Heliand*, a ninth-century work in Old Saxon that may have been intended to help ground Christianity in newly converted territory. Jesus is presented here as a powerful figure able to lead.

Pope Leo III crowned Charlemagne Emperor in 800, in an attempt to unite the two in restoring the authority of the Roman Empire and in support of the papacy. This drew on the Franks' willingness to intervene in Italy. In turn, Charlemagne's empire was divided by his heir, Louis the Pious, among his sons in 817, by the *Ordinatio Imperii*. Division was entrenched by the Treaty of Verdun (843), which created western, middle and eastern kingdoms, the first the basis for France and the last for Germany but, due to fortuitous deaths, Charles the Fat united all the dominions in 884–7, until a rebellion by his nephew Arnulf of Carinthia led to the collapse of his position. Arnulf was ruler of East Francia from 887 to 899. Charles the Fat's success followed by failure indicates the unpredictability of history.

Aachen

Very much on the edge of Germany, Charlemagne's capital and place of burial was an important, symbolic site for the medieval Empire. Kings of Germania were crowned in its cathedral from 936 until 1562, when Frankfurt-on-Main became the coronation city.

Charlemagne had consciously sought to emulate the Byzantine Roman Empire, with his use of a domed octagonal basilica the basis for the cathedral he built. His relics were placed in a gold shrine in the building when Frederick II was crowned in 1215, part of the process of endorsement by ritual and the white magic of relics. The cathedral holds both Carolingian and Gothic treasures, including Charlemagne's throne and the imperial crown. The later development of the Empire and of Germany, however, left Aachen distinctly marginal.

The Carolingians absorbed tribal duchies or vassal kingdoms that, in turn, took on a new form with the end of the Carolingian dynasty. These areas were Saxony, Franconia, Bavaria, Swabia (based on the Alemanni) and Lotharingia; the dukes in effect made them hereditary. However, internal division and external challenge made stability difficult to achieve. As a result, following the Edict of Pîtres of 864 – which loosened and delegated the royal right to build fortifications – aristocratic fortresses became more common to secure lordship, as with the counts of Schweinfurt in northern Bavaria. Their fortresses were destroyed by the emperor Henry II (r. 1002–24) after the overthrow of the family. Episcopal seats such as Würzburg and Eichstädt were also fortified.

The Ottonians

The run of Carolingian rulers in Germany ended in 911 with the death of Arnulf's son, Louis the Child. They were eventually succeeded by the Saxon or Ottonian dynasty under Henry the Fowler, Duke of Saxony, Henry I (r. 919–36), who subjugated the Slavs in 924–6 in what is now central Germany and advanced eastwards with new fortified centres; for example, Meissen in 928. His impressive son, Otto I, became king in 936, crushed the invading Magyars at Lechfeld near Augsburg in 955 and became emperor in 962. This was a key episode in the creation from war of the Empire, the first Reich.

Winning great prestige from his victory, which halted the damaging and wide-ranging Magyar raids, Otto established an effective governmental system that was continued by his successors and benefitted from the ritual potency of the Empire and from the support or acceptance of the ruling elite. Cooperation was seen in the imperial household, in personal fealty and patrimonial politics, with the 'good magic' of a monarch – notably military success, potent relics such as the Holy Lance and a secure succession – being important for winning support. The ruler, not the state, was foremost, and ritual – both lay and religious – and personal links were shaped and experienced accordingly. Carolingian and, even more, Ottonian kingship were particularly sacral and seen as an aspect of providential time, in that the idea of the *translatio imperii* represented the need to carry forward in the new Empire those aspects of Rome under which the Christian message had been propagated. The extent to which the Ottonian Empire also had a well-developed organisational system able to deploy large armies is controversial, with differences raised over the interpretation of texts.

This was not, however, a German state (a term that is very difficult to apply for the Empire), as Otto had added the kingdom of Italy in 951 and his successors competed there with Byzantium, which was the Eastern Roman Empire. In Germany, indeed, ideas of Germanness took shape after the Ottonian emperors began to take armies into Italy. The Ottonian and Salian rule of the Empire was, more generally, a framework for ideas of German national identity, ideas that continued to develop thereafter, in terms of the Empire, but also with reference to other factors, such as language.

Having focused on Italy, the Ottonians benefitted when Henry II consolidated the government of Germany and forged a strong state for his successors. Reflecting the newly important role of bishops in imperial elections, Henry II was also a prominent supporter of the Church, as was demonstrated by his backing of the new cathedral see at Bamberg, established in 1007. The early thirteenth-century *Bamberger Reiter* (*Bamberg Knight*) statue at the cathedral captures the desired fusion of authority and sanctity and may represent Henry, who is buried there. On the UNESCO World Heritage list, Bamberg is a very attractive city, which has the cathedral (1004–12; rebuilt after fire in 1081), the episcopal residence, and the town hall on an island in the river.

Relations with the Church remained a key factor in the interweaving of German and Italian politics, one that was marked in 1077 when the excommunicated Henry IV stood in the snow for three days at Canossa in Tuscany as part of a necessary reconciliation with Pope Gregory VII. This crisis was followed soon after by the German princes electing Rudolf of Rheinfelden as emperor. The collapse of Henry's authority shown through the Saxon rebellion of 1073 provided an opportunity for new solutions.

THE HOHENSTAUFENS

The Ottonian and then Salian (1027–1125) dynasties of emperors were succeeded by the Hohenstaufen dynasty in the person of Conrad III (r. 1138–52). Bringing the medieval Empire to a height, the dynasty was named after the Swabian castle of Staufen, the ruins of which survived Swedish destruction in 1632. The talented Hohenstaufens had been dukes of Swabia since 1079.

Meanwhile, Germany participated in wider developments, including the major and long-term expansion in population and economic activity that brought the 'dark ages' to a close and lasted until the climate downturn and plague of the fourteenth century. The focus was on expansion, with new towns sometimes marked by the name '*Neustadt*', as with Neustadt an der Weinstrasse in the Palatinate, founded in the early thirteenth century. Moreover, towns became larger, more sophisticated and more significant, both economically and politically. They were an important source of liquidity for rural society.

Greater activity brought wealth that helped underpin successive territorial dynasties as the major landowners, and was spent on a number of goals including both religious foundations and buildings, and also on political ambition. Thus, Germany saw splendid church-building as well as the foundation of important sites such as the house of secular canonesses at Quedlinburg in 936 and monasteries, for example the Cistercian houses of Ebrach (1127) and Eberbach (1135).

One of the most striking legacies of the period is Maulbronn abbey, a UNESCO World Heritage site in a remote part of northern Baden-Württemberg. Founded in 1147, this Cistercian abbey was an independent territory under the Empire until annexed by Württemberg in 1504. The monastery was dissolved in 1558 and replaced by a Protestant seminary established in its grounds in 1556. Part of the monastery, including Germany's oldest example of Gothic architecture, dating from about 1220, appears on the German 2013 €2 coin.

There were also major Templar houses, as at Augsburg and Bamberg. Religious commitment, moreover, led to crusading activity, not only in the Near East, but also in expanding Germany at the expense of Slavs to the east, with the Teutonic Knights conquering Prussia in 1226–1309. The Teutonic Order had many houses all over Germany, some of which can still be found in local names in the form of '*Deutsches Haus*'. A different aspect of religious violence took the form of the massacres of Jews notably, but not only, in the Rhineland in 1096, especially in Worms and Mainz, as part of the activism associated with the calling of the First Crusade.

German settlement to the east followed the advance of control, the Duchy of Pomerania, for example, being added in 1181. This was a fundamental change in the 'space' of Germania, one that was only reversed – and then only in part – in the twentieth century. Settlement was based, in part, on the iron plough and the introduction of grain, supplanting the earlier emphasis on grazing,

The Danes played a major role close to the Baltic, as did the Hanseatic League, a group of commercial cities centred on Lübeck that developed trade routes and helped finance economic development, notably grain production and trade. Other major Hansa centres included Bremen, Cologne, Dortmund, Hamburg, Brunswick, Magdeburg and Wismar and, with eastward movement, Stralsund and Greifswald from the mid-thirteenth century.

Nicknamed Barbarossa or Redbeard, Frederick I (r. 1152–90) succeeded his uncle, Conrad III, and was a vigorous ruler, but his position was challenged by the growing power of many leading aristocratic families, especially the Guelphs in Saxony, under Duke Henry the Lion. The latter was deprived of his lands in 1180 when the duchy was partitioned, with Westphalia and Brunswick-Lüneburg split from the Saxony that was to be the basis of the later Electorate. Similarly, Bavaria lost Austria, Styria and Tyrol, an outcome – finally confirmed after repeated conflicts in the eighteenth and early nineteenth centuries – that proved critical to the long-term shaping of Germany. Under Barbarossa, Charlemagne was canonised in 1165, a step that helped both local Aachen interests and also the image of the Empire.

Committed to maintaining imperial power in Italy, Frederick repeatedly led expeditions to the country, only to be defeated, weakening his position in Germany. He drowned on the Third Crusade. His successor, Henry VI (r. 1191–7), sought to make the Empire an hereditary monarchy, but what was known as the *Erbreichsplan*, although similar to the practice followed in other kingdoms, as well as the situation in German territorial principalities, was thwarted. In part this was due to opposition, notably raised by Pope Celestine III and Archbishop Adolf of Cologne, an opponent of Henry. His own competing commitments also played a role and he died early, at the age of thirty-two.

This death was followed by a dispute over the German throne, in which opposition to Henry's three-year-old son – the future Frederick II – interacted with power politics in both Germany and Italy. Philip, Duke of Swabia, was elected in 1198 by German princes sympathetic to the Hohenstaufen, while Otto of Brunswick, a Guelph and the son of the Saxon duke Henry the Lion, was backed by the opposing faction. Both were crowned in rival ceremonies and, in 1199, Pope Innocent III came down on the side of Otto. Conflict was followed in 1208 by the murder of Philip by Otto of Wittelsbach, the count palatine, an event that Innocent conveniently saw as divine judgement.

Otto of Brunswick, Otto IV, then became clear ruler, only to fall out with Innocent in 1210 over Italian interests. The pope, instead, turned to Frederick II. This led in 1212 to a civil war that was won by Frederick, who was re-elected 'King of the Romans', the title then used to describe an elected German king not yet given the imperial regalia in a coronation by the pope. Otto's defeat by the French in 1214 at Bouvines wrecked his position, as well as the plans of King John of England, and he was deposed by

Innocent, dying in 1218. Frederick was crowned emperor in Rome in 1220.

These conflicts had an effect across the Empire, including on the factional politics of cities such as Cologne. They could readily be replicated in any account of the medieval Empire, and throw light on the degree to which dynastic ambitions could not only support but also weaken the practices of compromise in legitimation that helped the Empire to function.

Frederick II (r. 1220–50) devoted most of his time to his interests outside Germany, notably those in Italy. Indeed, he did not visit Germany after 1236. Opposition, primarily from the papacy, challenged his position and, overcome in Italy, Frederick's heirs were unable to sustain the dynasty. His son, Henry, fell out with Frederick over German princely politics and, in 1234, revolted unsuccessfully. He was dethroned in 1235 and imprisoned, dying in 1242. Henry's own son, another Frederick, was made Duke of Austria, but died in 1251, allegedly poisoned.

Frederick II's next son, Conrad, became Duke of Swabia in 1235, but faced opposition from Frederick II's opponents in Germany and Italy. Conrad focused on Italy, where he died of malaria in 1254. His defeated son, Conradin, was executed in Naples in 1268, while Frederick's illegitimate son, Manfred, who had earlier acted as regent for Conradin, had been defeated and killed in Italy two years earlier. The male line of the Hohenstaufen dynasty was extinct with Conradin's death, and Swabia ceased to be a coherent territorial unit. This had long-term consequences for the political weight of particular regions, notably by helping ensure the leading position of Bavaria in southern Germany.

THE LATER MIDDLE AGES

The German interregnum continued until 1312. In 1273, Rudolf of Habsburg was elected, but he should be seen as King of the Romans, a position (used from the early eleventh century to reflect election by the princes) he held until his death in 1291, but he was never crowned emperor. Achieving the latter position in part depended upon being crowned by the pope, and Charles V, in 1530, would be the last to be so acknowledged.

Prior to Rudolf's election, foreign candidates played a major role, notably Richard of Cornwall, brother of Henry III of England, who was supported by the Guelphs, and Alfonso X of Castile, backed by the Hohenzollerns. Rudolf had to fight hard to establish his position and territories and found it difficult to bring peace to the Empire. Imperial power and authority were weakened as major aristocrats, clerics and cities all gained power, although they did not seek to break up the Empire, which, indeed, was seen as not only legitimate but also part of a sacred plan. Nonetheless, they competed for prominence; for example, the Wittelsbachs of Bavaria and the Luxemburgs of Bohemia struggled for control over the bishopric of Regensburg.

The attractive castles scattered across Germany were very much practically employed. Thus, the prince-bishop of Constance, Nikolaus of Frauenfeld, an ally of the pope, worked on Meersburg castle to resist a siege by Emperor Louis IV (r. 1328–47). He dug a 14-metre-deep ditch, a 28-metre-deep well and a subterranean passage to Lake Constance in 1334. The fourteen-week siege, in which one very primitive cannon was used, failed.

In the late middle ages, the capabilities of imperial government decreased greatly, in part due to the allocation of fiscal rights to prominent subjects. Combined with the small size and limited development of imperial government and the range of area over which it had scope and for which it had responsibilities, this ensured a degree of weakness that made it difficult to offer a basis for coherence comparable to that of rulers elsewhere in Europe.

Although the territorial princes were not supposed to act against the emperor, they enjoyed great political freedom and the extent of their autonomy was important for the sense of regional identity and, later, for the significance of federalism in modern

Germany. Their aristocratic position was grounded in regional holdings and alliances and the territorial princes perforce had a degree of responsibility for political order. The travelling emperor, who ruled from the saddle and lacked the fixed centre of consequential power comparable to London and Paris, was increasingly limited in his itineraries within the Empire.

The families that dominated the choice of emperor – the Habsburgs, Luxembourgs and Wittelsbachs – relied on their own possessions rather than those of the emperor. The first two families generally focused in particular on territories that, while not as distant from Germany as Italy, were not core German regions. Sigismund of Luxemburg (r. 1387–1437) was greatly weakened by his defeats at the hands of the Turks and the Hussites.

At the same time, recent work on Frederick III (r. 1440–93) has shown that this Habsburg, despite his concern with his hereditary lands and his bitter rivalry with his brother Archduke Albert of Austria, had some success in keeping imperial authority alive across the Empire – including in the distant north – not least as an arbitrator in disputes. He also raised troops for common purposes, such as the war with Duke Charles the Bold of Burgundy in 1475. Imperial jurisdiction and coinage also provided a sense of identity.

Meanwhile, there was no consistency in imperial assemblies which, through the territorial rulers that attended, were representational in a federal fashion, rather than having any equivalent to the knights of the shire, the county representatives in the English parliament. Yet, a lack of state building did not mean an absence of nation making, while the Empire itself worked in part as a series of interconnections drawing on a considerable ideological heritage, not least a German sense of the emperor's particular responsibility for the German lands. These numerous connections encouraged not only respect for the office of emperor, but also associations or leagues between those with authority, associations that provided strength and ensured arbitration, contributing as well to the larger-scale version in the shape of the Empire itself.

Nevertheless, the alliances signed to defend their interest could also act against other members of the Empire. Feuds, however defined, both disturbed the peace within the Empire and were used by major principalities to absorb smaller ones. Thus, the Dohna Feud of 1385–1402 led to the occupation of an imperial fief by the margrave of Meissen.

The Golden Bull, 1356

Named after its seal, this decree, issued by the Imperial Diet headed by the emperor Charles IV (r. 1346–78), fixed the imperial constitution in order to end the contestation caused by opposing elections, as had happened on a number of occasions, as in 1257 and 1314. Papal intervention in elections was rejected, as, on a longstanding pattern, only the prince-electors were to choose.

The seven prince-electors were individually specified and majority voting was established. Four of them were secular: the king of Bohemia (Charles IV), the count palatine of the Rhine, the duke of Saxony and the margrave of Brandenburg. Three were ecclesiastical, the archbishops of Mainz, Cologne and Trier. Although this element was to a large degree forgotten, the process of selecting the seven was heavily political, with the rivals of the house of Luxemburg from which Charles came – the rulers of Austria and Bavaria – both excluded from electoral status until 1526 (when the Habsburgs became kings of Bohemia) and 1623 (when the Bavarians gained the Palatine vote) respectively. The title 'king of Germany' was used between election and coronation. The role of choice by major princes helped validate the Empire and emphasise the link between emperor and Germany.

Defining the Empire

Any definition of the character of the Empire is open to debate. In his *De statu Imperii Germanici* (1667), Samuel Pufendorf referred to a *'monstro simile'*, while Montesquieu in *L'Esprit des Lois* (1741) and Edward Gibbon in his *Decline and Fall of the Roman Empire* (1776–88), discerned a federative republic, with a weak emperor. William Robertson, in his *Charles V* (1769), wrote of a 'regular confederacy'. The *Encyclopaedia Britannica* noted, 'Authors are at a loss under what form of government to range the empire . . . a monarchical state . . . a republic or aristocratic state . . . a monarcho-aristocratic state . . . an aristo-democratic state.' Crucially, this decentralised, but enormous, corporatist polity of particular privileges, territorial liberties and mutual rights was not a German nation-state, as it ranged far more widely geographically.

Louis IV's death in 1347 brought out another aspect of German history: he suffered a stroke during a bear hunt west of Munich. Hunting was a key element in elite leisure and socialising – as seen in paintings such as Lucas Cranach the Elder's hunting scenes from the early sixteenth century – but was also an illustration of the degree to which humans were in competition with animals. This was a matter not only of remote wooded and mountainous areas, such as the Harz, but also across Germany as a whole.

The social tensions of the late fourteenth century, following the plague pandemic of the Black Death, contributed to religious differences, but in the early fifteenth century the centre of religious dissent was Bohemia, with the Hussite movement, and not Germany. The period saw the replacement of the Luxemburg family in 1438 as emperors by the Austrian-based Habsburgs.

The Habsburgs had initially focused on Swabia, Alsace and northern Switzerland, before acquiring Austria in the late thirteenth century. However, they went on to preside over an Empire whose federal character did not match the degree of state strengthening seen, in particular, in France and Spain in the late fifteenth century. Thus, a strong consciousness of Germanness and German nationhood developed in a particular political context, although the multiple identities and loyalties of the Empire were also seen elsewhere, notably in areas that were to detach from it, such as the Netherlands and Switzerland.

There was external pressure on the Empire, with Matthias Corvinus, king of Hungary (r. 1458–90), taking part of Austria. Differently, and lastingly, the Swiss made gains from the Habsburgs and in 1499, at the end of the Swabian War of that year, forced the emperor, Maximilian I, to acknowledge their effective independence. Official recognition only came in 1648 through the Peace of Westphalia. The advance of France into the Burgundian inheritance from the late fifteenth century after the death of Charles the Bold, Duke of Burgundy, was to have major implications for the Empire west of the Rhine.

The background to the German divisions of the sixteenth century was already apparent, but the course of likely events was totally unclear. It was the same with the fate of territories within the Empire. Thus Brandenburg, one of the seven electorates, gained nearby territories in the fifteenth century – notably Neumark and Kottbus – but also, more briefly, held Ansbach and Bayreuth. Saxony was divided between two major branches of the Wettin family; the Ernestine – which provided the elector of Saxony – and the Albertine, which provided its duke. The Wittelsbach inheritance was divided between its Palatine branch, which provided the elector, and the Bavarian which, in turn, was divided after the death of Louis IV. This led to conflicts.

Geography played a role, but the working of these divisions was uncertain. Thus, the Wittelsbachs lost Brandenburg, which Louis had acquired.

Alongside the damage stemming from the Black Death and associated and subsequent social and economic crises, there was also growth. This was particularly apparent in the major cities that became not only key points in a far-flung commercial system but also important centres of education, culture and the arts. Augsburg, Frankfurt and Lübeck were each important examples of such activity.

Frankfurt, with its two major trade fairs, reflected the important combination of long-range trade routes and specific physical features – in this case a crossing point over the River Main. The first Frankfurt autumn trade fair to be recorded was in 1240, when Emperor Frederick II decreed that its merchants were under his protection. The spring fair followed in 1330. The fairs were important to liquidity and credit as well as to trade in goods. Frankfurt's links were particularly strong with Cologne and Nuremberg. In 1372, Frankfurt became an Imperial Free City under the direct authority of the emperor, who was elected there from 1562, Frankfurt replacing Aachen in the ceremonial role.

Till Eulenspiegel

A picaresque character from Brunswick who appears in print from the 1510s and is based on early fourteenth-century adventures involving joke playing. Excrement plays a major role in the stories, which reflect a theme in the humour of the period. In his novel *Hag's Nook* (1933), John Dickson Carr argued, 'In Germany even the legends have a bustling clockwork freshness, like a walking toy from Nuremberg.'

Another aspect in development was the combination of skill and patronage that produced a wonderful series of works in late Gothic style. Based in Dortmund, Conrad von Soest (c. 1370–c. 1422) made an effective use of colour and was important in the 'soft style' of late Gothic art. Prominent in Cologne in the 1440s, Stefan Lochner (c. 1410–51) also made brilliant use of colour in his religious scenes and offered a degree of realism in his presentation of figures.

A series of painters provided elements of a German renaissance, centred in cities and courts, that bridged the late medieval concerns with a new success in representation, including the use of light and depiction of landscape in the works of the Regensburg painter Albrecht Altdorfer (1480–1538) and the mythological scenes of Lucas Cranach the Elder (c. 1472–1553). The Nuremberg painter Albrecht Dürer (1471–1528) was very open to Italian influences but others, such as Matthias Grünewald (c. 1470–1528), were much less interested in Renaissance neo-classicism, as also were the singing tradition of *Meistersingers*, for which there were important schools at Augsburg and Nuremberg.

Gutenberg and Printing

In about 1450, Johannes Gutenberg (c. 1400–68) began using his first printing press in Mainz, where there is today an excellent museum devoted to printing. A goldsmith, he took existing techniques and machines, notably engraving the reversed letter in the mould, as well as using the metal punch and presses, and created a system of printing using metal movable type with the reusability of individual letters. He also invented the ink for printing and discovered the importance of using paper rather than parchment in the printing process.

Gutenberg benefitted from the limited number of characters in western languages and from the availability of information about the properties of tin, lead and antimony – the metals used for type. The innovation spread rapidly, helped by the reputation of the Gutenberg Bible (1455). Gutenberg's apprentice, Konrad Sweynheim, who fled after the sack of Mainz in 1462, introduced the first printing press to Italy in 1464–5 with another German émigré, Arnold Pannartz. By 1500, there were presses in 236 towns in Europe.

The sack of Mainz was an episode in the Baden–Palatine War of 1461–2, arising from a disputed election to the archbishop-electorate of Mainz. The destructive conflict showed how disputes over ecclesiastical territories preceded the Reformation. The count palatine, Frederick I, emerged from the war victorious over Baden and Württemberg, while his ally, Adolph of Nassau, who became the archbishop-elector, overcame opposition in the city of Mainz and removed the city's privileges.

The Empire continued to be a system capable of generating outcomes. In 1422, a *Matrikel* (register) of the mobilisation of the imperial army was established, fixing the contingents in men and money that had to be provided by each principality or free city.

Moreover, the ability of imperial institutions to discharge functions and the capacity of the system to create new responses were shown in 1500–12 by the establishment of the ten *Kreise* (Imperial Circles), which provided a valuable intermediate level for cooperative purposes between the Imperial Diet and the individual territories of the Empire, although the Swiss Confederacy, Bohemia and northern Italy were left out. Indeed, the Reformation crisis helped undermine the potential for imperial reform and the discussion of national identity seen over the previous half-century, notably as a result of the 1495 Diet of Worms and the related process of governance through consensual administration as well as new institutions.

Thus, it was shown that certain problems could be solved on a regional level, while others were discussed through the Reichstag or Imperial Diet, institutionalised on a more formal basis from 1489. Previous attempts at reform at Diets had failed, in 1434–8, but in 1495 agreement was reached for a common penny tax and a 'perpetual public peace' banned feuds. The imperial chamber court was established, although the tax was abandoned in 1505. These reforms established the constitutional organisation of the Empire for the next three centuries and were important for German 'deep history', as they demonstrated the significance of regionalism and the apparent possibility of a decentralised political and administrative system.

3

The Battleground of
Religion, 1517–1648

....

Let us start not with Martin Luther or Emperor Charles V, but with Franz Schmidt (1555–1634). Son of a woodsman in the town of Hof, part of the territory of Margrave Albert of Brandenburg-Kulmbach, Schmidt followed his father, who had been enlisted by the margrave to act as a hangman.

Executioner at Bamberg from 1573, Franz took on the same role at Nuremberg in 1578, marrying his predecessor's daughter and becoming a wealthy citizen. In his journal he recorded 361 executions including breaking on the wheel, burning, hanging and beheading. Infanticide was a punishment for young women, reflecting the values of the period – men who abandoned mothers were ignored. Schmidt also recorded the crimes – many thefts, including those of animals. He took on another job as a healer, focusing on this work after retiring as an executioner in 1617. This was his world, in which the following occurred.

Germany was the prime setting for the Protestant Reformation, with its founder and greatest propagandist, Luther, travelling from Wittenberg, Saxony – where he was famously said to have attached his ninety-five points of defiance to the castle church door on 31 October 1517 – to affirm his dramatic, uncompromising and egotistic independence of faith before Emperor Charles V at Worms in 1521. The key foundation moment of Protestantism, this was also to be treated as an important occasion for modern German history. This is a Protestant view, but it is not only one taken by Protestants; thus, in 1983, when East Germany celebrated the hundredth anniversary of the death of Marx, it also marked the five-hundredth anniversary of the birth of Luther. For the communists, he was a progressive German and thus a figure worthy of memorialisation. The Reformation and, thereby, Protestantism were annexed to the communist state, which was a way to root the latter in the German past.

Wittenberg was celebrated and remains an interesting destination, not least for the paintings and books on display in the town's museums. Committed to the concept of people reading the Bible, Luther translated the New Testament into Saxon German, which standardised High German, and reaffirmed his commitment that holy scripture should be readily understandable, thus reducing the need for an intercessory clergy. Luther also wrote a series of accessible pamphlets and his supporters encouraged their dissemination.

Presenting this central episode in German history was much more problematic for Catholics and this remained the case, reaching throughout society as in the names used for christening by Protestants and Catholics. In his *Geschichte der Deutschen* (*History of the Germans*, 1785–1808), the Catholic scholar Michael Ignaz Schmidt (1736–94) offered a critical reading of the Reformation that fed into established patterns of religious animosity. In turn, Walhalla was the neo-classical pantheon, constructed in 1842, in which Ludwig I of Bavaria (r. 1825–48), a German nationalist, sought to commemorate 118 German worthies in order to help demonstrate an exemplary national cultural past and, thereby, Catholic Bavaria's role in representing Germany. There was a vexed debate as to whether to include Luther among the worthies. He was finally accepted as such as a translator of the Bible into German and thus a national figure, rather than the founder of Protestantism. It is a sign of a very different public culture of history, that Walhalla is now essentially an impressively sited architectural curiosity.

The powerful assertion, in response to the certainty of sin, of justification through faith in the promise of Christ and the certainty of grace rather than winning salvation by means of good works, criticism of the Church, the specific challenges of financing via indulgences, a sense that change was necessary, the particular pressures in a sequence of issues and conjunctures and the emphasis on scripture not least in the context of the impact of the new world of print, all helped to turn Luther into a cause. So it also became within influential groups, notably important princes, nobles and urban circles, a wish to break from Rome. That the Reformation also rapidly took off in other countries indicated that it was not specifically German, and so also for the conflicts of the wars of religion that were widespread over the following 150 years, most notably with the Thirty Years' War (1618-48).

Yet there was a key German dimension and not only in the origin and early history of the Reformation. It had significance for an assertion of Germanness, as with Martin Luther's *To the Christian Nobility of the German Nation* (1520), an important work – written in German, rather than Latin – in which he called on the laity to champion the reforming role the Church was unwilling to take. The laity was given a role akin to that held by secular priests, not least by Luther challenging the Church's sole right to interpret scripture and that of the pope alone to call a general council of the Church or discuss spiritual matters.

The maintenance of religious control became a key element of defending order. Thus, catechising (instructing) the young, religious education, confirmation, confession, preaching, the nature of church services and the building and decoration of churches, were all central and divisive. The same applied to conversion, publications, censorship, marriage, christening, the household and poor relief. Doctrinal, liturgical and organisational issues became of greater significance due to their linkage with the quest for salvation. In modern terms, soft power was as much at play as hard and that remained true in confessional terms into later German history. Religious soft power is still at stake today. Indeed, there has been a religious dimension to much of modern German history.

Yet, other themes were also present and provided different patterns of identity. The Reformation depended on support from some (but far from all) princes, cities and peasants. The last contributed to the Peasants' War of 1524–5, a major conflict motivated in large part by social tension and economic discontent, notably generated by rising population and rents. To a degree, this was encouraged by the volatile atmosphere in Reformation Europe, especially the questioning of authority, although some peasant communities remained bulwarks of Catholicism.

In the early stages of the Peasants' War, which embraced other social strata as well, rulers were frequently forced to rely on fortified positions such as Würzburg castle. However, in 1525, the forces of princely power restored control, benefiting from their military practice and confidence in battle, including through the use of cannon and cavalry. Short of weapons and of the necessary experience, the peasants were slaughtered in large numbers, which reflected social contempt, the fear they had created and the lack of restraint in counter-insurgency warfare.

Tilman Riemenschneider, c. 1460–1531

A superb sculptor and woodcarver who spent most of his life in Würzburg, Riemenschneider, like other members of the town council, was imprisoned and fined in 1525 for failing to oppose the peasants' army. A visit to the Main-Franconia Museum in Würzburg provides an opportunity to see the largest collection of his works. They show a vivid late Gothic style with richly expressive figures, and I can still recall first seeing them as a child. There is also a collection of his works at the Germanisches Nationalmuseum in Nuremberg.

In the twentieth century, communist authorities in East Germany (1949–90), attempting to establish a pedigree for social revolution, cited the book on the Peasant's War by Friedrich Engels, Karl Marx's most prominent supporter. Describing the struggle as a proto-communist revolution played down other interpretations, notably relating to the Reformation, and suited the need of the East German government to present themselves as nationalists, not least by allegedly demonstrating that East Germany, rather than capitalist rival West Germany, was the true heir of the progressive German past and of a German past presented as progressive.

In practice, there was no simple class conflict in the early sixteenth century, as was shown by the Knights' War of 1522–3, in which Free Imperial Knights, under pressure from economic and political change, turned against the princes, only to be defeated. The statue at Bad Kreuznach to their leader, Franz von Sickingen, and his ally, Ulrich von Hutten, was erected in 1889 as part of the memorialisation of the past that was so important in the late nineteenth century.

The Anabaptists – who took over Münster in 1534, establishing a reign of terror over the ungodly, only for the city to be successfully besieged in 1535 – provided a different form of radicalism. Their 'New Jerusalem' turned out to be deadly for the disciples: the three cages on the steeple of St Lambert's Church contained the bodies of three executed leaders, displayed as an exemplary form of public education. The entire episode demonstrated the presence of very radical alternatives – including polygamy – to social norms, but also that few pursued them.

A different strand of religious violence was directed against Jews, for example with their expulsion from Regensburg in 1519, after which the gravestones were removed from the Jewish cemeteries. Separately, Luther was antisemitic, as well as critical of the peasants.

Augsburg

A prosperous city that stood out in the sixteenth century, on the main route between Germany and Italy via the Brenner Pass and a key centre of trade and finance. Its wealthy Fugger family were major contributors to the finances of Charles V. Dedicated to Charles, a bird's-eye map of 1521 produced by the Augsburg goldsmith Jörg Seld (c. 1454– c. 1527) was the earliest-known plan view of a city north of the Alps. Modern tourists can see the Renaissance wealth in the shape of Maximilianstrasse, the town hall, the Fugger funeral chapel in St Anne's church, the buildings for the poor in the Fuggerei, and the art of the period, notably by Dürer, Holbein and Cranach the Elder, in the cathedral and the art gallery.

Principally preoccupied by war with France and the Turks – the latter advancing as far as Vienna in 1529 – facing disorder in Spain and not without his own uneasiness about the papacy, Charles V sought to keep Germany peaceful but spent insufficient time there and, in particular, suffered from not cultivating the Imperial Free Cities and the princes.

After an attempt at religious reconciliation failed at the Diet of Augsburg in 1530, the Protestant princes created the Schmalkaldic League in 1531. There was a long history of German territories making attempts to cooperate. In the sixteenth and seventeenth centuries, they tended to have a confessional basis. It is possibly only with the benefit of hindsight that such leagues can appear somewhat anachronistic then and later, notably in the eighteenth century.

We need to be cautious about suggesting there was some sort of early 'golden age' of German autonomous action that was overtaken by the rise of non-German powers and their intervention in

German politics. Thus, in the 1550s, the French supported the German Protestants.

The combination of leagues and foreign intervention accentuated the already significant contrast between national identity and state-making; but that was not inevitable. Alliances like the Schmalkaldic League were banned. They claimed to defend the interests of a group of imperial principalities or cities, according to the constitution, but raised their own troops and, by doing so, deprived the empire of vital resources. They formed a kind of parallel organisation to the Empire and thus undermined the latter.

Anxious to avoid war, Charles continued to hope that a general council of the Church could reunite Christendom. However, negotiations at the Diet of Regensburg (1541) failed, and, at the Diet of Worms (1545), the Protestants rejected the suggestion that a general council be held.

Meanwhile, in 1529, Landgrave Philip of Hesse, a leading princely supporter of Lutheranism, created the first academic chair in history in Germany, at the University of Marburg. Moreover, Antonius Corvinus (1501–53), a writer and theologian in the circle of Philip of Hesse, identified him as a new Charlemagne. This was an aspect of the argument that the territorial German princes, especially Philip, were the true heirs of the Roman emperors, one that challenged the claims made on Charles V's behalf.

Hermann von Wied, the archbishop-elector of Cologne (r. 1515–46), sought a broad-church compromise at the local level, but the papacy and Charles V rejected this and he was deposed by Pope Paul III. Victory over France, a truce with the Turks and the defeat in 1543 of William, Duke of Jülich-Cleves-Berg – none of which was inevitable – enabled Charles to act more widely. He insisted that he was doing so against disobedient vassals, rather than Protestants, when he defeated the larger army of the incompetent Elector John Frederick of Saxony and Philip of Hesse at

Mühlberg in Saxony in 1547. The victory was celebrated in a triumphant equestrian portrait of Charles by Titian. Charles used Spanish troops but also benefitted from the support of Protestant princes, notably Duke Maurice of Saxony, who had attacked John Frederick in 1546, thus reflecting the emperor's ability to profit from feuds between related princely families. Exploiting his victory, in 1548 Charles dictated peace terms at the 'Armed Diet' of Augsburg and acted against Protestant territories, for example taking control of Constance, one of many cities where the Reformation had been introduced.

Had Charles been able to sustain and further this result, the history of Germany might well have been very different: the Reformation would have been more clearly seen in a pattern of medieval politico-religious disorders, while bullion from the new world could have been used to give force to the traditional universalist aspirations of the emperors. However, a failure to produce a lasting religious settlement, divisions between Charles and his brother Ferdinand and the opportunism of Maurice of Saxony led to a French-supported rising that drove Charles from Germany in 1552.

A compromise, the Peace of Augsburg, agreed with the Protestant princes in 1555, drawing on the Peace of Passau of 1552 – between Ferdinand and the princes – allowed Lutheran rulers to make Lutheranism the religion of their territories. This was the principle of '*Cuius regio, eius religio*' ('Whose realm, his religion'), a principle not extended to ecclesiastical rulers. If Protestantism had been practised from the 1520s, cities were exempted from the clauses on religious uniformity. In contrast, there was no universal right to religious choice, which put princes who converted to Calvinism in difficulties, as well as all people living in territories with a ruler of a different religion.

Charles divided the Habsburg inheritance, crucially separating Spain, Spanish America, the Low Countries and Italy – which went to his son, Philip II – from the Habsburg hereditary lands which went to his brother Ferdinand, who became emperor. To a degree, this course of action weakened the emperors, as the Austrian Habsburgs lacked the resources that came from the dominions that went to the Spanish Habsburgs.

Religion helped to unite as well as divide. In the late fifteenth century, politics and warfare in northern Germany were only loosely connected to events in southern Germany, which was indeed distant. From the 1530s, by contrast, every local or regional conflict in which opponents were involved from different confessional options assumed a far greater nationwide importance. Moreover, alliances were formed comprising members across Germany of a confessional group. Propaganda helped lead to concern about confessional fortunes across Germany. Luther was a master of printed propaganda and Catholic publicists copied this energy.

Religion also became crucial in Protestant takeovers and secularisations of ecclesiastical principalities. These were significant politically, notably as three of the seven electors were clerics, the archbishops of Cologne, Mainz and Trier, and territorially. Prince-archbishoprics included Bremen and Magdeburg, while prince-bishoprics included Augsburg, Bamberg, Constance, Eichstätt, Freising, Halberstadt, Hildesheim, Minden, Münster, Osnabrück, Paderborn, Passau, Schwerin, Verden and Würzburg. Between them, they controlled a large portion of Germany, especially, but not only, in the Rhineland, the north-west and Franconia. The wealth of the clerics can be grasped from the squarely massive palace built at Aschaffenburg in 1605–14 for the archbishop of Mainz.

Conflict related to secularisation became most critical in the archbishopric-electorate of Cologne in 1583–8, where Bavarian and Spanish intervention thwarted the Protestants following the conversion of Gebhard Truchsess von Waldburg, the archbishop-elector, to Protestantism – in part because he wished to marry Agnes von Mansfeld-Eisleben, a Protestant canoness, which he did in 1583. The Bavarian candidate, Ernest, the son of Albert V of

Bavaria, was victorious and already bishop of Freising, Hildesheim and Liège, with Münster following in 1584. His win helped strengthen the position of the Bavarian Wittelsbachs as champions of Catholicism and provided the background to a Catholic revival in the Rhineland, with proselytism matched by coercion. The Wittelsbachs were archbishops of Cologne until 1761, which gave them another electorate. Protestant anxieties were increased by such signs of the vitality of the Counter-Reformation and this led to a parallel process of reform and confessionalism.

Causes and episodes of dispute were matched by efforts to maintain and impose order. Feuds were outlawed in 1495 – the last noble to organise a warlike feud in Franconia, Wilhelm von Grumbach, was executed in 1567 and his patron, Duke John Frederick of Saxony, became the emperor's prisoner. Long in dispute with the bishops of Würzburg over territorial claims, Grumbach had attacked Würzburg in 1563 and was placed under the 'imperial ban'. A very different sign of imperial vitality occurred in 1597 with the institutionalisation of the Reichspost – the postal system – as an imperial prerogative. This became an important means for the dissemination of information and opinion and was linked to the development soon after of newspapers.

Confessional tensions increased in the early seventeenth century, with the formation of the German Protestant Union in 1608 and the prospect of war in 1609–14 over the contested succession between the heirs of the two sisters on the death of the childless ruler to the united Rhenish duchies of Jülich, Cleve and Berg. This issue recurred until the 1740s. John Sigismund, Elector of Brandenburg (r. 1608–19), made gains from the Treaty of Xanten of 1614, in the shape of the territories of Cleve, Mark and Ravensberg. Separately, in 1618, he acquired the Duchy of Prussia through marriage to Anna of Prussia, although that remained under Polish suzerainty until the 1650s and did not become a kingdom until 1701. Nevertheless, for the sake of clarity, Brandenburg is referred to as Prussia from here on.

In the event, the Jülich-Cleve-Berg crisis caused only a local war. Indeed, what became the Thirty Years' War (1618–48) began as a rising against the Habsburg position in Bohemia (now Czech Republic). The Bohemians rejected the authority of the Habsburgs, who had held the elective crown for nearly a century, and elected Frederick V, Elector Palatine. A rash Calvinist, he was defeated by the Habsburgs in 1620 and Bohemia was Catholicised by his rival, Emperor Ferdinand II (r. 1619–37), supported by the Catholic Duke Maximilian of Bavaria and the Lutheran John George I, Elector of Saxony. The struggle should not be seen in simple confessional, Protestant-versus-Catholic terms: John George played his part not only because Ferdinand offered him Lusatia, the area round Bautzen and Görlitz, but also because, like most Lutherans, he was hostile to Calvinists and, like most German princes, he was worried about violent disruption of the Empire and was loyal to both the emperor and the imperial constitution.

In turn, the Spaniards in 1620 overran the Lower Palatinate, helped by the ambitious Maximilian, to whom the electoral dignity (but not the territory) was transferred in 1623. The competition of the Bavarian branch of the Wittelsbach family with the Palatine branch was a prominent instance of the divisions between and within German ruling houses that were played out more widely across the Empire. Maximilian had already overrun the Upper Palatinate, authority over which he received from Ferdinand II. Ferdinand's commitment to Maximilian helped transform the struggle, making it more clearly one involving Germany and religion, and being presented in part as a struggle between the emperor and German liberties. Christian of Brunswick and Peter, Count of Mansfield, fought on behalf of Frederick V, both being repeatedly defeated and also causing great damage.

Albrecht Wallenstein (1583–1634) was a key military figure, a Bohemian military entrepreneur to whom Emperor Ferdinand II entrusted his forces. On his estates, Wallenstein produced bread, beer, clothing and footwear, and bred horses, all of which he charged to the emperor. Using Bohemian resources freed up by the suppression of rebellion and the consequent expropriation of land, he built up a large, imperial army. He exercised total control over the troops, receiving contributions and seizing supplies, in the process causing great damage to Brandenburg and other principalities. Their dukes deposed for rebellion, two duchies of Mecklenburg were given to Wallenstein.

By 1629, the Catholic powers had become dominant in Germany and foreign intervention in the shape of the Danes had totally failed: Denmark's Christian IV, who was also Duke of Holstein, had been heavily defeated at Lutter in 1626. Success led Ferdinand II to expand his goals, notably as far as the recovery of the north German prince-bishoprics was concerned. Yet again, the prospect of a very different Germany came to the fore, one symbolised by the Edict of Restitution of 1629, returning secularised church lands and enforced by imperial troops supporting themselves by 'contributions' – war taxation, which was a heavy burden. Yet, this edict did not amount to the extinction of German Protestantism. Moreover, alongside the desire of Ferdinand II to trade Wallenstein for support for the election of his son as King of the Romans, there was a justified sense that the general had built up an expensive army that was not under the emperor's control. Ferdinand II, under pressure in 1630 at the Diet of Regensburg, dismissed Wallenstein.

As with other conflicts, the war had many causes. These included constitutional factors, notably the role of the emperor, religious division, foreign intervention and military exigencies. None of these were new and there was no more inevitability in the course of conflict than there had been in 1546–52.

The situation was overturned by the anti-Habsburg intervention of the Swedes (1630) and French (1635). Swedish forces under king Gustav Adolphus landed in Pomerania in 1630, and Saxony defected from the imperial side in 1631. The Swedes defeated the main imperial army at Breitenfeld in 1631 and, in 1632, fought their way into Bavaria, capturing Munich, only to return northwards, fighting the imperialists under a recalled Wallenstein at Lützen, The Swedish king was killed but his side was victorious, although levying of contributions by the Swedes and the allied League of Heilbronn, founded in 1633, undermined their campaign that year in south Germany. The Swedes and their allies were totally defeated the following year at Nördlingen by a much larger Habsburg force composed of Austrian and Spanish units.

In turn, a German solution was found, with most German princes reconciled to the emperor: Saxony by the Peace of Prague of 1635, which dissolved the Heilbronn and Catholic Leagues and revoked the Edict of Restitution. The principle of *cuius regio* was re-established – although again not for Calvinists – which was an important aspect of the war as an episode in state building. A distrusted Wallenstein had been killed at the emperor's behest in 1634. By 1643, among the major German states, only Hesse-Cassel – a Calvinist territory under the regency of the widowed Landgravine, the effective Amalie Elisabeth – was still at war with Austria. The desire for peace was widely expressed in German pamphlet literature of the period.

In the latter stages of the war, alongside a reliance on garrisons guarding areas from which necessary contributions were raised, smaller field forces were used, including cavalry that, despite the latter costing more to hire and pay, provided important opportunities for wide-ranging campaigning. Although serious difficulties in the supply of men, money and provisions were important to the outcome of campaigns, they did not prevent campaigning.

Dominating north Germany – notably, but not only, Brandenburg (under the ineffective George William, r. 1619–40), from which they raised contributions as they chose – the Swedes had a logistical basis for operations to the south. For them, and others, areas seen as resource-rich attracted particular attention. An example was the French interest in Swabia in the 1640s. These contrasted with areas that were essentially ravaged rather than occupied, as Bavaria was by the French and Swedes, whose armies knew they could not overwinter. The ability of French and Swedish forces to advance far into the Empire – the Swedes to Bavaria and Bohemia – helped lead Ferdinand III to terms. Faced by frequent advances – notably by Sweden after its victory at the Second Battle of Breitenfeld in 1642 – it was necessary to bring Sweden and France into any settlement.

Signed at Münster and Osnabrück, the treaties that ended the war in 1648 are known as the Peace of Westphalia. The Austrian Habsburgs were left in secure control of their hereditary lands, while the Swedes gained much of Pomerania and the ecclesiastical principalities of Bremen and Verden, winning control over the estuaries of the Elbe, Oder and Weser. Prussian gains included eastern Pomerania, the prince-bishoprics of Halberstadt and Minden and the reversion to the prince-archbishopric of Magdeburg (which they gained in 1680). Prussia became, alongside Saxony, one of the two leading north German Protestant states. It also made more substantial gains between 1610 and 1680 than Saxony, even though, partly due to vulnerability to Sweden, it was more a victim of wholesale destruction in the Thirty Years' War.

Benefitting from peace coming before its descent into the civil war of the *Fronde*, France gained control over much of Alsace. The Upper Palatinate became part of Bavaria, which kept its electoral position, but the more prosperous Lower was restored to the Palatine branch of the Wittelsbach family, as was its electorate, so that there were now eight electors. In an important amendment to the 1555 Augsburg agreement, Calvinism was accepted as a permitted religion. Rulers in the Empire were allowed to ally among themselves – and with foreign powers – to ensure their preservation and security, but not to ally for offensive purposes and only on condition that the alliances were not directed against the emperor, the Empire, or the terms of the treaty.

Made guarantors of the peace, France and Sweden were given opportunities to interfere in German politics. This was taken further in 1658 when France sponsored the League of the Rhine, consisting of German rulers who allied with France and promised not to allow troops hostile to France to move into their territory. This protected France's eastern border, the league including the archbishop-electors of Cologne, Mainz and Trier, as well as the rulers of Bavaria, Brunswick, Hesse-Cassel and others. The league, which officially came to an end in 1667, demonstrated the practical difficulty of ensuring that the Westphalian treaties did not greatly limit the emperor; although, examined from another perspective, that settlement had simply accepted and codified the existing situation.

The War Recalled?

Written by Hans Jakob Christoffel von Grimmelshausen (1621–76) in 1668, *Simplicius Simplicissimus* is a picaresque novel offering a grim account of the Thirty Years' War in which the young protagonist loses his home as a result of troops seeking supplies. Popular in its time, the work continues to provide a modern reference point for the war, although the extent to which it was autobiographical – based on Grimmelshausen's period in Hessian and Austrian units – as opposed to drawing on hearsay and imagination is much discussed. The impact of the war was also seen in the work of another writer, the poet and dramatist Andreas Gryphius (1616–64), who sought to bring out the poetic possibilities of the German language.

It is difficult to disentangle the effects of war from the more widespread economic and population downturn that affected Europe (and the world as a whole) in the seventeenth century. This was a period in which the little ice age was particularly acute, with the cold weather affecting crops and diets, causing hunger and poverty and exacerbating the impact of disease. As a result, fantasies about feasts played a part in folktales, while the winter weather encouraged a reading of the springtime Good Friday as being redemptive. In part, the structural characteristics of local societies and economies were crucial to their very different demographic response to frequently similar experiences of war.

It is also necessary to distinguish between the actual devastation wrought by military action – most notably by the imperial forces storming Magdeburg in 1631 – and the eating of human flesh in Augsburg in 1635, and attendant pressures of the conflict. For many, the first stage of war was most damaging due to the *Kipperzeit*, a widespread and disruptive currency inflation. Wartime taxation hit purchasing power, depressed demand, affected trade and industry and damaged town economies, while the uncertainties of the period exacerbated anxieties about witchcraft. The spread of hostilities accentuated demographic and economic pressures, producing both immediate devastation and longer-term difficulties. The relative demographic 'weight' of France over the following 150 years was in part a consequence of the Thirty Years' War.

Apologising for the Past

Most of our contemporary 'history wars' – the often heated debates over the interpretation and meaning of historical events – relate to the last 110 years, but some relate to long-established tensions, notably that of Protestantism and Catholicism, while others refer to more recent concerns.

Thus, in 2020, Bishop Gregor Hanke of Eichstätt, long a centre of firm Catholicism, described the witch trials of the early modern period as a 'bleeding wound in the history of our church' and undertook to place a memorial plaque in the cathedral. In a campaign begun in 2011, over fifty towns have apologised. The degree of apology allegedly necessary is a matter of dispute, while the issue itself is part of the current critique of the Catholic Church.

Bamberg and Würzburg were other major centres of witch-burning, with Bishop Julius Echter von Mespelbrunn of Würzburg (r. 1573–1617) particularly active. He was also the founder of the University of Würzburg and a zealous supporter of the Counter-Reformation.

Witch-burning, however, reflected not only the bishop's own policies, but also the views across local society. There was also witch-burning in Protestant territories, such as the Imperial Free City of Nördlingen. As part of a far wider social engagement with occult elements and astrological meanings, witches were frequently blamed for disastrous weather, notably hail. There were other unfounded claims, for example of cannibalism, but they were less common.

At the same time, the religious and political compromises of the war lessened conflict within Germany for nearly a century. Moreover, the major efforts made by German rulers to fight France and the Turks in this period suggest that the war had not exhausted the Empire.

The Westphalian Settlement provides an opportunity to assess the Empire, which was long presented as an anachronism, a tradition encouraged by German nationalist scholars, notably from the nineteenth century. This reflected both the apparent failure of the Empire to resist French expansionism and the sense that a continued Austrian/Habsburg role in Germany through the Empire and the status of successive Habsburg rulers of Austria as emperor was redundant. Not only were they seen as unsuccessful, but also other forms of state development were presented as progressive. The inability to stop internal conflict and external devastation in the Thirty Years' War appeared to demonstrate this.

However, in recent scholarship, a different approach has stressed the ability of the Empire's federal structure to cope with many difficulties arising from confessional differences. Indeed, between 1555 and 1600, conflict within the Empire was less serious than in France, the Low Countries and the British Isles, while the protraction of what became the Thirty Years' War, notably beyond 1628, owed much to foreign intervention.

As with the Peace of Augsburg of 1555, the Westphalian Settlement should not be seen in terms of failure. Aside from bringing peace, it reflected a determination to make a federal system work and, in particular, to retain an imperial constitution with imperial mediating courts and an emperor unable to wield power comparable to that of some other sovereign rulers. Imperial princes willingly cooperated with him, in part as a consequence of a political culture that encouraged loyalty and provided reasons to remain obedient and to settle differences through mutual agreement. This position was very much taken by the electors of Saxony. They saw their leadership of the *Corpus Evangelicorum* (the Protestant body in the Empire) not as a cause for seeking chaos in order to foster Lutheranism, but as an opportunity to contribute to the Empire's stability.

The effectiveness of the *Kreise*, which continued until the end of the Empire, varied. Moreover, they were very much subject to the power politics of the local territorial states, with major rulers often attempting to ignore their injunctions. Thus, Bavaria very much dominated the Bavarian circle. Nevertheless, the *Kreise* provided a way to focus regional interests, to ensure that regional leagues did not become a disruptive model for German politics and to utilise the ambitions of territorial rulers in achieving wider goals. This was seen in Swabia where, in an area containing a large number of weak rulers, the *Kreise* played an important role in organising support for the defence of the Empire against France and the Turks in the late seventeenth century, with special taxes raised accordingly – the *Römermonat* and *Türkenhilfe*.

In reaction to the Thirty Years' War, there was a strong attempt to make the imperial system work, as well as a greater degree of elite cohesion within territories. Moreover, this effort paid off – as was seen in the firm resistance to French attacks in the Upper Rhineland in the mid-1670s and again against France in the early eighteenth century. One legacy is the Turenne monument, which marks the killing of the French general at the battle of Sasbach in 1675.

The pervasive element of social difference provided a fundamental context, as it did elsewhere, but more so than in Britain or the Netherlands. Symbolism was a continual reiteration of exclusiveness; the nobility, for example, had the sole right to certain forms of address, such as '*Fräulein*' for an unmarried young woman. Augsburg was typical in women's clothes varying according to their social position. In Frankfurt-on-Main, the merchants and principal citizens constituted a social world separate from that of the nobility, who would not admit them into their assemblies. Social distinctions protected the world of hierarchy; for example, with graded seating for the public concerts at Frankfurt.

The nobility dominated appointments to senior positions in the Church. In the cathedral chapter of the Catholic prince-archbishopric of Münster, each of the sixteen great-great-grandparents of the candidate had to have been noble. It was the same with Protestant states, where princely control was even more apparent as the key requirement: in Prussia, nobles received monastic and collegiate prebends from the government and, more generally, the Church fitted into the social order and into its patronage priorities.

Control over rural Germany varied greatly, in part as a result of the structure of rule and governance, with its highly distinctive privileges. There were about 350 families of Free Imperial Knights, exercising authority over about 1,500 small territories with a combined population of about 350,000. They possessed sovereign rights, including the rights to levy taxes, conscript troops and decree capital punishment.

Slavery was absent from Germany, having been denounced in the *Sachsenspiegel* compendium of laws written in 1220–35. Serfdom – forced labour based on hereditary bondage to the land – could be found across much of the Empire, but its character was not generally as harsh as that of serfdom in eastern Europe, notably Russia, although the burden could still be heavy. Labour services by serfs were generally performed for landlords east of the Elbe, while to the west of the river they worked for the ruler. In addition, dues were paid to the landlord for the land cultivated and to the lord on a variety of occasions, including marriage and death.

As was often the case in Germany, situations varied greatly by territory. In East Friesland, most land was allodial – not held under feudal tenures – and there was no tradition of serfdom. Moreover, all those possessing a small amount of land in freehold or tenancy or having a certain amount of capital could attend community assemblies and elect deputies to the Diet, where there was a third estate of independent farmers. The peasantry of nearby Friesian West Holstein and Dithmarschen (part of Schleswig-Holstein) were also in a strong position. Dithmarschen's peasants fought off would-be conquerors, notably in 1319, 1403 and 1500, only finally succumbing to Danish and Holstein attack in 1559. Despite that defeat, they continued to enjoy considerable autonomy.

Elsewhere in the Empire, the situation was less favourable, although generalisation is dangerous. Thus, in the Prussian territory of Minden, there were three groups of peasants: serfs, those tied to the soil by local custom, and free peasants exempt from labour services. In Hesse-Cassel, the type and extent of peasant obligations varied regionally and within the same community. Peasants were not bound to the soil, but could leave the state on paying a small fee. Like many German peasants, they enjoyed in practice hereditary tenure of the land they cultivated. Alongside burdens, lords could at least provide protection, including from the demands of the state. More generally, peasants' use of the imperial court system to press complaints has been put forward as an explanation for the relative lack of violent protest.

The peasantry, including the appreciable and growing numbers of landless labourers, notably in Saxony, Thuringia and Westphalia, faced different difficulties. Of the agrarian working population in Saxony in 1750, 30 per cent had little or no land and relied on wage labour. Yet, whether or not they controlled some land, there was a common dependence on an environment made even more difficult by the little ice age, with hard labour the fate of all; women as well as men.

To end the coverage of this period at this point would be to neglect the opportunity to discuss the importance of a non-subject – namely, Germany's failure to act as a significant player in European expansion. The sixteenth and early seventeenth centuries were very important in the creation of transoceanic European territorial and commercial presences. States seriously divided by civil war still managed to create a notable presence, particularly France. Yet, the significant part of the one-time Empire in this position was the United Provinces (Netherlands) which were, in effect, independent, a position confirmed in 1648. A smaller transoceanic presence was that of Denmark, which ruled a part of the Empire, that part not being of consequence in this respect.

The Hanseatic League had a major maritime presence in northern Europe and was well capable of engaging in conflict, but this period was one of decline rather than expansion. This also held true for Genoa and Venice. Indeed, city states that were not closely linked to major states, as Genoa was to Spain, found the period to be one of fewer opportunities and shrank, essentially until they held only regional significance.

Germany only reached the sea in the area of Hanseatic influence, but the potential role of its cities was lessened by the Reformation, which cut off any prospect of alignment with the emperor. Moreover, the cities were affected by Danish and, subsequently, Swedish expansionism, and by the protectionist role of German principalities.

In theory, the Hanseatic League could have gone the way of the cities of Holland and Zealand, becoming key players in a new Protestant federal polity, so that Hamburg could have emulated Amsterdam; but that was not feasible in terms of the local and regional power politics. Nor did it reflect the aspirations of the cities. As a consequence, there was no transoceanic-fuelled development of maritime Germany, although German financial and mercantile interests benefitted from the imperial activities of other powers; for example, the Welser family from 1528 in Spanish-ruled Venezuela. Another Augsburg family, the Fuggers, used their financial links with Charles V, who needed their ability to raise loans in order to invest in Spanish America, although that was not to be their key activity.

The histories of all countries involve turns not taken. The lack of foundations for a German overseas empire in this period was one of the most important of those roads untravelled and affected not only Germany's options in the wider world, but also Germany itself.

4

Baroque Germany, 1648–1755

'The government of Arenberg, a place in the diocese of
Cologne, having lately driven out two Osnabruck and one
Celle regiment that had taken quarters in their territory,
which they did by six thousand peasants whom they raised
upon them on a sudden ... this affront is highly resented by
those dukes ... they have given out orders to some new forces
to march into the same quarters who it is supposed will
severely revenge the disgrace put upon their companions.'

Roger Meredith, 1676

In her first play, *Die Pietisterey im Fischbein-Rocke* (1736), Luise
Gottsched (1713–62), an important figure in the development of
German theatrical comedy, has her heroine, Luischen, not daring
to defy her mother and marry her fiancé and instead resign
herself to her fate. Her wicked sister, Dorchen, laughs at her
concern with respecting parental wishes. Luischen is rewarded
when her father overturns her mother's wishes, while Dorchen is
promised a husband – but only when she agrees to behave. This
evasion of the problems of patriarchal authority was also symptomatic of a recognition of current realities.

POLITICS

There was a parallel of sorts with the political situation, one that
was later to lead to criticism when it was argued that the
Westphalian Peace Settlement kept Germany weak and prey for
external attack, notably by allowing territorial rulers to ally with
foreign powers, as in the French-backed League of the Rhine in

the 1650s. In addition, the Empire's constitutional structures were presented as anachronistic, involving archaic legal cases rather than effective decision-making. The four Austro–Prussian wars, of 1740–2, 1744–5, 1756–63 and 1778–9, supposedly exposed the fundamental weakness of the Empire, while its eventual destruction by Napoleon in 1806 was seen both as long overdue and as a fundamental stage in the evolution of modern Germany.

In practice, however, the extent to which these wars reflected and caused the breakdown of the imperial system is questionable. It is certainly important to distinguish between crises and breakdown. It is the durability of the imperial idea that emerges clearly, not least in response to what were seen as attempts by emperors to infringe the rubric and meaning of the constitution, as with successive oppositions – to Ferdinand II in 1630, Charles VI in the 1720s and Joseph II in 1785, the last opposition leading to the creation of a *Fürstenbund* ('League of Princes').

Alongside this durability, certain practices caused volatility. The clarification of rights and authority led to disputes. For example, the situation with regard to Hamburg was open and, in legal terms, poorly defined. Using the emperor as a mediator in legal disputes with German and foreign governments, Hamburg claimed to be an Imperial Free City when the king of Denmark demanded taxes from this obvious source of profit and, in contrast, a *Landstadt* (subject town) when the emperor did so, which caused repeated tension when there were attempts to clarify the position. Thus, in 1679, Louis XIV and the dukes of Brunswick blocked a Dano–Prussian attempt to coerce Hamburg. There were other Danish efforts in the eighteenth century and these led the city to appeal for support from foreign powers, such as Britain, as well as the imperial courts.

Hamburg was far from alone. In 1670–1, the Duke of Brunswick-Wolfenbüttel and the prince-bishop of Münster, who were on rival confessional sides, differed over the suzerainty of a Westphalian town, while the Imperial Free City of Cologne and the archbishop-elector of Cologne, whose territories did not include the city, also clashed.

Minor rulers suffered particularly harshly in wartime, notably from forcible billeting, compulsory contributions and recruiting. Thus, Hesse-Darmstadt was burdened with French winter quarters in 1744–5 and the electorate of Mainz was troubled by their exactions the following spring. In 1748, the landgrave of Hesse-Cassel informed George II, who had sought permission for his Russian allies to cross Hesse, that Hesse-Cassel had been affected by the nearly continual march of troops.

The division of inheritances was also an issue. Hesse in 1567 was divided among the four sons of Landgrave Philip, helping to establish a longstanding division between Hesse-Cassel and Hesse-Darmstadt – not least over the future of the weaker branches, Hesse-Marburg and Hesse-Rheinfels. Whereas the partitions of 1308 and 1458 had ended in 1310 and 1500, that of 1567 did not. Moreover, the Ernestine inheritance split into many branches. This was an aspect of a parcelisation or miniaturisation that helped affect practices and attitudes, including cultural assumptions. In contrast, in 1656, Elector John George I of Saxony gave his three younger sons principalities: Saxe-Weissenfels, Saxe-Merseburg and Saxe-Zeitz, but he did not grant independence and the branches died out by 1747.

Far from being prone to division, Hanover and Prussia were consolidated. The former brought together most of the branches of the divided Guelph inheritance – although Brunswick Wolfenbüttel was never included. The latter was the realisation of the Hohenzollern family diplomacy that brought Brandenburg, East Prussia, Cleves and Mark under one ruler, while its army maximised the war-making potential of the close links between the Hohenzollerns and the landowners.

Similarly, the extinction of branches of the Wittelsbach family in 1685, 1742, 1777 and 1779 led to a process of amalgamation. In part, this extinction reflected the extent to which Catholic clerics became ecclesiastical rulers, thus reducing the number of spare sons able to marry. Before he was appointed at Cologne in 1688 and to the prince-bishoprics of Liège and Hildesheim, Joseph Clemens, 1671–1723, had already become prince-bishop of Freising in 1684 and of Regensburg in 1685, both principalities that increased the regional power of Bavaria. Known as the '*Sieur des Cinque Églises*' because of his accumulation of titles, he was succeeded at Cologne by his nephew, Clemens August, who was also prince-bishop of Regensburg, Münster, Hildesheim and Osnabrück. His brother, Johann Theodor, was prince-bishop of Freising, Liège and Regensburg.

A sense of responsibility to descendants, as well as predecessors, was captured by the Duke of Holstein-Gottorp when he told a French diplomat in 1725 that he preferred to rely on providence and wait for helpful international developments, rather than to take any step that would render him contemptible to his succession. The dukes of Baden-Durlach devoted their efforts in mid-century to gaining the succession to the Duchy of Baden-Baden, whose male line was dying out and, in 1771, negotiated an acceptable agreement.

Circumstances played a key role, notably the end of lines that terminated independence for territories, as with the acquisition of East Friesland (1744), Ansbach (1791), and Bayreuth (1791) by Prussia. In addition, across their domains, the Prussian rulers increased their power over subordinate institutions. Yet, while, in Württemberg as in Prussia, institutional development and ruler–estate relations were fuelled primarily by fiscal requirements arising from competitive international relations, the dukes of Württemberg failed totally to emulate the rulers of Prussia. In part, this reflected differences in political culture and practice, as the dukes lacked the regional power of the Prussians and, if they could, most lesser German princes were not prepared to surrender the initiative to stronger neighbours. Moreover, a large proportion of the Württemberg nobility were Imperial Knights.

Confessional rivalry also played a role in the failure of the dukes of Württemberg, a Lutheran territory, where a Catholic succeeded in 1733. This was a period of continued religious tension. A confessional conflict in Germany had appeared imminent both in the 1710s and in the late 1720s. Count Frederick Schönborn, the imperial vice-chancellor from 1705 to 1734, sought to enhance imperial authority and to use it to further Catholic interests. In some respects, Frederick the Great of Prussia represented a Protestant counter-offensive, albeit one very much affected by Prussian interests. As a reminder of the number of elements at play in dynasticism, he had only succeeded to the throne because his two elder brothers had both died before the age of one. Wars with Austria permitted his presentation as a Protestant hero. In a major development in German identity, Prussia had taken this role from Saxony and Sweden.

A number of German princely families, including the electors of Saxony, the Electors Palatine and the dukes of Württemberg, converted to Catholicism, but crucially not the electors of Brandenburg (kings in Prussia from 1701) nor Hanover, which became the ninth electorate in 1692. Although those who converted could no longer change the religion of their territories, there was considerable unease, not least because of the experience of the Palatinate after the accession of Catholic electors. When Count Moritz-Wilhelm of Saxony-Zeist converted to Catholicism in 1717, he was expelled from his duchy by the diocesan chapter, as Zeitz was a bishopric converted to Protestantism. The conversion to Catholicism of Frederick, the heir to Hesse-Cassel, in 1749, led his father, William VIII, to force on him a succession agreement restricting his ability to appoint Catholics and removing confessional matters and the education of his children from his control.

With their bounds established by feudal, rather than geographical, considerations, individual territories were vulnerable to attack. Thus, Hanover lacked defensive frontiers: while most of it was between the Elbe and Weser rivers, the North Sea and the Harz mountains, there were also important sections that were more vulnerable west of the Weser or east of the Elbe.

The East Friesland Dispute

The problems of the imperial system, including the interaction of power politics and jurisdiction, were exemplified in the dispute over the long-anticipated end of the ducal Cirksena family. In 1691, a mutual succession agreement with Hanover was confirmed, but in 1694 Emperor Leopold I granted the ruler of Prussia a right of succession. Danish and Dutch interest in the area compounded the problem and a civil war broke out in 1724–7 between Duke George Albert and the powerful estates. The East Friesland issue embittered Hanoverian–Prussian relations and the exercise of imperial authority in the dispute fortified fears about Austrian intentions.

WAR

External pressure was a major element in the politics of all parts of the Empire, including those far from its frontiers. Thus, French troops joined the forces of the French-sponsored League of the Rhine in 1664 in ending resistance by the city of Erfurt to the overlordship of the archbishop-elector of Mainz. Under Louis XIV (r. 1643–1715), French influence and pressure reached an unprecedented level. The 1660s also saw active cooperation with the prince-archbishop of Münster against the Dutch. In part by offering subsidies, Louis persuaded many German rulers into his system concluding, for example, treaties with Bavaria (1670) and Cologne (1671), prior to his 1672 attack on the Dutch. Louis benefitted from these alliances when he crossed the Rhine and invaded the Netherlands from the east.

Moreover, Louis pushed France's frontier eastwards and not only at the expense of Spanish possessions. In Alsace, France replaced the ambiguous relationship established under the Peace of Westphalia of 1648 by more clear-cut control. The gains of Freiburg in 1678 and of Strasbourg in 1681 took France into a dominant position in the Upper Rhineland. In addition, in the early 1680s, the French, in the *réunions*, used claims to the dependencies of territories ceded to the French crown to seize much of the Empire west of the Rhine and south of the Moselle, a process showing contempt for all other views. Furthermore, 1679 saw a secret alliance between Louis and Elector Frederick William of Brandenburg-Prussia, the Great Elector, a product of Prussian anger with the emperor, and the extent to which the French invasion of Cleves had obliged Prussia to return gains recently made from a defeated Sweden.

Under the twenty-year Truce of Regensburg of 1684, Louis was left in control of his gains, but Austria's success against the Turks weakened his relative position. So also did the distrust stemming from France's construction of new fortifications in the Empire at strategic points, including Landau and Trarbach. In 1686, German princes created the League of Augsburg, designed to guarantee the public security of the Empire and stipulating military quotas. The league was formed under imperial sponsorship and was a vehicle for the revival of Austrian influence within the Empire, which constituted an obvious contrast to the French sponsorship of the League of the Rhine in the 1650s. Growing hostility towards France was linked to an increased tendency to rely on the emperor. In 1685, Maximilian II (Max Emanuel), elector of Bavaria (r. 1679–1726), married Emperor Leopold I's daughter, a key currency of German dynastic politics. Moreover, Louis XIV's moves against French Protestants helped lead Prussia to sign a treaty with Leopold in 1686 and, separately, to offer shelter to Protestants, a large number of whom moved to Berlin, where they became important for Prussia's population and for its economic and cultural dynamic.

Louis' quest to dominate what was called 'near France' had obvious implications for Germany. In 1685, the succession of a new ruler to the electorate of the Palatinate led Louis to advance claims on behalf of his Palatine sister-in-law. In addition, the apparently imminent death of another Rhenish elector, the archbishop of Cologne, encouraged Louis to seek the succession of a sympathetic cleric. These became important tests of determination and, in 1688, Louis decided that it was necessary to demonstrate his power and the vulnerability of the Rhineland.

A large army, under the ostensible command of the dauphin, besieged Philippsburg, the major imperial fortress in the Middle Rhine. Louis demanded the acceptance of his candidate in Cologne and acknowledgment that his gains under the *réunions* were permanent. While Philippsburg did fall, German resistance gathered pace. As part of a wider European move to contain French influence, the willingness of Brandenburg, Hesse-Cassel, Brunswick-Wolftenbüttel, Saxony and Württemberg helped to reassure William III about the security of the continent. He invaded Britain in 1688. Hessian troops moved into Coblenz and Saxons into Frankfurt. That October – underlining the extent to which imperial structures could not provide the solution – Hanover, Hesse-Cassel, Prussia and Saxony concluded a treaty of alliance for the defence of the Middle Rhine.

In order to intimidate their opponents and to strengthen their defences, the French devastated much of south-western Germany in 1689, touching off a guerrilla struggle in the Palatinate and accentuating the anti-French nature of German patriotism, prefiguring the later response to depredations under the French Revolution and Napoleon. The damage was still readily apparent to travellers in the 1720s.

The war, variously known as the War of the Palatine Succession, Nine Years' War, the War of the League of Augsburg and King William's War, broadened out, notably with British intervention against France. In the eventual peace, the Treaty of Rijswijk of 1697, Louis had to return many *réunion* gains, as well as Freiburg, and got his way over neither Cologne nor the Palatinate, although his position in Alsace was recognised. In the subsequent conflict, focusing on the succession to the Spanish Habsburgs – the War of the Spanish Succession – most German princes backed Austria, with Prussia and Saxony rejecting French approaches.

In 1702, the territories of two of Louis' German allies, the elector of Cologne and the Duke of Brunswick-Wolfenbüttel, were overrun. To retain the support of the third – the most important, Max Emanuel of Bavaria – Louis promised to support his gain of the Lower Palatinate and the Spanish Netherlands (Belgium). This threatened a complete change in the political system within the Empire, which Louis deemed necessary if the Empire was not, as he preferred, neutral.

Bavaria, however, was completely overrun in 1704 after the total Franco-Bavarian defeat by an Anglo-Dutch-Austrian army under John, Duke of Marlborough and Prince Eugene of Savoy at Blenheim. Max Emanuel took refuge in Brussels. Responding to pressure from John William, Elector Palatine, Joseph I and the College of Electors placed the electors of Bavaria and Cologne under the imperial ban in 1706, depriving them of their rights and privileges. In turn, John William was invested with the Bavarian territory of the Upper Palatinate in 1708, although he was not to retain this in the subsequent peace.

As a reminder of the independence of the major principalities, Saxony gave only limited support to the allies during the war because most of its troops fought the Swedes during the Great Northern War in pursuit of the elector's interests as king of Poland. This only changed in 1706 when the advance of Charles XII of Sweden forced Saxony to sign the Treaty of Altranstädt, after which the Saxon troops were offered to the Dutch in return for subsidies.

The Imperial Circles and the Austrians sought a strong German barrier against France. In 1709, they demanded, as a condition of any peace, the three bishoprics of Metz, Toul and Verdun, which the French had acquired in 1552, as well as Strasbourg. In 1710, under the pressure of serious defeats, Louis was willing to exchange Alsace for the restoration of the electors of Bavaria and Cologne, but Allied divisions and French resilience helped France get better terms. Austria wished to retain Bavaria, while the Imperial Diet at Regensburg declared in 1713 that the French proposals would 'tarnish the glory of the German nation', but, outnumbered, abandoned by allies and pushed back by the French – who captured the fortresses of Freiburg, Kehl and Landau that year – the Austrians had to negotiate. In 1714, under the Peace of Rastatt, France retained Alsace but not any posses- sion on the right bank of the Rhine. This was a repetition of earlier terms that gave them authority and normality. Separately, Max Emanuel was restored, but without any territorial gains.

The interplay of threat was important to Germany's develop- ing politics, with Austria now the key player. France maintained permanent embassies at only a few German courts, while no British envoy was accredited to Munich between 1726 and 1746. Important Anglo-Wittelsbach discussions in the winters of 1728–9 and 1729–30 had to be handled at Paris. Defeated in the Great Northern War (1700–21), Sweden was no longer a signifi- cant presence or problem. Indeed, Russia was now more of an issue, a Russian army under Peter the Great overwintering in Mecklenburg in 1716–17 in preparation for an invasion of Sweden that was not mounted. In 1719–20, returning gains under the Westphalian Settlement, Sweden ceded Bremen and Verden to Hanover and Stettin and part of Western Pomerania to Prussia.

By the late 1720s, concern about the emperor's absolutist and indeed autocratic tendencies helped lead some German rulers to turn anew to France: treaties were signed with the elector of Bavaria and Elector Palatine, in 1727 and 1729 respectively. The French helped overcome the division between the two main branches of the Wittelsbachs that had greatly assisted the Austrians during the War of the Spanish Succession. Seeking to combine the Wittelsbachs with Protestant rulers, French efforts looked back to seventeenth-century policies. In 1727, 1729 and 1730, moreover, threats to Hanover from Austria and her allies, notably Prussia, led to plans for the movement of a French army into the Empire to provide protection: France was allied with Britain–Hanover in 1716–31.

Meanwhile, Bavaria and Saxony manoeuvred around the Austrian inheritance, advancing claims based on marriages with the daughters of Emperor Joseph I (r. 1705–11), whereas his young brother Charles VI (r. 1711–40), who also lacked sons, sought the entire succession for his elder daughter, Maria Theresa, by means of a legal device termed the 'pragmatic sanction'. France presented its opposition to the latter as designed to thwart Austrian desire for more power in the Empire, language that reprised criticism of Habsburg universalism in the sixteenth and early seventeenth centuries.

In 1732, France signed a subsidy treaty with Augustus II of Saxony and offered the assistance of troops to any Saxon–Bavarian action against the Habsburgs. In the event, the war that broke out in 1733 was over the Polish succession and saw Saxony align with Austria and Russia. France declared war on Austria and operated in the Rhineland, but no further east, which was the essential precondition of any action by vulnerable Bavaria. In the event, Bavaria remained neutral and, despite rumours, the French did not move into Cologne to gain a bridgehead over the Rhine.

The peace that came in 1735 did not end tensions, which appeared imminent over the Jülich-Berg inheritance in the late 1730s. Nevertheless, it is unclear what would have happened when Charles VI died in October 1740 had Frederick the Great

GERMANY

not attacked Maria Theresa by invading her Duchy of Silesia two months later, launching the War of the Austrian Succession. Maria Theresa's refusal to cede Silesia led Frederick to sign the Treaty of Breslau with France in June 1741, winning French promises of assistance that also involved Bavaria. The Prussian alliance increased French options, offering an alternative or addition to a treaty with the Wittelsbachs. Trying to create a powerful league, France helped secure an offensive alliance between Charles Albert of Bavaria – who was to become emperor and receive the Habsburg provinces of Bohemia, Upper Austria and Tyrol – and Augustus III of Saxony-Poland who was to become king of Moravia and gain Moravia and Upper Silesia. Furthermore, Prussia was increasingly more powerful than Hanover in Germany and lacked the complicating factor of Hanover's British links. Frederick William I had disliked taking an exposed position and was instinctively more pro-Austrian than French, but Frederick the Great was far more assertive and readier to turn to France.

French troops crossed the Rhine in August 1741 and in September Bavaria and Saxony entered the French system, prefiguring the Napoleonic attempt to redraw Europe's borders. Charles Albert of Bavaria was crowned Emperor Charles VII, at Frankfurt on 12 February 1742, the first non-Habsburg emperor since 1437.

France, however, failed; because of Austrian resilience, Russia's refusal to enter the French system and the fickleness of its allies. Frederick had observed in September 1740 that an alliance with France would leave him exposed. At Britain's behest – and encouraged by Austrian successes that included the capture of Munich – he abandoned France in 1742. This left Saxony in a difficult position. In addition, Bavarian subsidy demands placed a heavy burden on French finances while, in June 1743, the main French army in Germany was defeated at Dettingen near Mainz by George II of Britain–Hanover.

In 1744, the French returned with the Union of Frankfurt; a league with Bavaria, Prussia, Hesse-Cassel and the Palatinate designed to secure Charles's interests. The creation of this league was seen as a means of preserving the balance of the Empire against Austria and also as a tool of the French, in their attempts to destroy the European balance of power. It did not, however, shake Austrian power. The French captured Freiburg and Frederick the Great invaded Bohemia. However, in 1745, Bavaria was overrun by the Austrians and Maximilian Joseph, the new elector, abandoned France for Austria. Determined to exclude Francis Stephen of Lorraine – since 1736 the husband of Maria Theresa – France backed Augustus III of Saxony for the vacant imperial throne; but Francis was elected Francis I while, following the Prussian victory at Kesseldorf near Dresden, Austria and Saxony signed the Treaty of Dresden with Frederick the Great.

In 1747, France created a new alliance with Prussia and Sweden, but British-subsidised Russian forces kept the last two powers quiet and the peace in 1748 saw France unable to do anything for Bavaria. Frederick the Great and France remained allies, but each mistrustful of the other. Nevertheless, the French sought a post-war, broader German alliance system, including the Palatinate, Württemberg and Brunswick-Wolfenbüttel. In the event, French caution helped to restrain Prussia in the early 1750s. Meanwhile, Saxony tried to turn France against Prussia and the Austrians were casting about for those willing to accept – even support – their reconquest of Silesia. In 1756, angered by closer Anglo–Prussian relations, the Austrians turned to France and signed a defensive alliance, the First Treaty of Versailles. That proved to be a key step towards the outbreak of the Seven Years' War – with France and Austria allies against Prussia, which had attacked Saxony en route to invading Austria.

RELIGION

Religious belief, meanwhile, was buoyant. In the Catholic states, the Counter-Reformation piety that had begun in the sixteenth century came to fruition. There was also little doubt of the intensity of popular religiosity, both in the countryside and in cities such as Cologne, Coblenz, Mainz and Munich. Religious life was characterised by numerous services, processions, pilgrimages and confraternities. In addition, in Bavaria, the Church owned much of the land. This was the era of the great south German pilgrimage churches and monastery churches, which remain wonderful places to visit. Key artists of the period included the architects Dominikus Zimmermann (1685–1766) and Balthasar Neumann (1687–1753) and the sculptor Egid Asam (1692–1750). Others included Matthäus Daniel Pöppelmann and Balthasar Permoser for Saxony, Enrico Zuccali and Joseph Effner for Bavaria, and Andreas Schlütter for Prussia.

Protestantism also benefitted from cultural activity – as in the work of Johann Sebastian Bach (1685–1750) – as well as popular commitment and enthusiasm. As with the Reformation, cities and courts became key settings and significant centres for publications. Thus, Bach's son, Carl Philipp Emanuel (1714–88) produced a '*Versuch über die wahre Art das Clavier zu spielen*' ('Essay on the True Art of Playing Keyboard Instruments', 1753) that reflected his sensitive mastery of the solo keyboard. Carl Philipp Emanuel, who moved away from the Baroque style of his father and the *galante* Rococo of Frederick the Great to an *empfind-samkeit*, a style supposedly presenting true and natural emotions, paralleling the development in literature with Lessing and Klopstock, left the service of Frederick to become director of music at Hamburg, succeeding Georg Philipp Telemann.

Pietism, a north German development, was an attitude rather than a creed. Seeking to revive Protestantism, it called for the development of spiritual gifts among the flock. Philipp Spener (1635–1705), court chaplain in Saxony and then a refugee in Berlin, argued that faith had to be dependent on active piety. Pietists stressed the role of preaching and education, especially of the poor, and emphasised the importance of individual conversion.

Pietists presented the state as an institution designed to discipline and improve society and, alongside the dynastic imperative of loyalty and service to the Hohenzollerns – notably in the army – this contributed to the particular political culture of Prussia, one that made state service a form of morality. Halle University, founded in 1694 – where August Hermann Francke (1663–1727) was a highly influential professor of theology – encapsulated this linkage. Although far less significant, enthusiasm was more pronounced at Herrnhut, a Saxon religious community developed by the Pietist Count Zinzendorf and part of the 'Great Awakening' seen in John Wesley and Methodism.

Traditional astrological and occult beliefs and practices continued to play a large role, anticipating Carl Maria von Weber's opera *Der Freischütz* (1821), based on a story from Johann August Apel's *Das Gespensterbuch* (1811–15), featuring Samiel, the Black Huntsman, magic bullets, the selling of souls and eerie orchestration. Meanwhile, growing up in a Calvinist home in Nassau, the enlightened Baden bureaucrat Johann Reinhard (1714–72) encountered a world peopled largely by witches and ghosts, where the devil was omnipresent. Vampires and the supernatural played a role in Gottfried Bürger's influential ballad *Lenore* (1773). More mundanely, in an instance of uncertainty, bad harvests in the early 1740s pushed the price of grain up at Aachen, Leipzig and Nuremberg, hitting purchasing power and leading to cuts in the price of textiles.

ECONOMICS, GOVERNMENT AND SOCIETY

Human action was also a problem, some of it stemming from the particularism arising from the multiple nature of German statehood. On the Weser between Bremen and Minden, there were twenty-one toll stations and on the Rhine between Basle and Rotterdam there were thirty-eight. These frequent tolls had an effect. The Oder–Spree Canal, finished in 1668, its sluices rebuilt with stone in 1702, was in part designed to move goods to Hamburg, but tolls hit the trade. Conferences of representatives from states along the route failed to lower the tolls in 1685 and 1711. Tolls particularly discouraged the movement of low-cost items and inhibited regional specialisation. In 1747, Frederick the Great interrupted Saxon trade with Hamburg by forcing all ships on the Elbe to unload at his town of Magdeburg and the goods to move overland through Prussia before being loaded on Elbe ships again. Protectionism, however, frequently meant helping some producers at the expense of others, as in 1749 when Berlin's production of quality fabrics took precedence over those from the Prussian town of Krefeld. There was no equivalent in Britain.

Protectionism hit the Imperial Free Cities, many of which declined, in part due to a lack of political strength vis-à-vis the consolidating territorial states, their rural industries and protectionist economic policies. Another cause was the strength of their guilds. This was true of both Aachen and Cologne. Territorial states sometimes founded new towns, such as Karlsruhe in 1719, which became the capital of Baden. Indeed, many towns depended on the numerous princely courts, Dresden for Saxony being a notable example. It was estimated in 1785 that the move of the Palatine court from Mannheim to Munich – upon the extinction of the Bavarian Wittelsbachs in 1777 – had led to the former losing a third of its population.

States also sought to control existing cities; part of a long-standing pattern. Under Frederick William I of Prussia (r. 1713–40), many of the powers of the old town councils were transferred to agents of the central government as royal officials came to administer police and judicial functions. Government changes were sometimes matched by social legislation that restricted the rights of townsmen. The contempt with which these townsfolk were held by some rulers and by much of landed society is revealed in the table of ranks drawn up by Duke Eberhard Ludwig of Württemberg, in which army lieutenants preceded the mayors

of Stuttgart and Tübingen. At the same time, the oligarchs dominating the powerful municipal governments of cities had every
reason to champion the traditional tax structure; it placed a heavy
burden on the villages, which they also sought to direct financially
through their role in economic networks, notably the distribution
and processing of rural products – for example, textiles.

As elsewhere, both urban and rural society were highly inegalitarian, although much depended on local character and culture.
Thus, the administrative activities of Coblenz, the capital of the
electorate of Trier, played a major role in creating the great
economic and intellectual gulf between the small number of
wealthy, high-ranking lay and clerical officials – a largely inter-
related elite, open to new ideas and keen to reform the town's
economic and welfare policies – and the merchants, artisans and
petty bureaucrats, with their conservative and protectionist views.
The third section, the economically vulnerable and, often, socially
isolated day-labourers, servants and paupers, were a common
feature of urban society.

Many cities were similar capitals, and this created a culture and
society heavily focused on princely courts that leaves its legacy
today. Thus, Arolsen in northern Hesse was, from 1655 to 1918,
the residence of the counts – from 1712, princes – of Waldeck-
Pyrmont, a family that long supported its position by serving in
the Dutch army. A secularised nunnery was their residence until it
was replaced in 1713–28 by a new Baroque palace, in which the
family still lives. The town was organised in a geometric fashion in
the Baroque style. Such communities were commonplace, whether
or not the local landowning family was princely.

Much of the aristocracy across Germany, whether or not it was
princely and therefore enjoying territorial rights, fulfilled its
sense of identity and role, as well as obtaining funds and developing connections, through armed service. There was no difference
between service to 'foreign' rulers or German counterparts.
Instead, often – although not invariably – a more important

contrast emerged from whether this service was carried out for co-religionists – which was more normal – or for those of a differing creed. Thus, Protestant princes and nobles served in Dutch, Danish, Swedish and British armies while their Catholic counterparts served in the French, Portuguese, Spanish or, in particular, Austrian armies. Indeed, as in Italy, a key element of Austrian influence in the Empire was provided by such military service. Correspondingly, the growing ability of Prussia to dominate such service, attracting many non-Prussian and even non-German nobles into its ranks, was both cause and an expression of its position and strength. The situation was to change with German unification, until which time a very different ethos had value.

This was particularly seen in the extent to which German princes served at the head of considerable contingents in imperial forces fighting the Turks, including Margrave Louis of Baden-Baden, George I of Hanover, Max Emanuel of Bavaria and Charles V of Lorraine. Louis was known as '*Türkenlouis*' ('Turkish Louis') due to his many victories over the Turks, notably at Slankamen (1691), while Max Emanuel captured Belgrade in 1688. And so it went for other families in earlier conflicts, as in Austro–Turkish conflicts of 1593–1606 and 1663–64 and in subsequent wars, notably in 1716–18, 1737–9 and 1788–91, although far less so by the time of the bloody Austrian occupation of Bosnia in 1878.

Indeed, crusading ideology and practice in the shape of conflict with the Turks was important to German identity into the eighteenth century as a central part of an Empire that still had a valid role. Family tradition helped maintain this significance, but it was transferred after 1791 to a different context; that of great power competition between Christian powers. Success against the Turks, notably the conquest of much of Hungary in the war of 1683–99, and of the remainder in 1716–18, ensured that 'Austria' (the Austrian Habsburg monarchy) had an important alternative to its role in Germany. This also occurred with the Austrian acquisition of Italian territories as a consequence of the War of the

Spanish Succession (1701–14). Moreover, imperial jurisdictional issues played a role in northern, but not in southern, Italy. At any rate, the declining relative part that Germany took in Austrian affairs was not matched for Prussia or Bavaria, although it was for Saxony and Hanover, both of which acquired non-German kingdoms – in Poland and Britain, respectively. Austria had gained access in the Balkans to an apparently open frontier, suggestive of that won by the western European powers across the oceans.

Linked to communities such as Arolsen, there was an innate conservatism; more so than could be found from the nineteenth century, however much the politics then was right-wing. Thus, in the manufacturing town of Nördlingen, an Imperial Free City from 1215 to 1803, 58 per cent of a sample of grooms at first marriage in 1701–3 followed the same occupation as their father. The adults in the town were divided into groups. Citizens, economically independent heads of households, were allowed to belong to a guild and carry on a craft, while non-citizens – who were socially and economically subordinate; mostly apprentices, journeymen, servants and casual labourers, few of whom married – mostly lived in the homes of their employers or in special hostelries for journeymen. While the son of a citizen enjoyed a hereditary right to that status, a non-citizen had to apply for membership. The nature of the community and the potential labour force were controlled in Nördlingen by the regulation of marriages. Special permission was required for a man under twenty-three or a woman under twenty to marry and outsiders wishing to marry into the community were expected to meet property qualification.

From 1725 to 1755, Aachen had a regime based on the guilds, which opposed schemes for mercantile change. Imports of competing goods, such as rough needles, were prohibited. In 1755–6, this government was brought down by the merchants and the 'mob' supported by a nearby ruler, the Elector Palatine.

There was a widespread effort in what became known as the 'cameralist' movement to improve administration through the use of information, but it hit obstacles. Frederick William I sought regular reports on Prussian harvest yields, price fluctuations and cattle breeding, but only his personal domains kept exact records. Frederick the Great's attempts to obtain methodical reports and statistical information were limited by the use of different provincial criteria, which made it difficult to establish comparable data.

In general, whatever the precepts of absolutism, rulers often appeared to have only a limited control of politics, policy and government. Due to the folly of rulers, this was particularly apparent in Württemberg. In the context of a very difficult international situation, the central administration of Prussia during the reign of Frederick I (1688–1713) was characterised by the influence of favourites, vacillating policy, corruption and the perception of monarchical weakness. Moreover, his successor, Frederick William I, in the instructions written for his heir in 1722, advised that the officials responsible for royal domains not be employed in their areas of origin. His dissatisfaction with the operation of central government led him to reorganise it.

While not having to confront the regional autonomy faced by the Austrian Habsburgs, provincial particularism was a characteristic of Prussia; the disjointed territories differed and lacked common history and tradition. In 1740, the Cleves estates unsuccessfully sought to restrict official posts to local nobles. Prussian administration, however, was responsive to local circumstances. The General Directory, an institution created in 1723 by Frederick William I to supervise military, police and financial matters, was arranged on a territorial basis, with a number of provincial boards under it. Their heads were given a large measure of responsibility, while the instructions drawn up for the General Directory in 1748 included variations for the western provinces.

Although sensitive to the diverse nature of his territories, Frederick the Great was determined to maintain his control. After he acquired East Friesland in 1744, he abolished the prince's privy council and issued a new list of *Drosten* – local nobles with some police and military responsibilities – altering their position to bring it more into line with Prussian government elsewhere. Distance, however, made supervision difficult. Daniel Lentz, given responsibility for the provincial government in 1748, was ordered to execute his instructions as he saw fit and Frederick himself did not visit the province until 1751. The Calvinist Prussian ruling house married frequently with Lutherans, part of their policy of becoming more prominent in international Protestantism and of seeking good relations with their largely Lutheran subjects.

Other rulers faced more serious problems. In Saxony, the estates retained the majority of their prerogatives, particularly in financial affairs. In 1711, the nobility of the prince-bishopric of Hildesheim thanked neighbouring Hanover for protecting them in their privileges and religion. Similarly, there was external intervention in other states, notably Mecklenburg and East Friesland.

Moreover, financial and other weaknesses of rulers encouraged dependence on foreign paymasters. In 1674, Ernst August of Osnabrück followed a well-trodden path when he agreed to provide six thousand troops in return for Dutch subsidies. In the eighteenth century, Hesse-Cassel frequently turned likewise to Britain. Some small principalities treated their armies as a form of income. In turn, in 1744, the French pressed their Bavarian ally to create a more efficient administration.

War repeatedly hit ruling families hard. Five of Landgrave Karl of Hesse-Cassel's sons served in the War of the Spanish Succession, two falling in battle. George I of Britain–Hanover lost three siblings to war. Charles, Duke of Brunswick, and Prince Louis Ferdinand of Prussia were killed fighting the French in 1806.

Intellectuals, whether or not in clerical positions, repeatedly stressed the role of the state. The mathematician and philosopher Gottfried von Leibniz (1646–1716), who became the founder president of the Berlin Academy of Science in 1700, was a Hanoverian official and publicist. He believed in the unity of knowledge and the need for power to be guided by an intellectual elite, and hoped to discover a universal scholarly language and to create harmony through mathematical and symbolic logic. Although, in theory, he believed in rule by the wise, in practice he supported hereditary monarchy and severely limiting the right of resistance to it. Christian Thomasius (1655–1728), professor of jurisprudence at Halle from 1690, sought authority enlightened by reason. Condemning torture and trials for witchcraft, and pressing for laws based on reason, he also argued that individual liberties should be enjoyed only at the ruler's discretion. Halle University reflected, as did Göttingen – founded in the electorate of Hanover in 1734 (opened in 1737) – the link between government and education. This emphasis contrasted with intellectual and historiographical traditions focused on Latin humanism and the history of the Empire.

RULERS

Rulers also celebrated the fame of their dynasties. In Prussia, references abounded to the Great Elector's victory over the Swedes at Fehrbellin in 1675 – in practice a relatively minor victory. This victory by his grandfather provided Frederick William I with an example of meritorious rulership that encouraged his militarism. Dynastic imaging thus offered the possibility of seeking – or, rather, selecting – the history required.

Acquiring new dominions outside the Empire made for status but not sustained greatness for German rulers of the eighteenth century. The attempt to upgrade a dynasty was very important, but was not possible within the Empire; there could be only one king. Thus, German dynasties sought foreign crowns. Prussia was an exception as the Duchy of Prussia was not part of the Empire: under the Golden Bull of Rimini of 1228, Emperor

Frederick II offered the lands conquered by the Teutonic Order to the Knights, providing imperial protection but not including them in the Empire. As a result, Frederick I, in 1701, could become king *in* Prussia (within the duchy), but not *of* Prussia (the entire Hohenzollern state).

The ruling houses of Hanover, Saxony, Hesse-Cassel and Holstein-Gottorp all acquired positions in Britain, Poland, Sweden and Russia respectively, but none succeeded in the long term in winning power for their German territories by this means. Max Emanuel fared no better for Bavaria in his efforts to gain from the Spanish succession. He was driven from Bavaria in 1704 and only subsequently achieved restitution of his territories in the eventual peace of 1714.

Even with the resources of Britain and Poland behind them, neither the Hanoverians nor the Saxons could play power politics successfully enough to limit Russia. This situation was driven home by Prussian threats. In 1740, Field Marshal Schwerin claimed that, if Frederick the Great was provoked by George II, there was little to hinder him from invading Hanover. George was well aware of this point.

Frederick the Great's approach to war was certainly not casual, whether to war as a courtly activity, a royal sport or a variation on hunting. He saw it as a duty best fulfilled through training and dedication, an attitude that he sought to disseminate in Prussia. His long poem, *The Art of War* (1749) revealed Frederick's belief in the need for detailed planning and cautious execution, a philosophy that was reinforced through confidential works of instructions for his officers. He led his army throughout his reign, not only winning spectacular victories (even though, in 1741, he fled from Mollwitz, his first battle), but also drilling the army and conducting major peacetime manoeuvres. Exposed to fire on several occasions, Frederick was bruised when a canister ball hit him in the chest at Torgau in 1760. This was part of an enduring pattern of rulership.

Frederick's success over Austria owed much to happenstance, not least in comparison with earlier Bavarian failures. In 1740, Austria was exhausted, her army in need of regeneration after her eventual failure in the Turkish War of 1737–9. In the wars of 1740–2 and 1744–5, Austria had to confront a number of other powers (including Bavaria, France and Spain), but Frederick had no other enemy except, eventually, a weakened Saxony. Austria's principal allies, Britain and Russia, refused to help her against Prussia and the British pressed her repeatedly to direct her attentions against France.

Saxon Weakness

'We have been long in pursuit of wild chimerical schemes ... and I believe it mortifies us a little to find that all our projecting yields us no more than our labour for our pains ... We are under a quack sort of management and have, I fear, but little taste or knowledge of other methods.'

James Scott, British envoy, reporting from Dresden on Augustus II's government, 1721

'It is thought there is not one good head at Dresden to govern the affairs. The elector is said to be weak, diffident and irresolute; both he and his ministers not a little imbued with the speculations and requirements which cost his father so much trouble. His government begins with setting up a declared favourite, whose greatest merit is his knowledge in dogs and horses but who, it is apprehended, has without the least tincture of affairs, no small share in them.'

Thomas Robinson summarising Austrian views on Augustus III, 1733

Conclusion

If in the eighteenth century, Germany was spared the eventual fate of Poland between 1772 and 1795 – namely, a partition by external powers: Austria, Prussia and Russia, into extinction – it was nevertheless increasingly affected by Russian power. This was the case with the movement of Russian troops into the Empire in 1716, 1735, 1748 and during the Seven Years' War. Combined with French aggression, this encouraged the argument that the German nation required greater strength. Moreover – until it became a Prussian territory in 1744 – the Dutch frequently intervened in neighbouring East Friesland in support of Emden in its opposition to princely demands.

However, in the eighteenth century, France – in a marked and important reversal of the earlier situation – largely ceased to make territorial gains in Germany, until after the French Revolution. In part, this was due to changes in French policy, with a lesser emphasis on territorial aggrandisement – although Lorraine was annexed in 1766 – but the success of resistance was important. This owed much to Austria, but British participation in a series of conflicts also played a major part, dramatically so in 1704 when John, Duke of Marlborough, marched his army to the Danube, going on to victory at Blenheim.

The long success of Austria into the mid-nineteenth century is a warning against any teleology based on Prussia, despite its long-term increase in strength. The revival of the imperial concept in the early eighteenth century ensured that it was far from clear that Austria and Habsburg power would be dissociated from Germany, despite the separate expansion of this power into the Balkans and Italy with gains from the Turks and from the Spanish Succession. Moreover, the Prussian achievement appeared precarious. Prussia was weakened by the Austro–Russian axis – both in peacetime, most obviously during the War of the Polish Succession (1733–5) and in wartime, especially during the Seven

Years' War. It was then Prussia that appeared to be heading for partition.

Samuel Pufendorf (1632–94) and Leibniz employed natural law as a guide to the conduct of international relations, presenting it as a permanent code of moral values implanted by God, accessible to reason and a necessary guide to state behaviour. Such theories remained important, influencing, for example, the thought of Christian Wolff (1676–1754). It was not so much that in some demonstration of an anachronistic character for the Empire, such writers had scant understanding of dynamic elements in international relations, the scope of change and the attempt by certain powerful rulers to match diplomatic developments to their growing power. Instead, they sought to reconcile these to the culture and practice of the Empire in a worthy effort to tempt power to embody order and justice.

However, Frederick the Great had no interest in being bound by the imperial constitution and helped launch its politics in a new direction in 1740. This represented an abrupt break with the longstanding search for consensus and discussion of reform that had characterised a strand of Germany's politics. Yet, looked at another way, it is solely because a line is drawn from there to the later politics of Prussia and Germany – notably the war with Austria in 1866 and the German occupation of Austria in 1938 – that a turning-point in 1740 appears apparent. By contrast, the history of Bavarian expansionism from 1620 to 1742 suggests that a different note can be struck. Moreover, Frederick always argued that he was willing to accept the Empire and that it was his rights that were threatened. In 1740–2, he claimed that he took Silesia as heritage and, in 1785, that he was seeking to protect the imperial constitution. This was a marked contrast to the war of 1866 which crushed the existing confederation and any sense of any alternative to Prussian dominance.

Again, to end on a note about Prussia is of limited value because it is Germany's wider significance in the world that is important.

German rulers understood the value of trade. Most were in no position to do much about it. The emperor Charles VI founded trans-oceanic trading companies, but, as he lacked German territory on the North or Baltic seas, he did so at Ostend and Trieste. The Prussians were more adventurous, establishing a trading empire that included an oceanic trading company, a small fleet and slave bases in West Africa and the West Indies. However, the company made no real profit, and the Great Elector's successor lost interest. The company was disbanded in 1711 and the colonies sold or lost.

The Great Elector's initiative was turned in a commercial direction by Frederick the Great, when, in 1751, in his new North Sea territory of East Friesland, he founded the Emden Company to trade with Canton (Guangzhou). The company did well, but was hit hard by the Seven Years' War, in which Emden was occupied by the French in 1757. The company was dissolved in 1765. This matched the Hanoverian failure at Harburg and the Danish one at Gluckstadt. Aside from the impact of war in Germany, the German states lacked the financial muscle for long-range trade, certainly that enjoyed by the British and the Dutch.

The situation was not to change until the 1880s, but the context and values of German imperialism then differed from the earlier commercial empire that was neither achieved nor even properly attempted. This contrast helped ensure a very different political culture to that in Britain and the Netherlands. The late nineteenth century was to see mercantile capitalism also to the fore in Germany, but the political context in the Prussian-dominated Second Reich was not as propitious as in Britain. That situation changed after the collapse of the Second Reich, but the economic opportunity was lessened by the chaos and poverty created by the First World War. The situation would not change until the massive economic growth that followed the Second World War and that later transformation was achieved in Germany without the profit and power being siphoned off to support an aggressive political order.

5

Enlightenment and War, 1755–91

'I sincerely pity them, they are such slaves as I have heard the negroes in the West Indies described. No uncommon sight to see them threshing corn, driving waggons, hoeing turnips, mending the highways.'

Adam Walker on the women he
saw near Füssen, Bavaria, 1787

Walker's observation is a reminder of the hard work and often oppressive conditions underlying the situation in this and other periods. This is true not least of the '*Aufklärung*' or 'German Enlightenment', which very much affected government, as well as leading to important advances, each contributing to an idea of Germany and its constituent territories as a rational project of meaning.

POWER

There was no need for the eventual collapse of the Empire, which, indeed, avoided the revolutionary breakdown that destroyed Bourbon France in 1792. Instead – prefiguring in some respects the impact of the Second World War – the memory of the Thirty Years' War (1618–48) remained strong and helped shape German political assumptions, encouraging the view that effective cooperation between German rulers was necessary to prevent the recurrence of such a calamity. Moreover, a multi-centred polity was less vulnerable than a single capital that could be subject to revolutionary disorder. However, the Empire would not in the end be able to survive the crisis caused by Napoleon and would not even be re-established in the same form after his defeat.

Meanwhile, Prussia and Austria were the dominant powers, and the relative size of the armies of other rulers declined. Saxony had a force of between twenty-five thousand and thirty thousand men in both 1700 and 1800, a peak paper strength, including militia, of about fifty-five thousand men in 1745 and a low point of about sixteen thousand men in the early 1750s. Bavaria kept a smaller peacetime army in the late eighteenth century than it had had at the start. Bavarian ambitions were undermined by the small size of its army: about eight thousand in 1726 and near twelve thousand men by 1745. French subsidies were required for Bavaria to maintain greater numbers. Alongside the peace, the end of British subsidies led to the cut in size of the Hanoverian army to fourteen thousand men in 1763. The forces of the jointly ruled electorate of Cologne and prince-bishopric of Münster numbered a maximum of about seven thousand in 1730 and 5,100 in 1792. In 1742, the army of the elector of Mainz was only four thousand strong. In 1779, John Moore, a British traveller, pointed out with reference to the margrave of Baden – whose army numbered fewer than three thousand troops, 'He has too just an understanding not to perceive that the greatest army he could possibly maintain could be no defence to his dominions, situated as they are between the powerful states of France and Austria.'

In Prussia, each province was ordered in 1693 to provide a certain number of recruits. This was achieved by conscription, chiefly of peasants. A cantonal system was established between 1727 and 1735: every regiment was assigned a permanent catchment area around its peacetime garrison town, from where it drew its draftees for lifelong service. The name of every duty-bound male was entered on a roll at birth, though there were a large number of exemptions. These included the nobility; localities (notably Berlin) and workers deemed important, such as

apprentices in many industries and textile workers. As a consequence, most common soldiers came from the rural poor.
Landlords were expected to serve but in a very different capacity.

The Prussian regiments were required to be up to strength for
the few weeks of the spring reviews and summer manoeuvres.
For the rest of the year – once over the initial training period –
native troops were allowed to return to their families and trades
and, even when stationed at the garrison town, they were permitted to pursue civilian occupations. In a similar fashion, artillery
horses were registered and then distributed among the peasantry,
with inspections to ensure they were cared for.

The cantonal system worked reasonably well, creating a
manpower pool deep enough to allow selectivity, a high participation rate among the population and, thereby, a degree of militarisation. It maintained a stable and predictable link between regiments and reserves of manpower in specific areas that generated
significant solidarity in companies and regiments for parish and
region and also encouraged a sense of obligation among the officers. Although different numbers have been suggested, Prussia
clearly had a far higher percentage of its population under arms
than other major powers. Moreover, as a whole, German peacetime establishments were proportionately higher than those of
the nineteenth century.

Although economically significant, Silesia, taken from Austria
in 1740–2, was not so major a gain as to lead automatically to
Prussia acquiring the role she did achieve under Frederick the
Great. Instead, the successful blending of elite and dynasty in the
service of the Prussian state – not least through the expansion of
the army – played a major role in the growth of Prussian power,
one that was to become the basis of the new Germany. The status
of 'great power' was for Prussia, however, problematic – as
Napoleon was brutally to demonstrate in 1806.

Indeed, it is too easy to allow the eventual outcome of Prussian
dominance to obscure its earlier situation: those who worshipped

power were certainly prone to this. In his *Friedrich der Grosse* (1983), Theodor Schieder (1908–84), a major historian from an active Nazi background who continued with his racism in the post-war world of West German academic history, described the Empire as anachronistic and the Habsburg monarchy as 'an hermaphrodite'. Instead, he presented Prussia as having a necessary sense of mission. Yet, in 1806, it was as much Prussian power as the Empire itself that fell victim to France. The subsequent redrawing of Germany's borders was at Prussia's cost.

Food

War certainly continued to hit hard, both in the Napoleonic period and during the *ancien régime*. The late eighteenth century was one of general population growth. Düsseldorf and nearby villages doubled between 1750 and 1790 and Berlin went from 55,000 in 1700 to 150,000 in 1800 – in each case due to a higher birth rate and immigration. However, the Seven Years' War (1756–63) cost Saxony a fifth of its population and Prussia a tenth. War, moreover, was to hit hard anew from 1792.

Many other factors were involved in population movement, social development and social strain. Economic opportunity was crucial. Thus, the cycles in the silk industry of Krefeld in the Rhineland were mirrored in the local marriage figures. More generally, good Rhenish harvests late in the century were matched by a relative absence of epidemics, as better nutrition increased resistance to disease and to the cold. Yet, in Coblenz, notwithstanding peace from 1763 to 1792, there was scant sign of a good late eighteenth century replacing an unfavourable earlier period, as there was in some other regions. Agricultural productivity failed to match the pressure of a rising population while, despite the goodwill of the authorities, progress in hygiene was limited and the old town, where the artisans lived, remained particularly unhealthy. More generally in the Rhineland, food prices rose and land hunger led to the subdivision of holdings and an increase in the number of landless labourers. As undernourishment was no longer so commonly eliminated by early death, it became the permanent condition of most people.

The possibilities for effective government action were revealed in Prussia. In the early 1740s, a network of royal granaries already existed and, despite a bad harvest, the onset of war and adverse climate, the Prussian government proved reasonably successful in preventing increases in destitution and unemployment, itinerant vagrancy and riots. A general edict in 1740 called upon all nobles and lessees of crown land to sell their grain stocks in the markets within two weeks – on pain of confiscation and at a price set by the government.

The Prussian system remained effective for the rest of the century. The grain stocks available in the public granaries, the policies of Frederick the Great and the social control exercised by landlords and government; all minimised the social responses to dearth – such as migration – that helped to raise mortality figures. The Prussian government believed in preparation and firm action to deal with food shortages. Thus, in 1790–1, the effect of crop failures in East Friesland – a Prussian possession from 1744 – was limited by the use of the royal depots. Furthermore, Frederick's system acted as a model for Hesse-Cassel and helped to minimise starvation arising from the serious crop failures of 1770–1. (The situation in terms of harvest failure was generally less favourable elsewhere, both in towns and countryside.)

Prussian administration was commonly held to be a model of efficiency. Focused on, and by, the *Kriegskomissariat* (general war commissariat), it was certainly more cohesive than its counterparts in many other states, had reasonably professional structures and conducted business quickly. Nevertheless, recruitment into administration was still greatly influenced by patronage, with even incompetent friends and relations helped out. Frederick the Great's attempts to make the somewhat unwieldy administration more efficient and more responsive to his wishes failed. As a result, he sought to bypass existing institutions and, especially after war ended in 1763, to create new administrative departments and arrangements directly answerable to himself, as with the excise in 1766. This taxation had the socio-political appeal of not weighing on landowners.

Across Germany, continuing pressures arose from the emergencies that reflected human vulnerabilities, many that were harder to confront than their modern counterparts. Cattle disease crippled Holstein's agriculture in 1764, while plagues of mice in 1773 and 1787 hit the harvests in East Friesland, where worms had damaged the dykes in the 1760s. It was not surprising that this created a climate of fear, with uncertainties fostering a sense of dependence on factors outside human control.

It can be all too easy, indeed, to let politics or culture dominate the other important aspects of life that had wider implications; for example, to treat agriculture as a constant element and to focus on other issues. But agriculture was the biggest source of employment and production; it was fundamental. Thus, in 1788, the Bavarian government rejected an Austrian offer to purchase two thousand horses with the argument that, although the money would benefit poor Bavaria, the true wealth of the state lay not in money but in agriculture, for which the horses were required. Indeed, the significance of agriculture persisted into recent times. It was only farm mechanisation after the Second World War that helped lead to large-scale migration to the cities, ensuring a supply of relatively inexpensive labour for industry.

Prior to that, significant changes still occurred in farming, notably in the late eighteenth century. The spread of iron mouldboards increased deep ploughing, while the more frequent use of clover and turnips as fodder, as in Prussia, enabled the rearing of more animals. Thus, in the Rhineland, clover spread, fallow was ended and the stall-feeding of animals increased, as did the numbers of livestock. In Baden-Württemberg, cash crops such as flax and tobacco spread, as did clover and turnips, meadowlands were improved, better breeds of animals were imported and live-stock numbers rose, increasing the supply of manure. In Baden, an attempt was made in the 1760s to abolish the three-field system by planting soil-renewing crops on the fallow.

Potatoes, which did not require much investment or particu-lar new skills, became especially important in Germany from the eighteenth century. By 1750, they were widely grown in the Rhineland; the subsistence crisis of 1771-2 encouraged their culti-vation, as in Swabia. Sir Benjamin Thompson (1753-1814), an American-born British scientist and social reformer who played a major role in the Bavarian government between 1785 and 1798, becoming Count Rumford in 1791, was a keen advocate of the potato and of maize. He sought to use the army to introduce agri-cultural improvements by establishing military gardens to publi-cise new methods of growth and crops. He also wanted army horses sent to peasants to be cared for until they were needed, but this was never implemented.

Even in the more marginal and remote agricultural areas, there were signs of improvement. In parts of Hesse-Cassel hith-erto lacking settled agriculture, villages were created thanks to government initiative. In the hill regions of the Eifel and the Hunsrück, slash-and-burn clearing and transient cultivation prac-tices were still to be found but, by the century's end, potatoes and clover were also being grown.

Little progress was made in Germany in consolidating the scattered strips worked by individual peasants, but agricultural improvement helped to lessen the acute pressure of a rising population, although there was also a need for imports, notably of sheep, cattle and oxen from Hungary. Indeed, Hungarian cattle blocked the roads near Frankfurt by the 1780s. Poland was a major source of grain. As part of a wider pattern of trade, north-west Germany supplied cattle to the Dutch cities, while part of the Black Forest suffered deforestation to provide timber, in particular for the Dutch shipbuilding industry, with the denuded slopes suffering serious erosion. More generally, trade on the Rhine rose, particularly after 1770.

People also moved in large numbers, many to North America, Hungary or Russia, mostly from Swabia and the Rhineland. Between 1760 and 1775, at least twelve thousand German immigrants reached Philadelphia. Facing under-population after the famine of the early years of the eighteenth century and the mid-century wars, Prussia's rulers followed a longstanding practice of the settlement of the eastern parts of Germany in actively encouraging immigrants and Frederick the Great relaxed laws accordingly. Thus, an edict of 1772 allowed foreigners to follow non-Prussian legal codes when settling in the province of Magdeburg.

INDUSTRY

Following another longstanding pattern, much industry was based in rural areas where water power was most readily available. Thus, in Württemberg, a trading company of merchants and dyers based in the town of Calw organised the weaving of wool in the duchy, while cotton-printing developed in mid-century in the Sulz area and came to employ over a thousand rural workers.

Moreover, technological innovation gathered pace. Friedrich von Heinitz, head of the Prussian mining department after 1776, built the first Prussian coke furnaces and introduced many innovations based on scientific principles. In 1779, the first steam pump for mine drainage in Prussia was installed, followed in 1783 by the first mechanised textile factory at Düsseldorf.

The number of academic posts and chemistry labs increased dramatically in 1720–80, thanks largely to government interest in promoting public health and industry. At the start of this period, in 1720, most German chemists would have also been practising medical doctors or teachers of medicine; by 1780 most specialised in pharmacy, technology and the teaching of chemistry. Trained chemists were more able and willing to conduct experimental research. The first German periodical devoted exclusively to chemistry, the *Chemische Annalen*, was found by Lorenz Crell in 1778. The *Journal der Physik*, established by F. A. C. Gren, followed in 1783.

Only patchy support existed, however, for free market capitalism and technological modernism, certainly less so than in Britain. On the whole, the Imperial Free Cities failed to keep pace with production technology. Thus, the Augsburg cloth-making and dyers' guilds vigorously opposed the establishment of cotton-bleaching and printing factories. By contrast in Prussia, Frederick William I reorganised the guilds in 1732–5, retaining them for regulatory and training purposes, while making them responsive to government interest. Protectionism, as practised by states such as Prussia, was also a major issue. Arguably, greater benefit came from the standardisation in 1773 of the twelve different ways of measuring common lengths in Prussia and from the re-coining in 1767 that followed the debasement of money during the Seven Years' War.

Frederick the Great had to counter the reluctance of Hamburg merchants – the principal source of north German mercantile capital – to invest in Prussia. In 1765, the government founded the Berlin Discount and Loans Bank to provide capital for merchants and manufacturers, while Prussian provincial governments formed credit institutions to help keep landed estates intact.

There were some improvements in communications in this pre-railway age. In 1780, the river Ruhr was made navigable, encouraging local coal production. In 1784, a three-metre-deep canal, between the North Sea at Tönning and Kiel was opened, while Frederick the Great built canals partly to move grain to the state granaries. However, in general, the situation remained one of simply limited change.

WOMEN

As elsewhere, most women had to work very hard, often outside the confines of the family, for example, dragging boats upstream to Mainz in 1789. Nevertheless, among the learned, a debate was had over the position of women. Journals written by women for women began to appear in Germany in 1779. Probably the most popular, Sophie von La Roche's *Pomona: For Germany's Daughters* (1783–4), argued for female education and considered the happiness of individual women at the same time as it stressed an ideology of service. Marianne Ehrmann, in her magazines in the early 1790s, presented men as partly responsible for women's current inferiority of position. Although the magazines did not call for fundamental alteration, they accepted change as a possibility, both for individuals and for women in general, and suggested that women should assert themselves.

Men, of course, sought to preside over the debate. In 1767, the Baden bureaucrat Johann Reinhard described a utopian world in which public heroes, both men and women, were honoured while, in 1784, the Prussian philosopher Immanuel Kant (1724–1804) argued that women were failing to become enlightened because they were supervised by those who did not wish them to become independent and, accordingly, exploited their timidity and need for comfort. His friend, Prussian civil servant Theodor Gottlieb von Hippel, had in 1774 produced a conservative treatment of marriage, stressing the subordination of women, but revised his position later. In 1792, inspired by his daughters, he published a study of women in which he argued that they were equal, adducing theoretical and empirical evidence, including the observation that, among the lower classes, women also carried out heavy labouring tasks. Claiming that marriage was a technique to ensure the social control of women and that enforced ignorance left them unable to compete with men, Hippel called for equal education. He also argued that equality of the sexes did not imply indistinguishability. Hippel's audience was the middling orders in which circumstances permitted such change as the education of women.

In practice, a number of territories had ordered the establishment of local schools and the compulsory attendance of both boys and girls. These were in Protestant states, followed, in the 1770s and 1780s, by several Catholic territories – such as Würzburg – as part of a widespread pattern of Catholic reform. The decrees seem to have been implemented, at least in Prussia, Württemberg and Saxony, where nearly every hamlet had an elementary school by the end of the century. Not all children attended, not least because of their need for immediate employment, but the availability of public elementary schools offered many German women the opportunity to receive a basic education. Yet, the education available generally directed girls to household tasks and only a small number of women were given an intellectual education.

Educational writers of the second half of the century, the so-called philanthropists, called for improvements, but emphasised the need for a different education for girls to prepare them to act as wives and mothers. These male writers argued that men and women should be equal in marriage but that such equality would come from their naturally different contributions to marriage, contributions that education should aid without obscuring the differences. Johann Campe's *Fatherly Advice for my Daughter* (1788–9) not only portrayed marriage, children and home as the proper destiny for women, but argued that the unfavourable social conditions of women derived from a divine plan for humanity. In 1787, Ernst Brandes (1758–1810), a Hanoverian civil servant and conservative writer, in his *On Women*, claimed that the blood of women was chemically different to that of men and that, because they allegedly had weak brain nerves (a widely held belief), they could not see connections between different ideas. For him, the rise of a female reading public was dangerous as it would lead them to neglect their domestic obligations.

Society

Social differentiation, as ever, was another element. In 1766, Johann Wöllner, an estate administrator and son of a cleric, married the only daughter of General Itzenplitz. Members of the general's family persuaded Frederick the Great to annul the marriage as a violation of established social barriers and Wöllner was accused improperly of winning the girl's hand.

Under Frederick's two predecessors, granting of titles had been fairly common, but he was more socially conservative, excluding bourgeois councillors from high office, seeking to end the granting of titles for money and generally unwilling to confer titles on commoners. He believed that nobles were the natural support of the administration and the army. Indeed, most of the adult male Prussian nobles served as officials or officers. The Académie des Nobles was founded in Berlin in 1763 to train young aristocrats as administrators and officers. Frederick also ensured that no noble estates could be sold without his permission.

Frederick was not alone in regarding nobles as a biologically superior group. In the Karlsschule founded by Karl Eugen of Württemberg in 1771, noble children were strictly segregated from those of the bourgeoisie. The large number of poems produced to commemorate the death of Prince Maximilian of Brunswick-Wolfenbüttel, who drowned in the River Oder in 1785 while attempting to rescue two peasants being carried away by flood waters, was a testimony to a heroic model of true nobility and individual bravery, not a suggestion that the elite ought to sacrifice themselves for the poor.

Of course, some measure of meritocracy existed, although women were excluded from most categories. Frederick II of Hesse-Cassel generally ignored family petitions for preferment in his bureaucracy, maintaining his resistance to pressures directed against the merit system by the aristocracy and helping to preserve his officials' professional standards. However, a quarter of the staff drawn from commoners who occupied his key middle- and upper-level positions in 1760-85 went on to become nobles, while nobles were still represented disproportionately in the senior ranks.

As a reminder of the variety of categories in which individuals could appear, Frederick II of Hesse-Cassel launched a major building programme in Cassel after the travails of the Seven Years' War. He rebuilt the palace and endowed it with a French garden and Chinese and classical Greek motifs, and constructed a new opera house where, by the late 1770s, seventy different productions – using many Parisian and Italian performers – were staged annually. Conspicuous consumption, in particular on court life and building works, placed a major strain on the finances of the electorate of Cologne in the 1740s and of Bavaria in the 1780s. It was an aspect in the political crisis in Württemberg and also helped weaken Saxony. In contrast, more frugal Hanover was helped by the absence of a project comparable in status to that of George III at Windsor Castle.

However, no major German state could emulate Prussia, where Frederick the Great, who had inherited a state treasury of ten million thalers in 1740, left more than fifty-one million to his successor in 1786, each figure reflecting periods of peace but also the strong internal position of the royal government, including the extent of its landholdings. Unlike France and Austria, Prussia did not have to devote a large part of its revenue to interest payments on the national debt. Indeed, its finances were crucial to Prussia gaining, and holding, the position of being a major power despite its limited resources.

Prussian success, however, had devastating implications elsewhere. The Seven Years' War exhausted Saxony, not least because it was repeatedly ravaged and exploited by Prussia, accounting for close to 40 per cent of Prussia's war expenditure. Furthermore, the devastation and debt enforced a retrenchment that terminated the role of Dresden as a great cultural centre. More generally, Saxony

– which had been politically and culturally superior to Prussia – was pummelled into second place and its attempt to take advantage of its Polish dynastic link was wrecked. After the Seven Years' War, the Saxon government had to focus on re-establishing the state. It also concentrated on issues ignored under the elector-kings of Saxony–Poland. As a result, there was, in Saxony, a degree of reform summarised as 'enlightened despotism'.

Public discussion of agrarian issues and the position of the peasantry became more pronounced in Germany from the 1770s, but change was limited. The Agrarian Society of Hesse-Cassel informed the government in 1782 that productivity would not increase significantly until manorial obligations were eliminated; a view that was to be vindicated over time. Such essentially pragmatic arguments for the improvement of peasant circumstances, entailing a commutation of their dues and obligations into financial rents, were accompanied in the 1780s and 1790s by claims for peasant emancipation on the basis of natural rights. The Osnabrück administrator and publicist Justus Möser argued that making all leaseholds by both freemen and serfs hereditary would increase their commitment to profitability. He was thwarted by noble opposition. The commutation of labour services for cash was begun in Hanover in 1753 and nearly complete by the 1790s; the electors of Bavaria also supported the policy, which was presented as an aspect of necessary social regeneration.

Other rulers were cautious. In his 'Essay on the Forms of Government and Duties of Sovereigns' (1777), Frederick the Great argued that rulers should imagine themselves in the position of peasants or artisans, but his moves against serfdom were limited in practice largely to the royal estates. Indeed, serf services were confirmed in the law code of 1794. Similarly, in 1765, Frederick II of Hesse-Cassel decided that hunting and forest labour services were being exacted too arbitrarily, yet he limited, rather than abolished, those services. He did not extend the decrees to noble estates. As in Prussia, the pace of legislation was not matched by comparable implementation, and an investigation in 1782–3 into peasant conditions revealed extensive abuses.

Despite the decree of 1773 that labour services would not be required, even if paid for, whenever the peasant needed the time for essential work, the practice was not ended. However, fearing peasant agitation, Margrave Karl Friedrich of Baden abolished serfdom in 1783. Four years later, Frederick Karl, archbishop-elector of Mainz, announcing his intention to abolish serfdom, declared that the fees due when a serf died or moved were too heavy. Nevertheless, payments were charged for redemption. This was very different to the situation of greater freedom in Britain, the Netherlands and, indeed, most of France. Moreover, far from being restricted to east of the River Elbe, serfdom was still widely practised in Germany.

In Munich, by contrast, Benjamin Thompson, in charge of the Bavarian army, convinced Elector Karl Theodor that a round-up of the poor would benefit the city. On New Year's Day 1790, the traditional day for alms-giving to the poor, Thompson used the army to register the deserving and non-deserving poor. To help keep track of the deserving poor, he had house numbers installed on buildings in the city. The state moved beggars to a workhouse, both clearing the streets and taking control of poor relief.

RELIGION

Religious direction and surveillance were relaxed in some areas and different groups were able to coexist, as in much of Swabia. Clemens Wenceslaus, archbishop-elector of Trier (r. 1768–1803), a Saxon prince who was also prince-bishop of Augsburg and a lavish spender on palace building, granted limited toleration of Protestants in 1783, although he also insisted that their clerics and places of worship be inconspicuous. Karl Friedrich of Baden provided funds to build a Catholic school and church in Karlsruhe. In the Rhineland, clerical influence decreased in the schools and their curricula became more practical, while theology declined in the reformed universities of Mainz and Trier and the new foundation of Bonn, all in Catholic territories. More weight was instead given to modern languages and sciences.

There was considerable interest in the educational ideas of Johann Basedow (1723–90) who founded the Philanthropinum school at Dessau in 1774. His work stressed the spontaneous development of children's benevolent and rational faculties, rather than conventional religious education.

Religious identity, however, remained strong. In 1782, Pope Pius VI was given a rapturous welcome in Augsburg and Munich, while in Cologne University the traditional curriculum and methods remained dominant. Yet calls for reform came from within the Church, reflecting both longstanding differences over church government and tension between German and Italian Catholicism. 'Febronius,' J. N. von Hontheim, vicar-general of the archbishop of Trier, in his *Present State of the Church and the Legitimate Power of the Roman Pontiff* (1763), presented a limited view of the power of Rome. At Coblenz in 1769, and in the so-called 'Punctuation of Ems' in 1786, the three German archbishop-electors challenged the authority of the papacy and asserted that only a general council of the Church could wield supreme legislative and judicial power. This, however, was a German Catholicism that was not in the long term to prevail.

ENLIGHTENMENT

An Ingolstadt academic, Adam Weishaupt, wishing to 'help reason gain supremacy', founded the Illuminati in Bavaria in 1776. Weishaupt hoped to influence rulers to use the schools and churches to educate the people, fostering concepts associated with Enlightenment circles, such as natural religion, although most of the rank-and-file members did not share his bold plans. Many members were nobles and officials and some were clergymen and, although the movement preached reducing social barriers, it practised social segregation in appointing to senior positions in the order.

The suspicions the Illuminati engendered arose not so much from their beliefs, which were more utopian than revolutionary, as from their secrecy and their attempts to increase their influence in Bavaria, a state which was generally resistant to fashionable opinion. The Illuminati were viewed as supporters of Joseph II, who shared their anti-clerical views and wished to take over the state. In 1785, all secret societies, including the Freemasons and Illuminati, were banned by Charles Theodore of Bavaria and, in 1787, evidence that purported to demonstrate a plot by the latter was published. The Bavarian foreign minister wrote of 'that abominable sect, which directly seeks to destroy religion and healthy morals and to overthrow the thrones of rulers'. Members who held official positions were dismissed. The treatment of the Illuminati demonstrated the fears that characterised several of the states of the period, leading to police action and persecution. In practice there were more serious challenges for states – the Illuminati were a relatively small group.

In Germany, the Enlightenment is known as the '*Aufklärung*', which Kant defined in 1784 as man realising his potential through the use of reason. With their own *lumières* (the French Enlightenment) in mind, French commentators would have applauded the German stress on education but they would have been surprised by the close relationship between intellectuals and governments, as well as the relative absence of anti-clericalism, in either Protestant or Catholic Germany. Kant, indeed, stressed the creative role of the monarch in the *Aufklärung*.

Academics and officials also played a major role, helping to make government appear to be the crucial pivot of social activity. The large number of opportunities presented by the numerous German governments provided employment for intellectuals, leading to social advancement and state recognition to a degree unknown in France. However, Frederick the Great maintained censorship and, in the 1780s, some of Kant's religious essays were not published. Yet, while criticising serfdom, Kant was opposed to ideas of popular sovereignty and the general will and, in common with most writers, accepted both the inegalitarian social hierarchy and the idea that servants should not enjoy political rights.

Intellectual movements rested on a broader pattern of intellectual engagement. There were fifty-seven German newspapers published in 1701 and 186 in 1789, higher numbers than in Britain, although they were to be found across a larger area. Readership was primarily urban, with Hamburg a particularly important centre, but peasants also read newspapers, some of which – such as the *Bote aus Thüringen* (*Messenger from Thuringia*, 1788–1816) – were produced especially for them. Although, crucially, newspapers lacked the political independence of their counterparts in Britain, the press played a major educational role, sometimes ostentatiously so, as with the *Deutsche Zeitung für die Jugend und ihre Freunde* (*German Newspaper for the Young and their Friends*). The distribution of newspapers was linked to the growth of postal networks.

Newspapers were published in German as part of a growing commitment in cultural and intellectual circles to the use of the language rather than Latin, Italian or French. Johann Gottfried Herder (1744–1803), a pupil of Kant who was superintendent at Weimar from 1776, very much pressed for the vernacular, as in his *Critical Forests* (1769). He placed great weight on the distinct nature of language as both a consequence and a way of sustaining national identity and as a product of the experience of its speakers. Herder's views extended to a positive endorsement of the people – the *volk* – not as a mob (a pejorative view, reflecting social exclusion), but as a nation. His ideas led him to regret the Reformation as having divided Germany. Under Frederick William II (r. 1786–97), the use of German revived at the Prussian court.

The Sturm und Drang movement was increasingly influential from the 1770s. It perceived nature as a creative force rather than a pleasing and inconsequential landscape. The human soul was a seat of passion rather than harmony and the feeling man of action was superior to the reflective scholar. The movement influenced the Weimar classicism seen in some of the work of Johann Wolfgang von Goethe (1749–1832) and his friend Friedrich Schiller (1759-1805), a prominent playwright. In his influential novel *The Sorrows of Young Werther* (1774), Goethe provided a complex hero driven to suicide by unrequited passion and the terrible power of total feeling. Romance ceased to be a game, as in many French novels of the period, or an opportunity for sentimental poses, as in their English counterparts, and became a cruel mistress. Goethe's *Werther* had a great impact and Schiller's first play, *The Robbers* (1781), was socially radical and full of melodramatic emotion.

Other art forms were also changing in the pre-revolutionary period. Karl Philipp Emanuel Bach (1714–88), the second son of Johann Sebastian Bach, had little time for his father's contrapuntal style and was one of the originators of the sonata form. In his numerous concerti, he influenced both Haydn and Mozart (1756–91), who also benefitted from the dynamic orchestral range of the Mannheim composers and transformed the piano concerto from a work of limited forces and devices into a dramatic interplay of piano and orchestra.

War

The conflicts of the period helped establish the relative position of the German states, bringing to fruition the developments of 1741–8 which had seen Bavaria, Hanover and Saxony clearly fail to become great powers. The first was overrun by Austria in 1742, the second forced into neutrality by the threat of French attack in 1741 and the latter was conquered by Prussia in 1745. As a result, all three had to accept the failure of their ambitions. This situation was not reversed and lesser rulers had to operate accordingly. In 1756, Saxony was rapidly overrun by Prussian forces, in 1757 Hanover by a French army, and Bavaria was not a significant independent participant in mid-century conflicts.

The Seven Years' War (1756–63), indeed, represented an opportunity for Austria to cut Prussia down to size, repeating what had been achieved at the expense of Bavaria in the 1700s and 1740s. Alliance between Austria and Russia threatened Frederick the Great with an attack that he sought to pre-empt by attacking Austria through its ally Saxony. This helped bring France into the war against Prussia and it also added the enmity of Sweden and of most of the Empire. In contrast, Britain – and, therefore, Hanover and its ally Hesse-Cassel – fought alongside Prussia and, from 1759, played a key role in thwarting French advances, notably winning a major battle at Minden that year. Hanover, however, did not make any of the territorial gains George II had sought – notably the secularisation of Hildesheim and Osnabrück.

The war proved much more difficult for Prussia than the conflicts of 1740–2 and 1745–6, but Frederick benefitted from a lack of cohesion on the part of his opponents and from France, after his victory at Rossbach in 1757, focusing on Britain.

Prussia found Russia a particularly fearsome opponent, which helped explain later Prussian worries. In 1760, Berlin was briefly occupied but, more significantly, Prussia was put under attritional pressure from which it was only rescued in 1762 by the death of Tsarina Elizabeth and the accession of the prussophile Peter III. This was the 'miracle of Prussia' that Hitler was fruitlessly to hope for in 1945. Prussia came out of the war without territorial losses.

When stressing the need for good relations to an Austrian envoy in November 1768, Frederick the Great might say, 'We are Germans,' but he also encouraged his nobles and his army to think and talk of a Prussian 'fatherland'. Indeed, ignoring the complaints of the princes of Anhalt, Frederick the Great sent in troops to gather recruits, leading the Bavarian foreign minister to reflect in 1773, 'It seems that the right of the strongest now determines all the moves of the great.' Under Frederick, and in a clear failure of the imperial system, Prussia bullied the surrounding princes – especially in forcible recruiting for her army – from which Mecklenburg suffered greatly. Prussian treatment of her neighbours repeatedly illustrated the degree to which strength bred strength, increasing the gap of relative power between states. In 1787, a Prussian invasion settled the political crisis in the Netherlands.

Meanwhile, in both Hanover and Saxony, a sense of political interest and identity was developing separately from that of their rulers, a process helped by the Saxon leader converting to Catholicism and his Hanoverian counterpart living in Britain between 1755 and 1821 (even then, George IV's 1821 visit was very brief). The implications of such developments for a sense of German identity were unclear. In Hanover, there continued to be a strong sense of identity.

The long list of might-have-beens continued over the Bavarian succession. Neither Maximilian Joseph of Bavaria (r. 1745–77) nor his successor, Charles Theodore of the Palatinate, had any direct heirs. Joseph II saw this as an opportunity to gain much of Bavaria. After Maximilian Joseph's death, he reached an agreement with Charles Theodore by which the latter ceded much of Bavaria while many of his illegitimate children were found posts in Vienna. Frederick the Great opposed this, concerned about the accretion of Austrian strength, as did Charles Theodore's heir, Charles Augustus of Zweibrücken, the elector of Saxony – who had his own claims – and France, which did not want its Austrian ally to become stronger.

The resulting War of the Bavarian Succession (1778–9) established anew that Austria and Prussia were the key powers in determining events. The Prussian attack in 1778 proved indecisive and the war was onerous for both Austria and Prussia but by the peace concluded in 1779, under French and Russian mediation, Austria gained from the Bavarian succession only the Innviertel in south-eastern Bavaria. Responding to Russia becoming a guaranteeing power of the status quo in Germany in place of Sweden under the Peace of Teschen of 1779, the British commentator John Richard observed, 'The Russians may now be considered as the arbiters of Germany, since it is evident that their conjunction with either power [Austria or Prussia] must overwhelm the other.'

Compared by Frederick the Great in 1781 to a chemist who kept politics in fermentation, Joseph II prefigured to an extent the attitudes of revolutionary France in the 1790s, although he proved less willing to push issues to a crisis. He was also generally more concerned about the situation in the Habsburg hereditary lands. Nevertheless, Joseph also pressed for what would have brought greater power within the Empire. In 1780, despite Frederick's opposition, Joseph's younger brother Maximilian was elected successor to the archbishop-elector of Cologne and prince-bishop of Münster. He assumed his roles in 1784 and thus created a Habsburg presence in the lower Rhineland to match that of Prussia at Cleves and Mark and of Bavaria in Jülich, Berg and the Palatine. However, Maximilian then had to flee from his capital Bonn in 1794 in the face of advancing French troops.

In 1784, Joseph began to press hard for the exchange of the Austrian Netherlands (Belgium) – which he ruled – for Bavaria. This was a reprise of the idea suggested in 1777 and it would have transformed German geopolitics. Charles Theodore was willing, but his heir was not. France refused to support Austria, while Russia was unwilling to intimidate Frederick the Great. The lack of international support proved crucial, but Frederick also formed the *Fürstenbund* ('League of Princes') in 1785. It was a measure of the suspicion aroused by Joseph that the German princes – who had traditionally backed the emperor or been wary of opposing him and had thus tended to isolate Frederick within the Empire, as had generally been the case during the Seven Years' War – were willing publicly to form a league against him. Many of the ecclesiastical princes were also unhappy about Joseph's critical attitude towards the Church and suspected him of being willing to support secularisation. The *Fürstenbund* proved more powerful than the last major league that was not reliant on external sponsorship, the Wittelsbach *Hausunion* of the 1720s. It represented a revival of the alliance of 1719–26 between Hanover and Prussia that had opposed the apparent determination of Charles VI to increase imperial authority.

To an extent, this was politics as normal but – also to a degree – it was an indication of acute strain in the Empire and this contrast reflects the complexity of assessing its character and trajectory. The *Fürstenbund* certainly marked an Austrian failure to weaken Prussia within the Empire. Austrian hopes of benefitting from the death of Frederick in 1786 in order to wage a war of revenge against Prussia were probably unrealistic but were to be dashed, anyway, by the Turkish declaration of war on Russia in 1787. This would involve Austria in Balkan conflict as an ally of Russia. Thus, an Austro–Prussian dualism in the Empire continued.

At a different level, the commonplace of dispute continued. Thus, in 1787, the prince-bishop of Freising and Bavaria contested both superiority over the county of Werdenfels, where the fortress had been owned by the prince-bishop since 1249, but had been enfeoffed several times, and also control over dykes on the River Isar. The following year the latter dispute went to the Aulic Council, the imperial court. In the event, Werdenfels went to Bavaria as part of the secularisation in 1802.

Austria and Prussia, having inconclusively fought in 1778–9, came very close to war again in 1790 as Prussia successfully tried to pressurise Austria not to make territorial gains in the Balkans. To many in Germany, this appeared more important than the early stages of revolution in France.

The Problem of Mapping Germany, 1762

In 1762, Walter Titley, British envoy in Copenhagen, attempted to secure a map that would throw light on the 'hereditary animosity and ancient grudge' that lay behind the Holstein-Gottorp dispute. On 2 March, he wrote to Edward Weston, an undersecretary:

'A map of the Duchy of Holstein, wherein the royal and ducal possessions are distinctly marked, is, I believe, one of the *Desiderata* of geography. I do not know that there is any such map extant; but if I should happen to meet with one, you may be sure to have it. In the meantime I can send you here, in a very few lines, a list of the territories properly belonging to the Duke.'

A week later, Titley wrote again:

'Having found one of Homann's maps, wherein the two several parts of the Duchy of Holstein were distinguished with colours, though not strongly nor exactly, I have spread a shade of deep burgundy upon all the possessions, which properly belong to the duke; and the three ducal cities (which were very obscurely exhibited) I have marked with a small black cross, that may possibly catch your eye and help you when you look them out. These possessions lie in four different parcels, entirely separated from each other by the intervention of royal or collateral territory. I am not satisfied with this part; it is blind and indistinct and the river courses seem not always well traced; however it is right, as to the ducal dominions and may serve your purpose perhaps, till a better can be met with.'

On 27 March, Titley wrote, forwarding another map:

'You have herewith another map of Holstein, which is somewhat better, as being more distinct, than the first I sent you. The several territories are distinguished by colours. Green denotes the royal parts and red the ducal. The yellow tracts belong to the bishop and chapter of Lubeck and what little appears of the territory of Hanover is marked with a shade of blue. In the first map I had inadvertently put the famous baillage of Steinhorst under the same colour with ducal Holstein; but in this it is restored to its proper sovereign and, I think, with interest, for there are a few villages added under the blue colour which do not really belong to it. A very accurate chart of this duchy, I believe, is not to be had.'

There had been a small-scale conflict in 1738 between Denmark and Hanover over who controlled Steinhorst to the south of Holstein. Titley's main difficulty – and one he seems not to have fully grasped – was that single maps in Germany, as opposed to specially composed atlases of base maps all showing the same area, were not a particularly good way of expressing princely territorial rights. It was usually beyond the ingenuity of even the most skilled cartographer – and Germany had excellent ones, notably the Homann publishing house in Nuremberg – to indicate on one map alone areas of mixed jurisdictions. Each would owe allegiance to various rulers for different aspects of their existence. When, on top of that, one adds the question of the interpretation of treaties, the inadequacy of single maps becomes still more apparent.

6

The Shadow of
France, 1792–1815

FRENCH VICTORIES

The French Revolutionary Wars began in 1792. After the invading Prussians were stopped at Valmy, the French advanced into the Rhineland while, in response to appeals for help from radicals in Mainz and Zweibrücken, the National Convention passed a decree declaring that the French people would extend fraternity and assistance to all peoples seeking to regain their liberty. The French were driven out by the Austrians in 1793 but returned anew and, in 1795, negotiated peace with an exhausted Prussia, which had become more interested in expansion in Poland and was also running out of money.

Under the Peace of Basle of 1795, Prussia accepted French occupation of the Rhineland, where often very violent French exploitation had already generated resistance as well as much disruption. In return, France promised gains for Prussia on the right bank of the Rhine and accepted a Prussian-led neutrality zone in northern Germany. Prussia did not fight France again until 1806.

Although the French revolutionaries presented the Rhine as a natural frontier, they advanced across it in 1795 and 1796. However, they met effective opposition organised by Austria which demonstrated its continued role, as well as major popular risings in the areas they occupied. In addition, in the 1790s, both the Reichstag and the *Kreis* system worked well, although they were hit not only by the persistence of the French challenge but also by its coincidence with Austro–Prussian rivalry.

In 1797, French successes in Italy led Austria to agree peace. The left bank of the Rhine was ceded to France in a recognition by the emperor that he could not protect the Empire. The Congress of Rastatt, intended to compensate secular rulers by letting them make gains elsewhere in the Empire, produced an impasse, but Austria's revived interest in exchanging Belgium for Bavaria was now redundant.

Rebuilding Munich

Munich was well fortified, its medieval walls supplemented under Maximilian I by new-style fortifications. However, under Elector Charles Theodore (r. 1777–99) different priorities came to the fore. The Englische Garten, the largest city park in Europe, was laid out in 1789–92 in the area north of the Schwabinger city gate and the Hofgarten (court garden), which lay within the outer defensive ring. In 1795, the elector declared that Munich 'is not, cannot be, and should not be a fortress' and announced his intention to create a new, 'open city', by razing the walls and removing any obstacles to the city's growth and planned expansion. This happened from the late 1800s.

War resumed in 1799, with the French defeated by the Austrians in Germany at Ostrach and Stockach and driven back across the Rhine. However, divisions in the second coalition combined with the new energy brought by Napoleon's takeover transformed the situation. Victories earlier in 1800 at (second) Stockach, Messkirch and Höchstädt led to the overrunning of southern Germany, with the key battle in Germany at Hohenlinden east of Munich, Jean Moreau decisively defeating the larger Austrian and Bavarian army under the inexperienced Archduke John of Austria.

Transforming Germany

Combined with Napoleon's triumph in Italy – notably over the Austrians at Marengo – the successes led to the Treaty of Lunéville with Austria in 1801. With this, the French annexation of the left bank of the Rhine was recognised. In 1803, after negotiations within the Empire, an Imperial Recess decreed that the area's secular rulers were to be compensated at the expense of the ecclesiastical states, minor principalities and cities. Thus, Jülich and the Palatinate, which, as a result of the merger of Wittelsbach lines, had been parts of Bavaria, were replaced by the gain of a number of prince-bishoprics, including Würzburg, Bamberg, Freising and Augsburg, while Prussia gained Münster. Only the electorate of Mainz was not secularised. Most Imperial Free Cities, very much a continuance of political culture from the later middle ages, lost their sovereignty.

As the ecclesiastical states had been great supporters of the imperial system, these terms, bringing great profit to the secularisers, augured the end of the Empire and helped to foster a political vacuum in Germany. They also exemplified the process of seeking the support of the defeated at the expense of others, a technique of divide and rule the French were to employ so successfully in Germany. They obliged German rulers to consider how best to confront Napoleon and to entertain reform, as well as policy changes.

Austria adopted a conciliatory approach towards extensions of French power. However, Napoleon continued his pressure, leading to a resumption of war in 1805, with Germany rather than northern Italy the central area of operations. Napoleon had built up his army in the peace years, in preparation for an invasion of Britain that he never ultimately launched, and he outmanoeuvred the Austrians, forcing them to surrender an army in Ulm. The French overran southern Germany and Austria before defeating an Austro–Russian army at Austerlitz.

Having initially refused to join the third coalition, Frederick William III of Prussia had secured Hanover from Napoleon in 1805, but Napoleon's exploitative and bullying treatment of Prussia led the indecisive Frederick William at last to enter the coalition, only to be defeated by the French at Jena–Auerstädt in 1806, the year in which the Hanseatic cities were occupied. Georg Wilhelm Friedrich Hegel referred to Jena as 'the end of history', in the sense of the chance of a new beginning. Subsequent battles, notably at Halle and Prenzlau, saw Prussian forces defeated, while the French occupied Berlin. Moreover, the impact of the war spread. The Prussians fortified neutral Lübeck, only for the French to storm it. Sweden's German possessions of Stralsund and Rügen fell into French hands in 1807.

Napoleon, meanwhile, reorganised Germany. The creation of the kingdom of Bavaria on 1 January 1806 violated the principle that there could only be one king in the Empire. In July 1806, Napoleon established an institutional basis for French intervention, the *Rheinbund* or Confederation of the Rhine, which linked France and sixteen southern and western German states, including Bavaria, Württemberg and Baden. Territorial gains helped make these rulers allies, with Württemberg doubled in size. This alliance was designed to limit Austrian and Prussian influence and also represented a rejection of the Russian intervention in German politics under the Peace of Teschen of 1779. Russia had mediated this agreement to end the War of the Bavarian Succession. Its capital at Frankfurt, the *Rheinbund* was also intended to give Napoleon, who assumed the role of protector, control over the forces and resources of the confederation's members and it backed him against Prussia later in 1806. There was no attempt to create an alternative to French direction: the Diet of the Confederation never met. This was truly an authoritarian system and different from the federalism of the Second Reich (1871–1918), let alone the First Reich.

Napoleon also had Francis II dissolve the Empire (the First Reich). On 6 August, Francis II formally abdicated his role as emperor and released all imperial states and officials from their oaths. Francis did remain emperor of Austria – a title he had assumed in October 1804. The German territories thereby became fully sovereign although, as a historical anachronism, the recently created elector of Hesse-Cassel (1803) kept his title until 1866, even though there was no longer an emperor to elect. In 1806, Napoleon also made Württemberg and Saxony into kingdoms, part of his strategy of building up an ally capable of opposing Russia in east-central Europe. It had fought on Prussia's side, yet Saxony was not treated as a defeated country. Indeed, Frederick August III/King Frederick August I also became duke of Warsaw, in a short-lived remake of the Saxon–Polish union.

In addition, Napoleon made his brother Jerome king of Westphalia in 1807 and this kingdom, the capital of which was at Cassel, included the part of Hanover not ceded to France, as well as Hesse-Cassel and part of Prussia. A modern-style constitution was issued for Westphalia, with serfdom and guilds abolished, Jews emancipated and all male residents given equal rights. However, censorship and French control were imposed and, in 1810, the northern part of the kingdom was ceded to France.

In the longest-occupied part of Germany, the Rhineland, there was an attempt to impose French structures, including over matters of the Church and language. As far as other Germans were concerned, the Rhinelanders became 'new French'. However, in practice, the Frenchification had limited effect, not least because of continuing dependence on local elites but also due to the maintenance of the German language and education. Instead, an additional complication was created, notably with the many mixed marriages, for the existing pattern of multiple identities.

A cynical exploitation of allies and a ruthless reliance on the politics of expropriation repeatedly became evident. In 1808, the French agreed to end their onerous occupation of defeated Prussia, but at the cost of the cession of its territories west of the Elbe to France, the permanent occupation of the major fortresses in eastern Prussia, a massive indemnity, a network of French military roads across the kingdom, the limitation of the Prussian army and its support in any conflict with Austria and the free transit of French goods. These were terms that for Prussia were far worse even than that for Germany in 1918, and, again, were the product of launching an advanced state into the unpredictable maelstrom of international conflict. The shock of defeat encouraged calls for German nationalism as with the *Addresses to the German Nation* (1808) by the Berlin-based philosopher Johann Gottlieb Fichte, with its theme of a common identity.

By 1808, the Confederation of the Rhine included thirty-six states, but some of its territories were then lost. French expansion played a key role. Hamburg, Lübeck, Bremen and Oldenburg were annexed by France in 1810, followed by Swedish Pomerania in January 1812. Meanwhile, given territory at the expense of an Austria defeated anew by France in 1809, Bavaria was obliged to cede land to Württemberg. The Austrians had received no help from other German rulers in that war, a major contrast to the situation that was to arise in 1866 when Prussia attacked Austria.

NAPOLEON DEFEATED

By 1812, Napoleon took with him many allied German units – including from Prussia, Baden, Bavaria, Berg, Saxony and Westphalia – when he invaded Russia, only to be totally defeated. The Russians established a Russian–German Legion from prisoners and deserters that eventually became part of the Prussian army. The states that Napoleon had bullied into providing troops and resources then moved against him, although at a very different rate.

Prussia was the key player and, on 30 December 1812, the army that had invaded Russia negotiated a truce with the Russians. Prussia was in a difficult position – under pressure from both France and Russia. In January 1813, Napoleon harshly rejected Prussian terms and ordered the continuation of Prussia's commitment to the war.

However, a wave of Francophobia in the army and part of the populace in early 1813 put pressure on the government, which, in February, negotiated an alliance with Russia. In March the two powers agreed on the liberation of Germany. Frederick William III summoned the Prussian people to fight for their king, fatherland, freedom and honour and promised a constitution, a promise he never kept. Suspicious of moving beyond the army, the king also came reluctantly to support a *Landwehr* (conscripted militia), in order to raise numbers. It soon contained twenty thousand men.

Napoleon fought back hard in Germany, aided by concerns about Russian and Prussian intentions among the German rulers, specifically their support for a mass insurrection. The Prussians themselves were concerned about Russian plans for Poland. Napoleon rebuilt his army and the new levies, both French and German, helped him drive his opponents out of Saxony in May 1813, winning victories at Lützen (2 May) and Bautzen (20–21 May). North Germany did not rise against him as had been anticipated. Saxony rallied to Napoleon in May.

Concerned about their intentions, Austria refused to join Russia and Prussia, but did stop fighting the former. Austria proposed an independent central Europe, neutral towards both France and Russia. Prince Klemens von Metternich, the talented Austrian foreign minister from 1809 to 1848 (and chancellor from 1821 until 1848) was hostile to Prussia and Russia. He hoped to reach an agreement with Napoleon and create a partnership that would secure Austrian interests and re-establish Habsburg influence in Germany. In particular, Metternich, who saw a powerful France as a counterweight to Russia, sought stability rather than territorial expansion.

Metternich offered Napoleon the left bank of the Rhine and co-guarantorship of a neutralised *Rheinbund*, but Napoleon declared all France's annexations inalienable. His refusal to understand that peace entailed compromise led Austria to declare war on 11 August 1813. The French were now heavily outnumbered, although Napoleon was victorious at Dresden on 27 August and the French regained Cassel on 4 October.

Napoleon's system collapsed, however, that month. Threatened with Austrian invasion, Bavaria – long a stalwart of French interests – allied with Austria, as did Württemberg, both demonstrating the great political skill of changing sides at the right moment. On 16–19 October 1813, Napoleon was heavily defeated at Leipzig in the Battle of the Nations. Germany was lost, as Napoleon was no longer in a position to assist and exploit Frederick August of Saxony, whose territories were now occupied by Prussia and Russia. The *Rheinbund* collapsed.

In 1814, Napoleon refused to surrender the Rhineland as the price of a more general peace and renewed peace talks with Austria failed. Prussian and Austrian forces advanced on Paris, where Napoleon abdicated on 6 April.

The 1814–15 Settlement

In the subsequent Peace of Paris of 30 May 1814, France was restored to her frontiers of January 1792 for, as with the peaces of 1697, 1714 and 1748, German hopes of regaining Alsace were not fulfilled. However, a territorial consolidation on France's borders greatly limited its chances of expansion. The kingdom of Sardinia (ruler of Savoy-Piedmont) was strengthened with Genoa, while Belgium and the Netherlands were united, although its ruler's hopes of expansion in the Rhineland proved fruitless. Most crucially, Prussia regained the German territories it had lost under Napoleon and gained much of Westphalia and the lower Rhineland, including Cologne, Coblenz, Münster and Trier, a major extension of Protestant rule over Catholics. It ensured that Prussia was now cast in the role of champion of German national integrity against France, as well as becoming coal rich.

The Prussian acquisition of so much more of the Rhineland and Westphalia than it had held previously led to a fundamental reorientation of Prussian policy westwards, not least as Poland was now stabilised as a largely Russian sphere of control, a situation that lasted until the First World War. Prussia was given an incentive to link its western and eastern possessions, first economically and ultimately through military and political unification.

Prussia's gains helped to substantiate Austro–Prussian dualism in Germany. Yet the Austrians were the predominant partner. The Holy Roman Empire was not recreated and nor were the ecclesiastical principalities. Germany was left with only thirty-nine states. Austria assumed the permanent presidency of the German Confederation on its foundation on 8 June 1815, a union of sovereign princes and free cities. Moreover, Austria regained the lands ceded to Bavaria and France, although not the Black Forest possessions lost in 1805. Partly as a result, Baden and Württemberg were both strengthened, each acquiring significant Catholic minorities. Bavaria lost some of its Napoleonic gains, especially the Tyrol and Salzburg, but it kept others, notably Ansbach-Bayreuth (from Prussia) and Regensburg and now, in confirmation of the 1803 settlement, it added Würzburg and part of the Palatinate.

Hanover, which had ceased to exist during the wars, being gained first by Prussia and then by France – before part was granted to the kingdom of Westphalia – was restored. It was enlarged, notably with East Friesland, Hildesheim and Osnabrück, all gains George II (r. 1727–60) had failed to obtain. It became the fourth largest state in Germany, after Austria, Prussia and Bavaria (and the fifth largest in population). In 1814 it became a kingdom, joining Prussia, Saxony, Bavaria and Württemberg. This was a testimony to British power and Hanover and Britain remained under the same monarch until 1837. However, Hanover's territorial gains were modest – far less than those of Prussia. Indeed, Hanover remained only a regional presence and even that came with weaknesses: Lauenburg was lost to Denmark. Far from Hanover absorbing neighbouring principalities, Hamburg and Bremen remained free cities (as did Frankfurt and Lübeck); Oldenburg (the ruling house linked to the Russian royal family), Brunswick, Lippe-Detmold and Schaumburg-Lippe continued to be independent.

Peace offered an opportunity for new alignments. Initially, Metternich had hoped for an alliance of Austria, Britain and Prussia to check both France and Russia and, as a result, had been willing to see annexations as the price of Prussian cooperation against Russia. However, when Frederick William III rejected this policy of his minister, Karl August von Hardenberg, Metternich changed tack, and, in January 1815, Austria, Britain and France concluded a triple alliance, agreeing to oppose – if necessary by force – both Prussia's wish to annex Saxony and also Russia's plans in Poland. Hostilities appeared possible, but in May 1815, Frederick William, who had particularly wished to gain Leipzig, backed down, although he was still ceded about 58 per cent of Saxony.

This compromise owed much to a focus on Napoleon, who had evaded control, returned from exile in Elba and regained power in France. He hoped to create a new league, including the minor German powers, but this was simply testament to his lack of realism. The major powers renewed their alliance against him and other territories agreed. Reacting to the revived threat, they allocated contributions to what might have been a long-term struggle. Thus, Austria and Prussia were each to produce 150,000 troops, while the Hanseatic cities were each to produce three thousand and Mecklenburg-Schwerin 3,800.

Napoleon aimed to defeat his opponents sequentially. Invading on 15 June, he attacked his nearest opponents, British and Prussian forces deployed in Belgium – the British army including Dutch, Belgian and many German units. The Prussians were hit hard at Ligny on 16 June and over ten thousand deserted because the army included many newly absorbed and dissatisfied Saxons and Rhinelanders. Fourteen thousand mutinous Saxon troops had already been sent home in May and a few were shot.

On 18 June 1815, in the battle of Waterloo, the German units in Wellington's army, essentially from Brunswick, Hanover and

Nassau, put up a brave resistance, helping Wellington defeat successive French attacks. Indeed, memorials were to be erected in Hanover (in Waterlooplatz) and Nassau. The arrival of Prussian forces under Blücher and Gneisenau against the French right at Waterloo, where there was bitter fighting at Plancenoit, spelled the end. Some of the Prussian troops sung the Lutheran psalm 'A Mighty Fortress is Our God'.

German units played a major role in the subsequent invasion of France, the Prussians inflicting much damage in response to their earlier humiliation in 1806. Major William Turner wrote from near Paris: 'Every town and village is completely ransacked and pillaged by the Prussians and neither wines, spirits or bread to be found.' The Prussians were also prominent in the occupation that followed. Austria, Prussia, Bavaria, Saxony and Hanover were also among those providing units – the Bavarian role was ironic given its recent position of ally of Napoleon. In the new peace terms, Saarlouis and Landau were ceded by France to Prussia and Bavaria respectively.

The Pont de Jena was not demolished as Marshal Blücher wanted, but Germany was now free to pursue its destiny without French intervention. Moreover, Prussia had regained a useful historic account in the identity politics that were advanced from 1813. Thus, in 1851, Johann Gustav Droysen produced a biography of Count Johann Yorck von Wartenburg, a Prussian field marshal, hero of the 1813 war of liberation and a conservative, a work that did not harm the National Liberal Droysen's efforts to gain an academic post.

At the same time, not all Germans were happy with the direction of travel. Goethe was a supporter of Napoleon, in 1828 describing him as a 'demi-god . . . in a state of continual enlightenment'. Napoleon had bestowed the Legion d'Honneur upon him in 1806, alongside the writer Christoph Martin Wieland (1733–1813) who, in 1767, had produced the first *Bildungsroman* or 'coming of age' novel.

Caspar David Friedrich (1774–1840), the most talented German Romantic painter, was born in then Swedish-ruled Griefswald. He studied there and in Copenhagen, becoming thereby part of the German–Scandinavian culture of the Baltic. Settling in Dresden in 1798, he was elected a member of the Berlin Academy in 1810 but, in 1816, he chose to identify more clearly with Saxony, applying for Saxon citizenship and, in 1818, becoming a member of the Saxon Academy. His superb, almost dreaming landscapes, provide a corrective to any account of the period focused primarily on battle and territorial change, but politics did affect his work. His nationalism was directed against the French during what conservatives were to call the 'war of liberation', liberals tending to prefer the term 'war for freedom'.

Indeed, the 1806–13 experience of foreign occupation, and the anger at cooperation with France, were to be far more unsettling than after 1945. In part, this was because the Third Reich, in destroying German alternatives, had left an emptiness and exhaustion that was different to the situation of the French-dominated Germany in 1806–13. The latter did not prevent other opinions from being advanced that, in its disintegration, provided full rein for the expression of nationalist views. Moreover, the damage and humiliation imposed by the French was to be more potent because it focused on Prussia, the major German state after 1815 and even more so after 1866.

There was also the extent to which, in ending foreign occupation and/or enforced cooperation, 1813 was a cathartic experience. This was to be a less conditional and contentious experience than in 1517, 1848, 1918–19 and 1933 and one that was not to be really matched until 1989. By then, liberation was perceived differently, but the experience had many similarities with that of 1813. So it was in the sense of aftermath not always matching the high hopes that had been held. What the legacy of this war would be, however, remained unclear.

7

Unification, 1815–66

....

'After fifty years of peace the Prussian state needs a good
baptism by fire ... much blood will be shed, but so it is
with the history of man as with the land we toil over: only
by our blood is it nourished.'

Albrecht von Stosch (1818–96), Prussian
general, on war with Denmark, 1864

AFTER THE WAR

The revolutionary and Napoleonic periods had led to crucial internal changes in German states that had been occupied or influenced by France. Although those areas had been gravely compromised by the burdens and humiliation of war – for example in
Bavaria – French hegemony had produced reform and secularisation. This had apparently offered a model for unification but,
totally flawed in its genesis by cooperation with Napoleon, that
model was set aside by defeat in 1815. This defeat made further
possible the discrediting of many German ruling houses for cooperation with France.

In place of the Napoleonic disorder, not least its incessant
change, came, not the restoration of the pre-1792 situation, but a
new conservative order, albeit with the Empire remaining a
significant memory and model which, indeed, was to influence
the Frankfurt parliament in 1848–9. By the quadruple alliance of
November 1815, the four great powers – Austria, Britain, Prussia
and Russia – renewed their anti-French grouping for twenty
years. Moreover, the new settlement for Germany sat within the
attempt to develop a practice of collective security through a

congress system, with Tsar Alexander I's 'holy alliance' of Christian monarchs – or, at least, those of Russia, Austria and Prussia – designed to maintain the new order. This provided no prospectus for radical change within Germany. In Prussia, concern about the *Landwehr* (militia), seen by aristocratic officers as a social threat, ensured opposition to the institution.

The King Goes to Hanover, 1821

No king of Britain and elector of Hanover had visited Hanover since George II in 1755. Indeed, in his *A Tour from London to Petersburg* (1780), John Richard noted, 'The Hanoverians do not mention England with any marks of cordial friendship. They seem to consider the absence of their elector as a disadvantage to them.'

In 1821, George IV, who had already become the first monarch to visit Ireland since 1690, travelled to Hanover, via a visit to Waterloo. In Hanover he was king, as a result of the Congress of Vienna. At Osnabrück, he was greeted rapturously by his subjects. George's skill in making himself agreeable to a new audience was demonstrated by his facility in speaking German. George enjoyed the short visit but was not terribly well. He reviewed the troops and visited Göttingen on his return route.

The interest of both Prussia and Austria in maintaining the new order helped discourage any post-war attempt at its overthrow comparable to that mounted in Italy, Belgium and Poland between 1820 and 1835. Indeed, despite tension in 1830, there were no large-scale rebellions prior to 1848 in either urban or rural Germany. In part, this was an aspect of social and political control exercised by landowners and governments over churches, education and policing; in part it was a reflection of divisions within the lower orders, not least differences in status and interest within both the peasantry and urban workers; in part it was due to ideologies of paternalism, order and subordination; and in part it was simply a matter of happenstance. Landowners' privileges were not weakened in the post-Napoleonic settlement, not least as the provincial estates (parliaments) continued to protect them.

Nevertheless, there was much liberal thought, largely through government, as a continuation of the pre-Napoleonic Enlightenment but, more directly, as an evolving product of a process of reform in government associated with the conflicts of the Napoleonic period itself. This was related to the idea of rationally based policies and, to a degree, to the materialism of science and economics; a form of utilitarianism, secular in motivation, but with a broader background.

In response to the post-Napoleonic redrawing of boundaries, new governmental systems needed to be introduced, notably for Prussia in the Rhineland, where Catholics endured the disruption of being put under a Protestant state. This became part of the more sustained crisis of German Catholicism from the 1790s, one that was to last until the post-Second World War partition of Germany ended Protestant Prussia's ascendancy. The importance of religion made this crisis more significant, but it was only part of a broader disruption in established Christianity. Liberal biblical scholarship was a related strand, challenging the literal inspiration of scripture and designed to help explain faith in a rational fashion. David Friedrich Strauss (1808–74) contradicted the historicity of supernatural elements, as well as Christology in the Gospels, in his *Das Leben Jesu* (*The Life of Jesus*, 1835–6). As a reminder of the varied reaches of history, he also wrote a major biography of Ulrich von Hutten, a key figure in the early Reformation.

Literature

Amid the high drama of politics, it is important to note that life went on. Ernst Theodor Hoffmann (1776–1822) had politics thrust upon him in 1806 when French victories made his Prussian civil service post redundant. He didn't regain his career until 1814, only to get into trouble in 1822 for satirising the Commission for the Investigation of Treasonable Organisations of which he had been a founding member in 1819. Written and published in 1819, *Die Brautwahl* (*The Choosing of the Bride*), features the pompous chancellery private secretary and the attractive young heroine Albertine who 'will in any event not remain single: she is much too pretty and much too rich for that'.

Elsewhere, as an expression of a growing awareness of a common German heritage, the Hanau-born Brothers Grimm – Jacob (1785–1863) and Wilhelm (1785–1859) – produced a dictionary, *Deutsches Wörterbuch*, published from 1852 and collected *Volksmärchen* (folklore), their *Children's and Household Tales* being published in two volumes in 1812 and 1815 and their *German Legends* in 1816–18.

CUSTOMS UNIONS

The major effort at state-directed change originated in an attempt to cope with economic problems by organising a custom-free zone that would overcome toll barriers and enable Germany to protect itself against British industrialisation.

Prussia played a key role with a *Zollverein* (customs union), but the endeavour succeeded in large part due to comparable interest by many other states. Württemberg saw such a zone as an opportunity to develop a union of states that neither looked to Austria nor Prussia and, in 1828, founded the South German Customs Union with Bavaria. A Central German Union, focused on Saxony, Hanover and Hesse-Cassel was similarly established. However, as exemplifying an aspect of the failure – both economic and political – of the other states, the Prussian-based union proved most successful and, after a series of accessions, the three customs unions merged in 1833–5. The *Zollverein* came formally into existence in 1834. Other states joined, including Frankfurt (1836), Brunswick (1841), Oldenburg (1854) and Hanover (1854), although Hamburg and Bremen did not do so until 1888.

Spa-Gambling at Baden

A very individual direction was taken by Baden-Baden where, encouraged by the government, new spa buildings were constructed from the 1820s and the railway arrived in 1845. Gambling was a key element of the city's success. It became Europe's summer capital and an extension, in part, of French high society.

The *Zollverein* did not cause unification, but it indicated a powerful drive in that direction associated with reform, a weakness of territorial states as they were too small for new economic needs, and a marginality on the part of Austria. Anxiety in the early 1830s and 1840s about war with France encouraged German rulers to look to Prussia for protection.

REVOLUTION IN 1848

Austrian marginality was further demonstrated during the Year of Revolutions – 1848 – for Austria faced a series of major crises, including in Vienna, Prague, Austrian Italy and Hungary. Those in Italy and Hungary proved especially intractable and the Austrians were unable to play a key role in either Germany and Denmark. In part, that also reflected the refusal to convert the Habsburg monarchy into a personal union in return for being awarded the German crown when it was offered.

Instead, it was Prussia that took action. Invading Schleswig-Holstein on behalf of the rebels against the Danish attempt to increase control, the forces raised under the authorisation of the German Confederation failed to exploit their military successes. The war ended in a stalemate: British, Russian and Swedish support for Denmark led Frederick William IV of Prussia to back down. He was concerned anyway about the direction of German liberalism, and in 1849 refused to accept the crown of a new, united nation that a national assembly, called in Frankfurt in 1848, had offered him as part of its plan to form a modern national constitution. The Hohenzollern dynasty had a strong sense of purpose and a commitment to Prussian strength, in both government and the military. The national assembly matched neither its image nor its prospectus.

Across much of Germany, 1848 saw movements for reform characterised by a liberal nationalism that relied heavily on the urban middle class and had only limited popular support. The movements drew on and accelerated a process of politicisation involving group activity and publications, such that the number of newspapers in Berlin rose from 118 in 1847 to 184 by 1850. The theme of 'the nation' was crucial to the liberal cause, rather than preservation of the independence of the existing territories. 'Germanness' was presented in the Frankfurt Assembly as a multifaceted abstraction, with no one individual marker. In part, there was an attempt to subsume the fact of Prussian power into a federal solution, with conservatives strongly wanting to maintain both existing states and a link with Austria.

The army under the future Wilhelm I overcame liberal opposition in Prussia in 1848, and the use of regular troops against popular uprisings became widespread in Germany. Well-disciplined Prussian forces, benefitting from the use of railways, helped put down poorly led uprisings in Baden (where they won a victory at Rastatt), Hesse, the Palatinate, Saxony and Württemberg. Prussian forces also drove the assembly from Frankfurt. The Prussian 'needle' rifle, with its high rate of fire, was employed to devastating effect. Radicals fled abroad, including Richard Wagner, who went to Zurich. The revolution had failed because of divisions over its goals and methods, a lack of impetus and the (eventual) strength of opposition. Readily apparent in Frankfurt, the divisions helped ensure that much of the reforming enthusiasm and energy was dissipated in internal differences.

A keen admirer of Prussia, who had lived for much of the 1820s in Berlin, the choleric Ernest I of Hanover (r. 1837–51), George III's very martial fifth son, had come to the throne when William IV died without legitimate issue. His niece ascended to the British throne as Queen Victoria but the law forbade female succession in Hanover. Thus, the dynastic link with Britain came to an end – one of the major might-have-beens of German history. A British king in Hanover would have radically altered the script of Prussian success in 1866.

A reactionary, Ernest revoked the liberal 1833 constitution, thus demonstrating the unsettled nature of political trajectories, and overcame radical tendencies in Hanover during the Year of Revolutions. Indeed, not only did German unification under Prussia not have to take its subsequent form and direction, but Prussian identity, and that of other states, were more contingent than much of the criticism directed against Prussia then, and subsequently, would suggest.

Beer Gardens

A feature of German life that developed in nineteenth-century Munich. Most establishments originally let customers bring their own food. In many now, only food sold on the premises is allowed. Classic dishes include sausages, grilled chicken and fish, soft pretzels and pork. It is common to share the tables. Very much part of Bavarian culture. Strongly recommended.

TOWARDS UNIFICATION

The 1848–9 crisis underlined the value of Prussia to other rulers but Austrian army mobilisation proved more effective in the 1850 attempt by Prussia to create the Erfurt Union – a federation of German states under its leadership. Moreover, the Austrians enjoyed Russian diplomatic and Bavarian military support. The Prussians backed down in what became, in German nationalist history, the 'humiliation of Olmütz', one of the major non-wars in German history.

Although Prussia had attacked Austria in 1740, 1744 and 1778, they had also backed down on earlier occasions when war had appeared very close, notably – but not only – in 1726, 1785 and 1790. However, the context was now very different, due both to the much more public character of politics and to the expectations created by the crises of 1813 and 1848–9. In 1850, Prussia agreed to the Austrian demand for the revival of the Austrian-led German Confederation.

The crisis showed the significance both of non-German powers in any confrontation between Prussia and Austria and of effective mobilisation. These lessons were to be well learned by Prussian planners, with the army improved by Count Helmuth von Moltke, appointed chief of staff in 1857 – a post he held until

1888. Meanwhile, the Crimean War (1854–6) saw the Austro–Russian alignment breached, a weakening of Austria that provided Prussia with opportunities. Moreover, Austria was heavily defeated by the French in Italy in 1859, which was an important enabler of German unification.

Planning Berlin

Unlike the contemporary reconfiguration of Paris by Baron Haussmann, James Hobrecht's 1862 plan for Berlin did not involve redeveloping the historic centre. Instead, guidelines for expansion included standardised housing blocks, orbital distributor roads and main radial roads. The density of the development was to be balanced with regular squares and open spaces. Although some of his ideas were not fully implemented, the plan did form the foundation upon which the city expanded in the late nineteenth century. An impressed Mark Twain praised Berlin as the 'Chicago of Europe'. This was a key instance of a rebuilding of one of Germany's major cities and Berlin provided a model that was implemented elsewhere.

Moltke brought important organisational improvement to the Prussian army. The Prussians sought to control conflict by treating it as a process in which the systematised application of planned pressure led to predictable results. To do so entailed adapting Napoleonic ideas of carrying out continuous offensives to the practicalities of the industrial age, which now included the use of railways.

There was also significant state-building in domestic affairs, with the 1850s seeing a lessening of feudal practices related to the role of guilds and to aristocratic rights over the peasantry. This was a conservative process of reform without disruption, one that was conducive both to capitalist enterprise and to state activity, focusing on infrastructure improvement – notably in railways, telegraphs, public health and policing. At the same time, repression increased, in the shape of surveillance, manipulation of the press and legal measures. This stabilisation of Prussia under Minister President Otto von Manteuffel (r. 1850–8) was not focused on war, but it was to make easier the tasks of Wilhelm I, Moltke and Bismarck.

Italian unification in 1860 greatly encouraged German nationalists. Wilhelm I was regent of Prussia from 1858 as a result of his brother Frederick William IV having a series of strokes. He became king in 1861, ruling until 1888. Like his army and bureaucracy as a whole, he was a conservative, who had spent his earlier career in the army. The key political issue at his accession related to the control of the army budget by the Prussian parliament (*Landtag*). By default, the finances constrained the army's size. The deadlock between government and parliament was broken by Wilhelm appointing Otto von Bismarck to office in 1862. Bismarck rode roughshod over the rights of parliament using the implicit threat of force and, to a degree, parliamentary democracy was overthrown.

Prussia's aims, inspired and directed by Bismarck – Minister President from 1862 to 1890 – and by Moltke, were focused specifically on the creation of a Prussian-dominated Germany. The failure of the liberal revolutions of 1848 ensured that German nationalism was increasingly focused on Prussia. In 1863, Christian IX of Denmark issued a new constitution that incorporated Schleswig into Denmark. The following January, an Austro–Prussian ultimatum required the abrogation of this constitution. Danish refusal led in February to an Austro–Prussian invasion of Schleswig and the defeated and outnumbered Danes had to accept the Treaty of Vienna of October 1864, placing Schleswig-Holstein under joint Austro–Prussian control.

The unsettled nature of this condominium and of the political situation within Germany, however, was exacerbated by domestic problems in both Austria and Prussia. This encouraged their rulers to war in 1866. In the Seven Weeks' War, of June to August, the Prussians gained the initiative, thanks in part to their more effective mobilisation and deployment plans, benefitting from a better rail system. Invading Bohemia, the Prussians outmanoeuvred and defeated the Austrians. By the Treaty of Prague that August, Austria paid an indemnity, withdrew from the German Confederation, which was dissolved, and recognised the annexation of its allies in north Germany. The two-power system in Germany, with Austria the senior partner, in part an echo of its earlier position, had gone. Rather than seeking *revanche* in Germany, Austria increasingly pursued a Balkan destiny, which made it possible to negotiate a dual alliance with Prussia in 1879.

The Prussians also defeated Austria's German allies, who had over 100,000 troops between them. Although the conflict's swift end greatly diminished possible consequences, this was a civil war in the short, medium and long terms. The Hanoverians, under General Alexander von Arentschildt, defeated the Prussians, under Edward Moritz von Flies, at Langensalza on 27 June. However, due to the Hanoverian army being cut off from all supplies and outnumbered by a rapidly assembled Prussian force, they had to surrender two days later, before they could unite with their Bavarian allies. As a result, the Prussians overran Hanover and Hesse-Cassel. Other Prussian forces advanced to Nuremberg and Frankfurt, although the Bavarian garrison of Würzburg resisted attack.

Prussia gained no territory from Austria in the resulting peace, but its annexation of Hanover, Hesse-Cassel, Nassau, Frankfurt (which had been neutral in the war) and Schleswig-Holstein, made it dominant in northern Germany as well as unified with its Rhenish territories. In November 1866, the defeated king Johann was allowed to return to Saxony, in large part because Bismarck was sensitive to public opinion and the unpopularity of Prussia in the region. Moreover, Saxony was now very clearly subordinate.

In contrast, George V of Hanover was unwilling to follow the Saxon example. Instead of negotiating, he backed anti-Prussian activism – including a political party, newspapers, and a military force based on that which had operated during the occupation of Hanover in the Napoleonic era. Hanover, indeed, was the German state most hostile to Prussification. George went into exile in Vienna, his claim being inherited by his son, Ernst August. In 1913, his son, another Ernst August, married Wilhelm II's daughter Victoria Louise. The claim continues to this day in the family but without political consequence.

In the 1850s, Bavaria, Saxony and Württemberg had seen themselves as leaders of the middling states and accordingly able to provide a 'Third Germany'. Their competition, however, helped to weaken the chance of reforming the German Confederation as a basis for unification. Rapid Prussian victory in 1866 ended this idea. Württemberg had mistakenly hoped for a Prusso–Austrian stalemate. Instead, concern about France helped Württemberg turn after the war to alliance with Prussia. This finally ended what might have been a liberal basis for unification, or at least one with a more significant Third Germany component.

Prussian dominance was underlined in 1867 when the North German Confederation was formed: it incorporated the remainder of north Germany into a federal state which was very much controlled by Prussia. Moreover, it introduced new administrative divides, as with the province of Hesse-Nassau created in 1868 from Hesse-Cassel, Nassau and Frankfurt. These reorganisations lessened the prospect of opposition. Barracks were built in such newly incorporated towns as Marburg. Yet far more than coercion was involved. Indeed, the major territorial changes in 1795–1814 had left many people with only limited engagement with the territorial states that also had to adapt in 1866–71. Different Germanies had become a reality from the 1790s and into the 1800s, ensuring that multilayered identities would be refocused once more.

Leopold von Ranke

Professor of history from 1825 to 1871 at the University of Berlin, which had been founded in 1810, Ranke had clear political and historical preferences for the development of a strong Prussia. His professionalism operated very much within that context. Ranke was very hostile to the 1848–9 radical revolution and, in 1849, claimed that only military force kept the peace in Berlin. He applauded Frederick William IV's eventual move towards a more conservative approach to politics.

Although other writers, such as Alexander von Humboldt (1767–1825), did not make the nation-state central to their vision of historical development, it was a theme that became more significant in the nineteenth century. Thus, Johann Gustav Droysen – who taught in the University of Berlin from 1859 to 1884 – produced his *History of Prussian Politics*, which served, in his view, as German by destiny and vice versa. Whereas liberals presented Frederick the Great as enlightened, conservatives emphasised his role as a great war leader.

NEW LANDSCAPES

The railway, and its bridges and cuttings, was the most obvious technological manifestation, but it was not the only one. Steamships were important for sea and river travel, but also ensured local requirements such as dredging and the provision of coal. Indeed, the sight of steam and smell of burning coal became part of the German landscape and experience.

Growing industrialisation of the landscape occurred, notably in the Ruhr. Rural industry had been powered largely by water, wind, animals or humans and was essentially small-scale. Much of it was down to households. Steam-driven industry brought not only factories but also worker housing, and rural areas suffered deindustrialisation. The contrast between rural and urban areas became much more marked.

CONCLUSION

The path of German history in the nineteenth century might suggest unification, but certainly not its form or end. This was made abundantly clear by the contrast between 1871 and the unification attempted in 1848. As in 1806, these were new forms of German federalism. It was unclear how soon south Germany would follow the formation of the North German Confederation, but the war of 1866 suggested that local resistance and intervention by Austria would be ineffective. Whether Napoleon III could thwart Prussia was uncertain, but the direction of travel appeared clear. Meanwhile, economic and cultural changes over the century were helping encourage unification, notably movements across territorial borders in search of work, the creation of new routes, nodes and networks with the train and the increasingly national stance of many political, cultural and economic movements, institutions and tendencies. However, the extent to which this nation-building was due to unification or a cause of it, is a matter of conjuncture. German institutions and patriotism long preceded this conjuncture and they could lead in different directions.

It was possible to admire German music and universities, while disliking the social and political forces that had created Bismarck's Prussia. Masculinities could be formed through war, the commemoration of wars and military service, but that was not the inevitable pattern. Again, that remains a persistent feature in the assessment of German history.

Social Dynamics in Germany According to Marx and Engels

'In Germany, the petite bourgeois class, a relic of the sixteenth century, and since then constantly cropping up again under various forms, is the real social basis of the existing state of things. To preserve this class is to preserve the existing state of things in Germany. The industrial and political supremacy of the bourgeoisie threatens it with certain destruction; on the one hand, from the concentration of capital; on the other, from the rise of a revolutionary proletariat ... The communists turn their attention chiefly to Germany, because that country is on the eve of a bourgeois revolution that is bound to be carried out under more advanced conditions of European civilisation, and with a much more developed proletariat, than that of England in the seventeenth and of France in the eighteenth century and because the bourgeois revolution in Germany will be but the prelude to an immediately following proletarian revolution.'

The Communist Manifesto (1848)

Their assessment was wrong.

8

A New Great Power, 1867–1918

WAR

The new political order was quickly demonstrated in renewed war, this time with France in 1870–1, the most difficult of the German Wars of Unification, but still a major triumph.

France's smaller population and lower growth rate reduced the recruitment pool for its army, which underlined the damage done to France by Prussia's success in overcoming its German opponents in 1866. Despite serious failings in battlefield performance, a well-organised German mobilisation and conflict style ensured that the poorly commanded French were conclusively defeated and notably so in the battle of Sedan, which led to the surrender of Napoleon III. The Germans pressed on to besiege Paris and overrun much of northern France, frequently behaving badly towards civilians.

A harsh peace was imposed, notably with the annexation of most of Alsace and much of Lorraine, a significant loss of territory, industrial raw materials, industrial capability and defensive depth protecting France from attack from the east. Moreover, German troops remained in France until a large indemnity was paid in 1873. These terms ensured that there would be no postwar reconciliation of France and Germany to match that between Germany and Austria after 1866, although the expectations of German public opinion left Bismarck few options.

Victory enabled Prussia to transform her hegemony within Germany into a German empire ruled from Berlin, an achievement greater than any goal of Frederick the Great. In November

1870, the North German Confederation and the south German states united to form a new state, originally called the German Confederation. In December the name 'German Empire' was adopted and its existence was proclaimed symbolically in Versailles on 18 January 1871. The Prussian dynasty presided over the other German dynasties, none of which was of imperial rank, although Bavaria, Saxony and Württemberg were kingdoms. Bismarck became chancellor of the German Empire from 1871, holding the post until 1890. Bavaria, Saxony and Württemberg, however, continued to have control of their armies as part of the structure of the new Germany, which retained the constitution of the North German Federation of 1867. The federal system, which Bismarck keenly supported, focused authority on the emperor, but was also a response to the civil war of 1866.

Politics

It would be simple then and maybe a relief to the reader, to move to peacetime; to economic expansion, social development, democratisation and cultural activity, before resuming consideration of international relations and conflict with the run-up to the First World War (1914–18). Those topics, indeed, require attention, but a key part of their context was the continued competition between great powers and the related preparedness for war. Yet, astute management, notably by Bismarck, did lessen the risk of conflict; he was conscious of divisions within Germany and of the growing pressure of public politics in a period of increasing democracy and declining deference.

Under the 1871 constitution, the Reichstag was elected by universal male suffrage, but the government was responsible to the emperor. Moreover, the power of Prussia was entrenched in the federal council (*Bundesrat*), which had the ability to block constitutional change, while the power of the aristocracy was entrenched in the *Herrenhaus* (upper house) of the Prussian parliament.

Sceptical about the Reichstag, Bismarck feared economic growth and social change, but successfully negotiated the resulting uncertainty, producing effective expedients that held disunity at bay. He was helped by the tensions between middle-class liberalism and working-class socialism and used this to help find space for conservative outcomes, not least in the context of the male suffrage introduced between 1867 and 1871. Similarly, Bismarck pursued stability in Europe, seeing the two orders as linked.

Fear of organised labour encouraged the development from the 1870s of police forces, which drew heavily on veterans. This was an aspect of the multifaceted conservatism of the period and its ability to create, mould and engage with new practices, processes and institutions. As a result, there was not some simple process by which a redundant *junker* (landholding) class resisted attempts to push it aside in favour of a rising middle class and ascendant working class. An element of this situation existed, but it was also one of a long-established resilience and remoulding of traditional patterns, including landholding, albeit one that was to be unknit by its eventual involvement in a protracted conflict. This happened as a consequence of the effect of more traditional elements, but industrialisation was also part of the situation – as expressed by Krupp's rapidly-expanding Essen works. It would be Germany's largest company, not only a key supporter for the military but also a significant exporter.

Bismarck recognised the difficulties created by an inability to convert German military prestige into European hegemony, not least as a result of strong French interest in regaining Alsace-Lorraine. As well as unsuccessfully threatening France in 1875 with renewed attack, Bismarck sought alliance with Austria and Russia, first with Austria in 1879 and then in 1881 in the *Dreikaiserbund* (Alliance of Three Emperors: Austria, Germany and Russia). However, as a result of the Balkan crisis of 1885, this alignment did not last. Instead, a less potent alliance system left

Germany more exposed to competition: she was unable to retain Russia's alliance and the Reinsurance Treaty, which Bismarck had negotiated with her in 1887, lapsed in 1890. An arms race left the potential combatants at a higher level of preparedness than in the 1860s, but polarised between two roughly equal blocs: the Triple Alliance (of Germany, Austria and Italy) and a Franco–Russian alliance. Growing Russian strength worried German observers and, to a degree, helped to secure political support for the government within Germany.

Meanwhile, the memorialisation of victory became a key component in what was a militarised society, certainly by comparison with Britain, the USA and France. The large number of men in uniform was another aspect of militarism, as was cities vying to host garrisons. Columns of victory, triumphal arches, commemorative statues and war memorials were all erected, with celebrations held accordingly, including Sedan Day. Presented as proof of national capacity, the 1870–1 war was also portrayed as a unifying experience that superseded others, such as the role of Hanoverians and Hessians at Waterloo. Musical compositions, such as Johannes Brahms' *German Requiem* (1868), celebrated national identity.

The *Kulturkampf* ('Culture Struggle') of 1871–8, in which Bismarck, a devout Lutheran, was allied with the anti-Catholic Liberals, saw repeated criticism of the claims of the international Catholic Church. This was a longstanding Prussian stance and another aspect of the emphasis on nation, as well as obliging the Catholic south to conform to Protestant norms. About 36 per cent of the population was Catholic. Far from being passive, the papacy was very much directing Catholicism in an anti-modern and anti-liberal direction. In turn, Church control over education was challenged, notably by the Prussian School Superiors Act of 1872. The Jesuits were expelled from Germany. Further restrictions on the Church, particularly the May Laws of 1873, overturned the Catholic Church's control over clergy and laity and many of the former were imprisoned. Under the Congregations Law of 1875 about a third of monasteries were dissolved. However, the implementation of such laws was often thwarted, not least by popular opposition. The Catholics proved more united than anticipated, with Bismarck's attempt to create a separate Old Catholic Church largely unsuccessful. In contrast, Protestant divisions occurred over policy. The police were not up to the task of controlling Catholic society, and there were not the funds available to replace the Church's role in education and health.

The episode revealed the state's weakness in the face of a lack of support. Moreover, once the Catholic Centre Party became powerful, Bismarck drew back from the *Kulturkampf*, in part as an aspect of a reconciliation with conservative opinion: in 1878 he abandoned the struggle and the Liberals. Instead, Bismarck allied with conservatives in passing anti-socialist laws in 1878, a course that also helped to win the support for the new system of elites in newly incorporated territories, such as Saxony. In the face, however, of growing labour activism and of the great depression of the late nineteenth century, these measures did not end socialism. Bismarck instead sought to limit the growth of the socialist movement in the 1880s by associating the government with social welfare, including public insurance, thus creating the roots of the welfare state.

Suitable Medieval Forbears

The Second Reich, created in 1871, had potent medieval forebears. In 1879 Wilhelm I lent strong support to the reconstruction of the Goslar imperial palace built by Henry III (r. 1017–56). The large-scale historical paintings in the great hall depicted the glorious past when Salian emperors lived in the town. Large bronze statues of Barbarossa were part of the equation. Artistically indifferent, the entire project reflected a yearning for historical significance as the

---

Second Reich – in fact a Prussian enterprise – sought to accumulate suitable antecedents. In 1874, Wilhelm erected a monument over the grave of Emperor Lothair I (r. 817–55) in Prüm.

Preparedness for conflict clashed with views on domestic politics. Bismarck sustained the traditional position of the Prussian monarchy and a tax structure that benefitted landowners. In turn, in another attempt to control society, Moltke rejected the 1889–90 plan of Verdy du Vernois, the minister of war, to introduce unrestricted conscription, fearing this would create too many left-wing soldiers and middle-class officers. In 1890, in a speech in the Reichstag, Moltke voiced his concern about 'people's war', the radical social changes leading towards it and the lengthy struggle to which it might lead.

The distant past, meanwhile, was packaged in a way that extolled German greatness, as in the *Spruner-Menke Historical Atlas* (1880). In maps covering the thirteenth century, Germany was split into two – southern Germany, including Lorraine, and Switzerland – and there was also a town plan of Strasbourg. This was an accurate reflection of the Empire of the time but also, to a degree, the consequence of an attitude that did not emphasise the territorial limits of Germany. Droysen's *General Historical Atlas* (1886) included no economic history, but plenty of war – notably for 1864–71 – as well as a map showing how seventeenth-century France had extended its power in Alsace, a vital prelude to the *revanche* of 1870–1. The lesson was clear: the Austrian-led Empire had been unable to defend Germany, but its Prussian successor was more victorious and more German. The leading secondary school atlas, *Putzger's Historischer Schul-Atlas*, also devoted space to the Wars of Unification.

Creating the nationalism for a new Empire worked well when it aligned with existing loyalties, both to the current dynastic states within the Empire and to a sense of place that was expressed in German through the idea of '*Heimat*'. In part as a result, but also building on earlier practices, there was an overlapping and interaction of multiple identities, including of religion, place, dialect, family and occupation. *Heimat* stressed local identity but could do so within the context of a Germanness that was at once national but also an expression of ideas of home. This was an effective strand of nationalism. A *Heimat* movement came to be significant from the 1890s with its institutionalism in museums of local history and in other forms of localist heritage, not least the evolution of 'peasant costumes'. This was very much a small-town and rural Germany, a focus for tourism and culture.

The relationships between identities could also confuse the processes of rhetorical affirmation that were so important to national politics and thus the divisions they could encapsulate. There were more specific clashes, as in the legal action taken against the Social Democratic Party (SPD), which included the imprisonment of its leaders. Wilhelm II described the SPD as lacking a 'fatherland'. In fact, although the SPD used Marxist language, it pursued politics and power by democratic means. The increase in SPD support – about a third of the national vote by 1912 – provoked conservative alarm but the SPD, while particularly strong in Saxony – known as the 'Red Kingdom' – was unable to win the support of all urban industrial areas. Indeed, in the Ruhr, the Catholic Centre Party proved particularly successful.

Ludwig II of Bavaria, r.1864–86

Young and immature, Ludwig was an introverted recluse, spending heavily on the semblance of power, notably building Neuschwanstein Castle. He provided a Gothic revival character for Bavarian monarchy, one that also underlined its historical roots and prestige, particularly with reference

---

to Emperor Louis IV, the Bavarian (r. 1328–47). Debts caused tension with his ministers and, in 1886, accused of being unstable, he was deposed and his uncle made regent. His body was found soon after in Lake Starnberg; officially he had drowned, but possibly he had been murdered or killed in an escape attempt that went wrong. His uncle remained regent until his death in 1912; Ludwig's younger brother, Otto, was regarded as incapable due to mental illness. Otto was deposed in 1913 to make way for his cousin, Ludwig III, who was in turn deposed in November 1918 as part of the German revolution.

Neuschwanstein, near Füssen, is more impressive from a distance. Incomplete at the time of the death of Ludwig II, the palace was swiftly opened to paying visitors. Ludwig also built the lesser-known Herrenchiemsee Castle, as a copy of Versailles. It included a hall of mirrors two metres longer than an earlier version at Neuschwanstein.

Economic Transformation

At the same time, Germany was also changing radically in economic terms, notably – although not only – through indus-trialisation. By 1913, it was producing about a third of the world's manufactured goods. Good fortune was part of the equation. Germany sat on top of the biggest coal deposits in continental Europe, while the introduction of railways brought particular benefit to parts of Europe furthest from the coast and from navigable waterways, and, therefore, in particular, to Germany.

Economic opportunity affected demographics, with a signifi-cant increase in the population, from 41.1 million people in 1871 to sixty-five million in 1910, by which time the French were heavily outnumbered. Population moves reflected economic developments, notably the rapid expansion in the Ruhr and that of already major urban centres, especially Berlin and Hamburg. The working-class radicalism of Berlin appeared to be a particular challenge to the government. Hamburg offered a different set of values, not least maritime and oceanic.

Britain had led the way in the 'metal-bashing' industries and textile production of the first stage of the Industrial Revolution but, by 1914, Germany had forged ahead of Britain in iron and steel production and, indeed, produced two-thirds of Europe's steel. It was also particularly successful in the second stage of the Industrial Revolution, with new, or newly used, resources becoming especially important, in the shape of chemicals – especially those based on coal and oil by-products – and electricity. Indeed, Germany led the world in the chemical industry, producing about 85 per cent of the world's dyestuff output by 1913.

Protectionism was important to industrial growth, as was the governmental support of cartels. The resulting market integration aided market concentration, investment and vertical integration. Risk was lessened. Cartels proved particularly useful in steel production, which increased 10.4 per cent annually from 1879 to 1913. The cooperation of industry with government-funded research facilities was also crucial. Government was committed to economic growth, not least with Wilhelm I backing technological advances. German industrial concerns benefitted from the creation of a national market and transport network, from highly talented entrepreneurs and from many aspects of societal change – including the very high literacy and organisational capacity from which Karl Marx and Friedrich Engels had hoped for a different socio-political outcome. German universities had developed a very strong research tradition.

Moreover, new products, such as cars, pharmaceuticals and telephones, provided opportunities for existing and developing industrial sectors. Germany proved especially successful in electrical engineering and optical goods. By 1913, 12.2 per cent of Germany's gross national product was exported, although this was a smaller percentage than Britain's 14.7 per cent.

Mercedes

A German automotive marque and a subsidiary of Daimler AG which, in 2019, sold 3.3 million vehicles, the company's origins were in Daimler-Motoren-Gesellschaft. It first delivered a Mercedes car in 1900, which was named after Mercedes Jellinek, the daughter of Emil Jellinek, a Leipzig-born entrepreneur who financed DMG to produce the car. He joined DMG's board of management. Intended as 'the car of the day after tomorrow', it was meant to fulfil Jellinek's wish for a more stable car that could go faster.

Manufactured in Stuttgart, the car had electric ignition, a low centre of gravity, a long wheelbase and a wide track and did well in races, reaching 37 m.p.h. in 1901. Sales rose and, in 1902, the company began to use the DMG trademark for its entire automobile production.

In 1926, DMG merged with Benz to become the Daimler-Benz company. Strongly helped through financial and moral support as well as innovative ideas from his wife Bertha, Carl Friedrich Benz produced the first effective motor car in 1885, the three-wheel Benz Patent Motorwagen, manufactured in Mannheim. In 1888 this became the first commercially available automobile. Cars designed for 'mass' production followed from Benz in the 1890s, as did the first truck and the first motor bus, both in 1895. In 1899, when it was the largest automobile company in the world, Benz became a joint-stock company. The 1926 merger reflected the economic crisis of the 1920s which hit sales.

The number of kilometres of railway grew from 11,089 in 1860 to 33,838 in 1880 and 63,378 in 1913, the annual average output of coal and lignite in million metric tons rose from 41 in 1870-4 to 247 in 1910-14; for pig-iron the figures ran from 2.7 in 1880 to 14.8 in 1910; and for steel 2.2 in 1890 to 6.6 in 1900 and 13.7 in 1910. The total length of navigable waterways doubled between 1875 and 1914, with electric and steam towing an important factor. In 1906, a new series of canals was authorised.

At the same time, economic expansion helped to cause pollution and was achieved by a workforce that mostly endured low pay, poor working and living conditions and little leisure. Moreover, traditional links between place and community were disrupted by national patterns of economic change and social identity.

German growth and dynamism, not least in science, technology and social policy, led to an international reputation for the excellence of German solutions. The British national efficiency movement looked to German models and there was much interest in the German education system. At the same time, there was scant attention paid to copying German militarism, which rested on conscription.

German Railways

A very different Germany was created by the rail network. It speeded up existing routes for passengers and freight and created new openings, both within and between existing territories. These have retained their significance to this day, linking cities and breaking through existing physical barriers.

Early railways mostly ran within states, notably the first long-distance routes – Nuremberg to nearby Fürth (1835), Berlin–Potsdam (1838), Brunswick–Wolfenbüttel (1838) and Leipzig–Dresden (1837–9). The system greatly expanded in the 1840s and with that came economic opportunities for manufacturing and commerce. Initially dependent on British expertise and technology – a British-made locomotive was used in 1835 – the Germans rapidly developed the necessary skills and works and this helped encourage more general industrial expertise.

The first international mainline joined Magdeburg to Leipzig in 1840. By 1842 there were nearly a thousand kilometres of track and, in 1846, the Berlin–Hamburg railway provided an important link for the major port. Berlin to Frankfurt followed in 1852 and Berlin to Munich the year after. Tunnels and bridges provided important opportunities, notably Cologne's Cathedral Bridge in 1859.

Nationalisation of the private railway firms became more significant and, indeed, close to uniform by 1890, as did use of the rail system to support and profit from industrialisation as well as nationalisation. It was not until 1920 that the Deutsche Reichsbahn, a national company, was formed from the state railways.

EMPIRE

Colonialism enjoyed brief popularity with Prussia in the late seventeenth century, but in 1717 the two forts the Brandenburg Company had on the Gold Coast were sold to the Dutch. In the 1840s and 1860s, there was renewed talk of the value of colonies and a navy and these ideas became far more significant from the early 1880s, which was the period of what was known as the 'scramble for Africa', and a new arena for the ongoing Franco–German competition.

The Colonial League was founded in 1882 and the Society for German Colonisation in 1884. Germany went on to become a major colonial power in Africa and the Pacific and this was linked to navalism. Conquest resulted in the death of many Africans, notably in the Herero–Nama war in German South-West Africa (Namibia) in 1904–8, and the Maji Maji War in German East Africa (1905–8). The former conflict led to the deployment of a very large force, 70,000 strong. The Germans killed their opponents in large numbers, driving the Hereros into a waterless desert and treating the prisoners sent to labour camps with such great cruelty that over half of those in the camps died.

The Maji Maji War saw scorched-earth policies to deal with native opposition and about a quarter of a million Africans died of famine. The extent to which there is a link between that violence – some of it highly genocidal in consequence – and the planned racial genocide later seen in the Holocaust has been a matter of great contention. Also, although not on the same scale, serious atrocities were committed in German New Guinea on behalf of German economic interests.

Imperial activity had implications in Germany but resulted in fewer consequences for ideology, culture and politics than was the case in Britain, France, Italy, Portugal and Spain. There was no significant immigration from colonies then or later. However, empire was brought home by a range of institutions, including Berlin's Botanic Garden and Botanical Museum. Other museums benefitted from seized artworks.

Popular culture reflected its own engagement with the outside world. The most-read author, Karl May (1842–1912), wrote adventure and travel literature, mostly set in America and the Orient, which he claimed to have visited. May identified himself with his most popular figures, Kara Ben Nemsi and Old Shatterhand, the latter friend to Apache chieftain Winnetou. May was heavily influenced by James Fenimore Cooper. While nowadays presented as an early proponent of the idea of ethnic equality, May was very much a child of his own time and his German protagonists were Catholic missionaries endorsing the German character. Read by Wilhelm II, Hitler and Adenauer, May – whose stories were filmed with great popular success from the late 1960s – remains very popular, with new film versions of his work being made from the late 2010s.

Like Moving Through a Giant Toy Set

Begun in 1887 and opened in 1895, the 98-kilometre (61-mile)-long Nord-Ostsee *Kanal* (or Kiel Canal) ran from Brunsbüttel at the North Sea mouth of the Elbe to Kiel-Holtenau on the Baltic. Originally known as the Kaiser Wilhelm Canal, it was widened in 1907–14 to take battleships, opened to all vessels under the Versailles treaty of 1919 – an international status repudiated by Hitler in 1936 but reimposed after the Second World War – and in 1948 was renamed. I was struck by the eleven high bridges across the canal that made me feel as if I was in a giant toy shop, a kind of expanded trainset at Hamleys in London, most notably with the cantilever Rendsburg High Bridge, from which a transporter bridge, or gondola, is suspended. Erected in 1911–13, the bridge had long elevated embankments and access bridges in order to enable the railway to make the gradient. The gondola was badly damaged when a cargo ship collided with it in 2016.

The social and economic changes, as well as colonial expansionism, challenged ruralist notions of a German *volk*, especially those that drew on an almost mystic relationship with a supposedly primeval landscape of forests and mountains. To a degree, Wagner's operas were a product of that relationship. Ludwig Ganghofer (1855–1920), a very popular writer, not least with his personal friend Wilhelm II and through his patriotic First World War writings, set his homeland novels in the Bavarian Alps.

The traditional military and social elite that felt threatened by modernisation used militarism to defend its privileges. In an increasingly volatile situation, urbanisation and the large-scale internal immigration it reflected, mass literacy, rapid industrial-isation, secularisation, democratisation and nationalism were creating an uncertain and unfamiliar world. Reflecting the atavistic roots of Prussian militarism, the regime and other anti-democratic groups sought to impose their view of order on the flux.

In some respects prefiguring Hitler, the mediocre, difficult and endlessly self-regarding Wilhelm II (r. 1888–1918) compounded the problem by concentrating power on himself and his sycophants, not least through destabilising ministries by his appointments, policies, use of ministerial reshuffles and crass interventions in foreign policy. Leo von Caprivi, chancellor in 1890–4, was succeeded by Chlodwig, Prince of Hohenlohe-Schillingsfürst (1894–1900), Bernhard von Bülow (1900–9), and Theobald von Bethmann Hollweg (1909–17). There was also a sharply political dimension, with the socialism of working-class activists regarded on the right as a threat to an ability and willing-ness to fight, and thus justifying anti-democratic measures, as with the electoral reforms of 1895–6.

Richard Wagner (1813–83)

Born in Leipzig, Wagner was both a composer of music and a librettist who sought to bring his skills together to produce a total work of art with great dramatic force. The lavishness of the harmonies and the reiterated use of *leitmotifs* leads to a feeling of luxurious, chromatic exuberance but also, in combination with the length of his works, of languor leading to boredom.

With funding from Ludwig II of Bavaria, a major supporter, Wagner also built an opera house, at Bayreuth, dedicated solely to the performance of his own works. Opened in 1876, it was the site of the premiere of his complete four-opera cycle, *Der Ring des Nibelungen*, in the same year. The orchestra pit is hidden to maintain the focus on the drama.

Written between 1848 and 1874, *Der Ring* was referred to by Wagner as a stage festival play. The four parts are *Das Rheingold*, *Die Walküre*, *Siegfried* and *Götterdämmerung*. This somewhat mystical grand opera was similar in theme to his more Christian *Parsifal* (1882) but different from others of his works, including his comedy *Die Meistersinger von Nürnberg* (1867) and his love story *Tristan und Isolde* (1865).

Wagner was a movable feast, emotionally and politically, lacking in purpose outside himself and his vistas. As well as his sometime nationalism, he also had sometime revolutionary inclinations. Wagner's works were praised by Hitler, a great fan, and the composer was antisemitic.

On Germanness

From Friedrich Nietzsche's *Beyond Good and Evil* (1886), prompted by Wagner's overture to *Meistersinger*:

'Something German in the best and worst sense of the word, something manifold, formless and inexhaustible in the German fashion; a certain German powerfulness and overfulness of soul . . . this kind of music best expresses what I consider true of the Germans: they are of the day before yesterday and the day after tomorrow – they have as yet no today.'

Nietzsche, in his essay 'Attempt at a Self-Criticism' (1886), complained about a Germany 'making the transition to mediocrity, democracy and "modern ideas"!' In 1934, Hitler, a fan, was to donate 50,000 Reichsmarks of his own money to building a memorial hall to Nietzsche.

There was a particular spatial dynamic: the wealth and political activism of industrial advance concentrated in the west,
much of the military elite basing their positions on landholdings in the agrarian east, where they felt threatened by Russia.
The relative wealth of this landholding elite diminished, both
within Germany and, as a result of increased transoceanic
trade, globally.

Improvements in German agriculture, notably in rye and
sugar-beet production and through new techniques, could not
fully counter this trend, not least because they largely benefitted
producers with the most fertile soils although, notably in the
1880s, these improvements helped facilitate migration to the
towns. Nevertheless, the development of sugar-beet production is
a classic manifestation of the relationship between German history
and that of distant areas. The cultivation of modern sugar beets
dated from Frederick the Great's attempt to ensure sugar supplies
from beets cultivatable in Germany. Beetroots were the original
source and the first factory opened in 1801. Responding to British
naval power, Napoleon rapidly followed suit in encouraging
production. By 1840, about 5 per cent of the world's sugar came
from sugar beets but, by 1880, with production concentrated in
Germany, but also spreading, notably to Russia, the figure had
risen to over 50 per cent. For British markets, German producers
were closer than those in the Caribbean and the price for sugar
from the latter fell dramatically.

Social categories have to be handled with care. The landholding elite was far from identical, both within regions and between
them. Thus, the conservatism that prevailed in Brandenburg was
not matched in Westphalia. Yet, in contrast to Britain, there was
not the mixing of landholders and successful middle class that
helped ensure a more stable and successful conservatism.
Moreover, the landowning elite was particularly powerful in the
government, both that of the Empire and of Prussia, and this
helped thwart reform.

A growing sense of instability encouraged the perceived need to respond by the use of force. Anxiety about the strength of Russia combined increasingly from the 1890s with a bellicose nationalism and fervent patriotism, a belief that war was a natural state and a conviction that it was honourable as well as necessary to fight and die for the country. War was seen as a tool of policy and a strong armament industry provided a key enabler, including companies such as Krupp.

Germany and the Birth of Geopolitics

Geopolitics as a self-conscious intellectual tradition rested on the realist theory of international relations and on the geography of states, as developed by Friedrich Ratzel (1844–1904), a professor of geography in Germany and the country's leading political scientist. He influenced a younger scholar, the Swede Rudolf Kjellén (1864–1922), who actually coined and defined the term 'Geopolitik'.

The key element in geopolitics was an approach to state competition in which the territorialisation of space was presented as an expression of conflicting political drives and, as such, held in tension by them. Ratzel, who was trained in the natural sciences, and who had served in the Franco–Prussian War of 1870–1, explained international relations in the Darwinian terms of a struggle for survival, arguing that Charles Darwin had failed to devote due attention to the issue of space. A Darwinian explanation appeared modern and relevant, a form of universal explanation that contrasted with more conventional accounts of international relations. In particular, it stood against the apparently more mannered, more historical and more limited nature of an explanatory pattern that looked back to the classics.

War, to Ratzel, was natural. He also saw states as organic, although accepted that such a term was a simile. Ratzel thereby largely ignored divisions within states, as well as the play of individual political and military leaders who, in practice, provide the key for understanding geopolitical pressures. In his *Anthropogeographie (The Geography of Environmental Influences on Human Society)*, published in two volumes, one in 1882 and the second in 1891, and his *Politische Geographie* (1897), a systematic analysis, Ratzel stressed the close relationship of people and environment.

The struggle for space was central to *Die Erde und das Leben (The Earth and Life)*, 1902. In this, Ratzel deployed the concept of '*Lebensraum*' ('living space'), that had been devised in 1860 by the biologist Oscar Penschel in a review of Darwin's *On the Origin of Species*. Focusing on '*Lage*' ('position'), '*Raum*' ('space') and '*Raumsinn*' ('sense of space held by the group that dominates the state'), Ratzel emphasised the role of environmental circumstances in affecting the process and progress of struggle between states.

Politische Geographie treated war as a normal process. Its second edition, which appeared in 1903, was entitled *Politische Geographie oder die Geographie der Staaten, des Verkehres und des Krieges (Political Geography or, the Geography of the State, Traffic and War)*. Ratzel's book was to be recommended to Hitler.

Ratzel was also much engaged in German maritime and colonial expansion, supporting the development of a large fleet and the establishment of overseas bases as the means to secure Germany's 'place in the sun', a reference to the tropical location of many colonies, notably in Africa and Oceania. Such a policy was highly provocative as far as other international powers were concerned.

Faced by what was seen as the threat of Russia, the German military regarded the path to success as resting on an initial, rapid defeat of France. A war on just one front could then be prepared. Overconfidence blinded policymakers to strategic realities.

There was also an ambition to become a world power with the ability to overthrow Britain and this was particularly attractive to Wilhelm II. As a result, Germany built up the second largest navy in the world, which helped ensure British hostility. A powerful Anglophobia saw British liberalism and capitalism as a threat to German culture.

THE FIRST WORLD WAR

In 1914, the Germans backed Austria in the Balkans crisis that developed into war, opportunistically seeking to use it to change the balance of power in their favour and further Wilhelm II's determination to be the leading ruler in Europe. Germany's leaders were willing to risk a war because no other crisis was as likely or could be planned to produce a constellation of circumstances guaranteeing them the commitment of their main ally and the support of the German people.

Having played a key role in causing the outbreak of hostilities, the Germans then proved very poor at fighting it, failing to knock out France with offensives in 1914, 1916 and 1918 or Russia in 1915, although she succumbed in 1917. Bringing the Americans into the war that year by resuming unrestricted submarine warfare was also a stupid mistake based on a serious misunderstanding of American and German capabilities. However, such an analysis assumes a rationalist balance of risks and opportunities that ignores the role of an ideology of total war and a rejection of the idea of compromise. This was part of a more widespread legitimisation of violence and militarisation of both society and options. There was also a determination to find a way to victory.

The war placed major strains on German society, but that did not lead to a search for a compromise and peace. Instead, with the politicians, including the SPD, unwilling to be effectively critical, the army became the directing pivot of state and economy, in effect gaining power in a military dictatorship in 1916. Neither Wilhelm II nor the Reichstag was in a position to exercise control. However, the military also were not up to the challenge. Manpower shortages affected both the army and the economy, creating competition between the two. Due to a lack of miners, coal production fell in 1917, affecting the rail system, which, from 1916, was also under great pressure due to the focus on steel production to manufacture armaments. The cumulative impact of such shortages was a decline in the economy and its growing atomisation, hindering attempts to coordinate and direct production.

Serious food shortages greatly damaged civilian morale and reduced energy and resistance to disease. Food rationing was introduced in April 1916 and became a contentious issue, in large part because potatoes were in short supply. This helped lead to an emphasis on turnips – and the 'turnip winter' of 1916–17 – and to food shortages and labour unrest, including in Düsseldorf in the summer of 1917. Malnutrition became a serious problem. Food protests in which women played a major role were frequent in Berlin and other cities.

Germany also had no equivalent to the support provided to Britain and France by the Americans. Winning territory and resources from Russia in 1918 appeared to offer a panacea, but there was no realistic strategy for victory and pressing the German domestic population harder helped undermine public backing for the war.

The failure of the spring offensives on the Western Front in 1918, combined with the success of Allied advances, led to a crisis in the German army and the loss of fighting resilience and unit cohesion. Officers felt they could no longer rely on their troops, many of whom deserted, surrendered or avoided combat.

The Allies mounted a successful assault on the Hindenburg Line near Cambrai on 27 September which came alongside a sense of crisis emanating from the impending collapse of Germany's alliance system. Erich Ludendorff who, with Paul von Hindenburg, directed the military, recommended an armistice on 29 September to preserve the army and allow it to repress radicalism. He put the stress on Bulgaria's decision to seek an armistice, which threatened Turkey, Austria and the grain and oil obtained from Romania.

The news of this decision reached Germany on 28 September. Allied successes against the Germans on the Western Front were probably more important, but it was preferable to blame the Bulgarians. On 2 October, however, the Supreme Army Command, in a briefing to the leading politicians in the Reichstag, emphasised the situation on the Western Front, notably the shift in troop numbers as a result of US reinforcements. Allied tanks were also mentioned.

Ludendorff saw an armistice as the basis for an honourable rather than a dictated peace. To that end, following the resignation of the cabinet on 30 September, a new government based on the majority parties of the Reichstag was appointed on 3 October under the chancellorship of the moderate Prince Max of Baden, heir to the Grand Duchy of Baden. This action was designed to appeal to President Woodrow Wilson and to meet domestic pressure for change. In the USA, making a speech to Congress, Wilson made a distinction between the German people and the Hohenzollern dynasty of Wilhelm II and the high command. This opened a way to negotiations on the basis of political change in Germany. In contrast, already manoeuvring for the post-war politics in a situation that he knew to be highly volatile, Ludendorff saw an armistice and the subsequent peace as a way to discredit the left.

On 4 October, Max of Baden approached Wilson to make peace on the basis of the fourteen points that the president had outlined to Congress on 8 January. Wilson was playing a key role in the negotiations and demanded, via a note of 14 October, that Germany be transformed into a liberal-constitutional state and that the armistice terms be such that Germany be unable to renew hostilities. Suspicious that Wilson was trying to act as an arbiter, Britain and France were particularly insistent on the latter point. The Allied leaders and generals initially thought that the conditions offered to Germany would be judged unacceptable and that the Americans would have to help them win an outright victory but, on 17 October, the German war cabinet accepted Wilson's terms. Ludendorff and Hindenburg, however, were unwilling to do so. On 24 October, Ludendorff denounced the proposed terms and said that Germany would fight on. He was dismissed two days later.

The strains of war had created a political crisis in Germany. The mutiny of the sailors in the High Seas Fleet on 27 October proved a key precipitant for rebellion across the country. It also thwarted the German naval command's plan for a final sortie to begin on 29 October, leading to a fight to the finish with the Grand Fleet. Combined with Wilhelm II's decision on 29 October to leave Berlin for the military headquarters at Spa, a counter-revolution was suggested by this plan, although it was in fact devised without Wilhelm. The idea was to reach an outcome that would justify post-war political support for the navy's position. In the event the naval mutiny prevented the fleet from sortieing and it was to sail forth only to surrender – nine battleships and five battlecruisers entering the Firth of Forth to do so on 21 November, escorted by the Grand Fleet in an impressive display of British naval power.

POLITICAL CHANGE IN GERMANY

In practice, by late October, support for the war in Germany and confidence in victory had largely collapsed. The impetus now came very much from those demanding political change, notably with the establishment of radical councils across Germany. The Social Democratic Party used this development to press for a new political order, including the democratisation of state governments. Max of Baden cooperated with the political parties, notably the Social Democratic Party, the largest in the Reichstag, in both establishing a new means of government and politics and in helping transform the constitution into a British-style system.

Aside from developments within Germany, there was to be a new political order in its conquests: on 3 November, Wilhelm II established a civilian government in the east, bringing to an end the military administration by the High Command Eastern Front (*Ober Ost*) established for Hindenburg and Ludendorff in 1914.

Thoughts of a German sphere in Europe, however, fell victim to the crisis at home. The Allied advance robbed the army leadership of confidence and created a sense of inexorable failure, while revolution began in Germany with sailors mutinying in late October. Under pressure from Max of Baden and from Wilhelm Groener, Ludendorff's replacement, Wilhelm II was driven from the scene on 9 November in the face of incipient revolution. Max of Baden unilaterally announced Wilhelm's abdication of the imperial and Prussian crowns, and the renunciation of Crown Prince Wilhelm. Moreover, the new provisional republican government, established that day under Friedrich Ebert, the Social Democrat leader since 1913, was eager to end the conflict. They hoped to prevent a deterioration in the situation that might open the way to a more radical outcome, as in Russia in 1917. The Social Democrats who dominated the government found Wilson's demands, from his 'Fourteen Points' speech, to be acceptable.

Wilhelm fled to Doorn in the Netherlands, where a plot to capture him and charge him with war crimes was unsuccessful. Until his death in 1941, Wilhelm always hoped for the restoration of his family. He made a move towards the Nazis in 1928, in common with other members of the old elite, became an even

more clear-cut antisemite and saw Hitler's victories as a vindica-
tion of his policies of the early 1910s. However, unlike Hindenburg
– who was a monarchist – Hitler was not interested in a return of
Hohenzollern rule. Wilhelm did not live long enough to see a
second failure for Germany.

In a sense, Russia in 1917–18 became Germany in 1918,
although there was no comparable social collapse. Groener
believed peace to be necessary, not least to allow the army to end
hostilities and maintain social order. Indeed, on 10 November,
Groener and the first chancellor of the German Republic, Ebert,
agreed on such a focus. Groener was to help the infant Weimar
republic resist left-wing risings in 1918–19, notably in Berlin and
Munich.

A German delegation crossed the front line on 7 November
1918 and met the Allied commanders under Marshal Ferdinand
Foch in a railway carriage stationed near Compiègne. The delegation was obliged to accept largely French-dictated armistice terms,
notably the handing over of much of their military *matériel* –
including all submarines – the evacuation of all their conquests in
western and eastern Europe, as well as Alsace-Lorraine; Allied
occupation of German territory as far as the Rhine and partly
beyond it (a demand that originated with Foch) and the continuation of the crippling Allied naval blockade until peace was signed.

French leaders felt that the disaster of 1870–1 at the hands of
Germany had been avenged. It had led to chaos within France,
including the Paris Commune and its very violent suppression in
1871. It seemed already apparent that the same could, and maybe
would, occur in Germany.

9

Chaos, 1919–45

....

Europe went to war in 1939. It is easy to trace this resumption of hostilities back to the failure of the Versailles peace settlement of 1919 and the deficiencies of the League of Nations, and thus to see the Second World War as the sequel of the Great War (or, as it became, the First World War). In part, it was a product of the factors that had caused and sustained that conflict and, more particularly, of the business left unfinished at its unsatisfactory close.

Focus on the reparations demanded from post-war Germany – 132 billion gold marks (less than 21 billion was paid) – as an aspect of its war guilt, proved a particular source of liberal (and German) criticism in the 1920s and 1930s. It ignored German reparations from France after earlier victories and the terrible damage done by German forces to, for example, Rheims, on which some of the money was spent. Instead, the criticism encouraged the view that the peace settlement had been mainly retributive. It was argued that a mishandled, if not misguided, total war in 1914–18 had led to a harsh peace, the latter a consequence of the former.

This verdict, which contributed to the critique of Allied diplomacy as dishonest, selfish and short-sighted was, in fact, an inappropriate judgement of peace terms that were certainly far less severe than those to be imposed on Germany in 1945. Those terms did not, of course, meet comparable criticism. Germany lost territory after the First World War: to Poland, (neutral) Denmark, Belgium, France and Lithuania. Notable was the loss of

Alsace-Lorraine to France, but talk in France of a Rhineland separated from Germany led nowhere.

The victors adapted to practicalities as well as to ideological concerns: Germany had not been overrun by the Allies while, as a result of her earlier defeat of Russia, she still occupied large territories in eastern Europe. Japan was to be occupied in 1945 despite being in a similar territorial position to that held by Germany at the time of the November 1918 armistice. This was true, at least, as far as land power was concerned; although crucially not at sea where Japan, an archipelago, had lost its fleet, and nor was it true in the air. The use of atomic bombs would provide an equation of power in favour of the victors not present in 1918.

Claiming the Past

Germany sought to appropriate and control the memory of the Polish victory of 1410 at Grunwald/Tannenberg over the Teutonic Knights by recording Tannenberg as its major victory of 1914 over Russian forces invading East Prussia. Tannenberg was not, in fact, the central site of the extensive 1914 battle, but it provided the necessary historical revenge, as well as suggesting that the modern Germans were the heirs of those presented as the noble, self-sacrificing, crusading Teutonic Knights. After the First World War, the victory was used by, and on behalf of, the generals who had been victors, Hindenburg and Ludendorff, to propagate myths about their real and potential roles as national saviours.

In 1918, moreover, the victorious powers were determined to try to prevent the spread of communist revolution from Russia to Germany. Prefiguring western discussion in 1944–5 about Germany's future, commentators warned of the ideological threat from the east. On 2 November 1918, while commanding the advance of the British First Army, which captured the city of Valenciennes that day, General Henry Horne wrote to his wife, 'I think we must not be *too* severe with Germany, in case of there being a breakup there and we shall find no government to enforce terms upon! Bolshevism is the danger. If it breaks out in Germany it might spread to France and England.' Thus, the First World War and the communist revolution created the rationale for anti-Soviet appeasement of Germany and, in the late 1930s, set the western Allies up to ignore Stalin's (highly problematic) offers to help contain Nazi Germany.

The terms of the 1919 peace were designed to prevent Germany launching new wars and thus to provide collective security for Europe, notably western Europe. Under the supervision of the Inter-Allied Military Control Commission, the size and equipment of the German military were seriously restricted in all branches. The Saarland – its valuable coalfield administered by France – was governed by France and Britain under a League of Nations mandate, until 1935 when it was returned to Germany as the result of a plebiscite. Under the mandate and due also to its role in the mining industry, France had a strong position within the international governing commission, but this scarcely equated to territorial expansion. Germany also had to accept an occupied zone along the French and Belgian frontiers and a demilitarized zone beyond, the net effect of which was to end the possibility that the River Rhine could provide a strategic defensive frontier for Germany.

As a result of the loss of overseas colonies, all of which had been conquered by the Allies, Germany became the first post-colonial power. No decision-makers wanted the colonies back, but the public was nostalgic. At any rate, Germany had no opportunity to gain more transoceanic colonies and this further strengthened its already strong focus on Europe.

Germany was also to be stigmatised both by a 'war guilt' clause, which was highly unpopular in Germany, and by the insistence that German officers be tried for war crimes, especially the murderous treatment of Belgian civilians in 1914 and the consequences of indiscriminate submarine warfare. The Allies wanted war criminals extradited for trial before an international tribunal but, in 1920, agreed instead to the German request that the trials be conducted before the supreme court in Leipzig. A list of 853 alleged war criminals was submitted by the Allies, but only seventeen were tried, in 1921–2. In the end, only ten were convicted and neither the Germans nor the Allies were satisfied. Concerned about the honour of the army, the Germans argued military necessity for their actions in 1914 and the theme of disowning responsibility has remained strong.

To argue from Versailles to the rise of Hitler is inappropriate; Hitler certainly rejected Versailles and the international system it sought to create. However, the responsible realpolitik of the 1920s that entailed compromise and benefitted from the idealistic currents of that decade's international relations focused on another German. This was someone far more prominent in the period, Gustav Stresemann, the talented foreign minister from 1923 to 1929, a centrist who died that year of a stroke aged fifty-one. Counterfactualism has its limits, but to subtract the failure, protectionism, misery and extremism produced by the depression from the 1930s is to suggest that the 1920s order could have continued, in part, because internationalism, liberalism, democracy and free-market capitalism would have retained more appeal, with the electorate and the government.

In rejecting this order, extremists turned to a politics of grievance based on anger with the verdict of the First World War. Its presentation thus played a prominent role in the politics of the 1930s, building on the anger already expressed in the 1920s mostly, although not solely, by the defeated. History mattered. While there was a left-wing critique of the war that blamed an oppressive and incompetent army establishment, a sense of the army having been betrayed by the left was important to Hitler's arguments. He also benefitted from the First World War in the shape of the anger about reparations and the misplaced belief that Germany was guiltless in starting the war and that it had lost because of traitors at home.

ESTABLISHING THE WEIMAR REPUBLIC

That theme was present from the start of the post-war period, with ideological rivalry to the fore as – in an accentuation of the wartime emphasis on only one legitimate outcome – radical attempts to seize power were violently contested by right-wing paramilitaries, the *Freikorps*, many of whom were veterans eager to assuage through violence their anger at defeat and to find a role for themselves; although most veterans did not join the *Freikorps*.

The Weimar Republic, established in 1919 with elections returning a clear majority for the democratic parties – notably the German Democratic Party (the pre-war left liberals) – was under pressure from the start. The attempts to seize power present an impression of chaos, which was certainly the case for a number of years.

This impression was compounded by post-war economic disruption, including high inflation. Moreover, many families grieved their war dead – about two million – and there were fresh losses due to the 1919 flu pandemic. The war also left many injured, in body and mind. Territorial losses led to refugees and bitterness and were given further political weight by plebiscites in contested areas. Social chaos also owed much to the search for a new German identity. Everything imaginable was being promulgated, with the loudest voices coalescing into street violence. Many mistrusted any form of authority, while at the same time there was a lack of confidence.

Fears of revolution led many moderates to compromise with the *Freikorps*, as was later to be seen with greater impact with the Nazis. In practice, the fears were exaggerated, but the success of revolution in Russia and, briefly, in Hungary encouraged caution as well as paranoia. Politics came to be seen as civil war, and, therefore, civil war as politics, a process that made (many) civilians combatants and encouraged a response accordingly.

In 1920, the unsuccessful, poorly planned, far-right Kapp Putsch in Berlin (and elsewhere) and the failed, far-left Ruhr Uprising occurred. Both were suppressed, but the subsequent 1920 elections saw gains for both far-right and far-left parties and a serious drop in support for the democratic parties, notably the SPD. The party was clearly linked to the army that had brutally suppressed the violent opposition of 1920 with actions that included the execution of prisoners and the killing of bystanders. This connection helped to divide the SPD from more radical workers. At the same time, there was an inherent difference in method between the two.

Chaos in Berlin had led the politicians debating the new constitution to take refuge in Weimar, where the national assembly was convened. The Organisation Consul terrorist movement, a group of former *Freikorps*, killed at least 354 people in 1920–2, including the ministers of finance (1921) and foreign affairs (1922). The communists were defeated in 1920 and Hitler also was a failure, his attempted Beer Hall Putsch in Munich in 1923 rapidly suppressed. The attempted coup was designed to emulate the seizures of power carried out by Mustafa Kemal and Benito Mussolini and twenty people were killed in the action. Hitler was arrested and imprisoned at Landsberg prison, rather than being deported to his native Austria. Hitler thereafter only used violence as part of his drive to control opinion. He didn't attempt to mount another coup, a course the army leadership would not support. Also in 1923, the army acted against the SPD–communist government in Saxony.

THE WEIMAR REPUBLIC

Weimar, a period of both hope and despair, faced particular difficulties as an expression of the recurrent theme of German state-building which began in the 1800s. However, its challenges were not as great, in many respects, as those faced in the 1800s or after the Second World War.

There were the difficulties of grounding a parliamentary democracy, of operating a federation of states, of abandoning monarchies, of coping with defeat and severe economic and financial dislocation, of confronting the revolutionary expansionism of communism and of creating not only structures and processes but also the sense of legitimacy and of national unity. Weimar produced a republican system (and a parliamentary practice accordingly) and granted votes for women.

The crises of the early 1920s had a clear regional component. Although every region contained activists from across the political board, areas of particular strength also existed, particularly in Bavaria (for the right) and Saxony (for the communists). Yet, the system did not break down completely and Prussia – the state that contained 60 per cent of Germany's territory and population – proved more stable than Bavaria or Saxony.

The powers of the central government increased under Weimar, especially with regard to finance, but Germany remained a federal state with the *Bundesrat* renamed the *Reichsrat*. Each with its own government, the *Länder* continued to be responsible for police, justice, local government, education and much else.

Ludendorff was involved in Hitler's 1923 putsch but, however conservative, most of the army backed the government, largely because it stood for political and social stability and because they hoped to revive Germany's international position. This support for Weimar was more significant than the *Freikorps'* hatred for Weimar. Moreover, the economy had not suffered fundamental losses as part of the 1919 Versailles peace settlement, while the reparations that were paid were understandable as Germany itself had imposed reparations on France in 1871 and had now lost. In 1923, crisis was in part a matter of the French occupation of the Ruhr because of differences over reparations and of the hyperinflation it helped provoke, but it did not lead to a wider conflict nor to Rhineland separatism.

By 1925, a considerable degree of stability had been regained and the Weimar Republic appeared resilient, a point that was subsequently to be derided by those who pressed for the chaos masquerading as order of the National Socialist state. The mark was stabilised in 1923–4. Stresemann proved a master of realpolitik, offering a new iteration of Bismarck's method in a very different context. In 1926, Germany joined the League of Nations. Social welfare included the introduction in 1927 of universal and contributory unemployment insurance.

The legacy of failure in the face of the subsequent rise of Hitler long contributed to a negative portrayal of Weimar. The problems of the 2010s have encouraged a more sympathetic assessment. There has never been any doubt, however, about the strength of the cultural life of the period, nor of its contribution to global cultural developments. Particular significance is attached to the Bauhaus movement in architecture, to music (as with Kurt Weill's *Threepenny Opera* of 1928), to painting (as with the stark and bitter realism of Otto Dix and George Grosz), to atonal music with Arnold Schoenberg and to cinema (as with Fritz Lang's expressionist films, notably *Metropolis* in 1927). However, these developments did not necessarily attract public approval and the vibrancy of the cultural life included other themes and styles. Weimar faced the strain of the Versailles settlement and the crises of inflation and later the slump. These encouraged many, but far from all, to turn to extremism.

Part of the culture of the Weimar years was driven by confronting the aftermath of the First World War, including Ernst Jünger's *Storm of Steel*, Remarque's *All Quiet on the Western Front* and the most successful novel of the late 1920s, *War*, a book written by Arnold Vieth von Golsenau under the name Ludwig Renn and based on his military experience. Golsenau turned to the communists, was imprisoned under the Nazis, emigrated, served in the Spanish Civil War and later lived in East Germany.

Change and the Shoe

As in other countries, individual products provided a focus for consumerism and the development and expression of social differences. And so it was with the shoe, which for long was for most of the population simply utilitarian. The rise of mass urban living, youth culture, sales linked to fashion and female commitment to shoes ensured from the 1920s that there was a rise in the range of models. The same was true in cosmetics. This put pressure on manufacturing and retail processes, encouraging nationwide machine production and retail chains. These changes in turn were later refracted through the perverted and violent rationalisation of the Nazi regime, not least in the recycling of shoes from victims in the concentration camps, as well as the brutality of shoe testing on prisoners in the Sachsenhausen camp.

Castle Skull

'The steamer moved down the Rhine . . . the current is so swift that these little steamers made remarkable speed. There is a flavour, there is an old dangerous twilight charm, about the warrior Rhine when it leaves its lush wideness at Bingen. Thence it seems to grow darker. The green deepens almost to black, grey rock replaces vineyards on the hills which close it in. Narrow and winding now, a frothy olive-green, it rushes through a world of ghosts.'

John Dickson Carr, *Castle Skull.*
A Rhineland Mystery (1931)

Carr had visited the area in 1930.

THE RISE OF HITLER

The economic and social strains stemming from the slump that began in 1929 put pressure on liberal democracies across the world, including in Latin America and Japan as well as across Europe. In Germany, the coalition government headed by the Social Democrat Hermann Müller collapsed in March 1930, marking the end of stable government. There was already economic and political strain and problems over liquidity. Political radicalisation had happened prior to 1929, not least a movement to the right in the Centre Party.

The two major illiberal challenges, each of which greatly gained electoral support, were communism and fascism and the latter very much focused on the movement's leader. Although Hitler, a malign master of inconsistency, made several statements explicitly rejecting the personality cult, he made many more accepting and promoting the cult of himself. National Socialism, in practice, was based on the pivotal figure of the *Führer* (leader) and the linked cult, as well as on a confused – indeed, incoherent – mixture of racialism, nationalism and belief in modernisation through force.

This *mélange* appealed to a significant tranche of the population; Nazi popularity rested on far more than a rejection of Weimar and its real and alleged failures. Its electoral support spanned all social groups and regional perspectives, ages and genders. At the same time, there were particular areas of strength, notably small-town and Protestant Germany, as in Holstein and Thuringia. The Nazis could also draw on the strength of pre-First World War, right-wing, strident Germanic nationalism, racism, and bitter antisemitism. Much increased both by the response to the war, with the national mobilisation it had brought, and by the post-war crisis, these provided seeds for later extremism. Nazism was *völkisch*, with a focus on a general nationalism and a strong antisemitism.

In the political manoeuvres of 1930–3, the Nazis – who did well in the September 1930 Reichstag elections, becoming the second largest party after the SPD – benefitted from not being the Communist Party who, on 13 per cent, became the third largest party. Conservatives were prepared to accept the Nazis in order to thwart the communists, who also suffered from very poor relations with the SPD and from the interventions of Stalin.

As the right manoeuvred, however, Hitler was far from the obvious or initial choice as chancellor. Hindenburg, who had succeeded Friedrich Ebert of the SPD as president in 1925, appointed the Centre Party's Heinrich Brüning as chancellor after Hermann Müller, the SPD chancellor since 1928, resigned in March 1930 because he was unable to put together a politically acceptable solution to the problem of funding rapidly rising unemployment payments. In turn, Brüning's deflationary policies hit both society and economy without bringing stability. Unemployment continued to rise and, with the government unpopular and lacking a majority in the Reichstag, Brüning used Hindenburg to issue presidential emergency decrees.

This authoritarian democracy remained subject to political tensions, including in his relationship with Hindenburg. They disagreed about how best to respond to the Nazi challenge, and how far to move to the right. Banning the Nazi paramilitary SA, a murderously violent nationwide movement, in April 1932 proved contentious, as did Hindenburg's refusal to accept the distribution of land to unemployed workers.

Although no Reichstag elections were due until 1934, Brüning was forced to resign on 30 May 1932 by Hindenburg, being succeeded by the conservative Franz von Papen, a protégé of Hindenburg's authoritarian adviser General Kurt von Schleicher, who had intrigued against the former chancellor. Papen ruled by emergency decrees signed by Hindenburg. The ban on the SA and SS was lifted in June and, in July, Papen overthrew the SPD-dominated regional government of Prussia, while wages and unemployment pay were cut in September. In the Reichstag election of 31 July 1932, the Nazis won the largest number of seats with 37 per cent of the vote, compared to 18 per cent in 1930 and 2 per cent in 1928. The SPD won 22 per cent, the Communist Party 14 per cent and the Centre Party 12 per cent. Instability led on 6 November to another election in which the Nazis, with 33 per cent of the vote, lost seats. The Communists won 17 per cent and the SPD 20 per cent. Papen, who still could not rely on Reichstag support, was forced to resign by Schleicher, who insisted that the army could not support the government.

In December 1932, Hindenburg replaced Papen with Schleicher himself, then the minister of defence, which led Papen to plot with Hitler. In January 1933, Papen persuaded Hindenburg that he could keep Hitler under control if the latter replaced Schleicher. The army had made preparations for the declaration of a state of emergency by Papen when he was chancellor. This was a step designed to combat communist disorder, Nazi paramilitary activity and a possible general strike that might have stopped Hitler's rise to power. In the end, there was no such action. When Hindenburg refused Schleicher's request for a state of emergency, he resigned.

A new government was formed on 30 January with Hitler as Chancellor. Papen was vice-chancellor and his supporters were in the majority in the cabinet. However, these individuals failed to resist the seizure of power and authority by Hitler and were politically marginalised, as were the monarchists who had similarly looked for opportunities.

HITLER IN POWER

Hitler consolidated his position in 1933, employing terror against political opponents and exploiting the opportunities offered by the arson attack on the Reichstag on 27 February to suspend civil liberties, attack the communists and introduce mass arrests. Concentration camps, the most prominent being Dachau, near Munich, opened in March 1933. They were established as detention centres for 'protective custody', meaning detention without trial. There were about 3,500 prisoners by the summer of 1935 and the system soon expanded, with major camps including Sachsenhausen, opened in 1936, and Buchenwald in 1937. Helped by its appeal to many of the young, violence was at the heart of Nazism, a creed that required the destruction of alleged enemies, and that aggression was deployed across the country to establish the Nazi order. Domestic dissidence, it was claimed, had to be prevented to strengthen Germany for war.

Cabaret

A very successful 1966 musical about the hedonism of Weimar Berlin was turned into a dynamic, successful 1972 film, having been based on a 1951 play *I Am A Camera*. This was itself adapted from Christopher Isherwood's semi-autobiographical novel *Goodbye to Berlin* (1939), which is set in 1931. The film made the most impact. Its Kit Kat Club provides an energetic setting, but the rise of the Nazis becomes the deadly theme, with their violence, their takeover of the cabaret and the scene in a beer garden in which 'Tomorrow Belongs to Me' is revealed as a Nazi theme song and intimidating pledge.

Isherwood had gone to Berlin to teach English. His novel *Mr Norris Changes Trains* (1935) also described, from the viewpoint of Berlin, the end of Weimar, the Nazi takeover, and those who were pleased by it:

'They smiled approvingly at these youngsters in their big, swaggering boots who were going to upset the Treaty of Versailles ... they thrilled with a furtive, sensual pleasure, like schoolboys, because the Jews, their business rivals, and the Marxists, a vaguely defined minority of people who didn't concern them, had been satisfactorily found guilty of the defeat and the inflation, and were going to catch it.'

Hitler, moreover, turned on others on the right with violence. He had not followed the advice of his ally Ernst Röhm who wanted to transform the Nazi *Sturmabteilung* (SA) movement, of which he was the head, into a militia-type army that would incorporate the professional military and remove their independence. This form of Nazi revolution was unacceptable to both Hitler and the army and Hitler did not want rivals. Röhm was murdered and the SA severely weakened in what became known as the 'night of the long knives'. Hitler also used the violence of 30 June to 2 July 1934 to murder those suspected of involvement in a conservative conspiracy against the Nazis, including Schleicher, who was manoeuvring for position. Schleicher's wife was also killed. The conspiracy against Hitler had sought to exploit military unease with the SA, but had failed to win the backing of Hindenburg.

Hitler was resolved to control the army. After the death of Hindenburg on 2 August 1934, Hitler combined the office of the president with that of the chancellor which he already held, and thus, as head of state, became supreme commander of the armed forces. At the suggestion of the army leadership, who thought it would bind Hitler to the army, an oath of unconditional loyalty to him as *Führer* was taken by every officer and soldier in the armed forces on 2 August. This oath was underlined in subsequent army education sessions. Moreover, the armed forces now addressed Hitler as '*Führer*'.

Hitler needed the army to support his aggressive policies, his determination to tolerate no other views and his dissatisfaction with the attitudes and reliability of his senior military advisers and of the army leadership in general. At the same time, Hitler promised the army the key role of providing the means to achieve German greatness. Moreover, these men were basically sympathetic to the Nazi regime, although wary of the SS and initially trying to retain their autonomy.

Nazi popularity among Germans can be explained because the

movement promised a revival of greatness. In addition, Nazism appeared committed to opening up social mobility and removing barriers to privileges for the middle and working classes, especially when it brought about full employment by 1936. Leisure, notably thanks to the Strength Through Joy organisation, also played a part. The 'national socialism' that the Nazis offered was different to that of the other conservative parties and, separately, the SPD.

This particular faith in a German community helped to maintain hostility towards those stigmatised (unfairly) as lacking national identity and loyalty and certainly left out the large numbers of Jewish Germans who had fought in the First World War. Democratic pluralism was presented as inherently wrong, as was communism. The push and pull of propaganda played a role, with the two elements linked in the response to the spectacle of the Nazi regime and the ritual incantation associated with Hitler.

An emphasis on race led to the dehumanisation of the racial outsider, with Aryans and non-Aryans (the 'blood enemy') treated as clear-cut and antagonistic categories; indeed as superhumans and subhumans. A stress on the Aryan *volk* challenged the culture of Weimar, with its individualism and notions of progress and liberty in terms of its celebration and protection of the self. These were now associated with a castigated liberalism. Moreover, the focus on the Aryan ensured that serious regional, political, institutional, religious, social and economic differences and divisions within Germany were deliberately downplayed. This was an extreme accentuation of the process by which, in 1871, the Prussian state had created the Second Reich, overlaying earlier and very long-established identities and loyalties.

More crudely and vigorously, the Nazi agenda of national strength and renewal and racial consciousness answered to the same historical awareness and set of references. A focus on apparent external threats was linked to the goal of a necessary depoliticisation that, in practice, was a by-product of a totalitarian drive. There was a meshing of national and racial themes in presenting beliefs about Germany's historical role and destiny, notably in eastern Europe. The present was to be employed in taking forward a vision of the past that was at once national and racial. There was a strong millenarian flavour to the project as well as its extremism in both language and implementation. A permanent state of emergency was the essence of the rhetoric.

Drawing on the strengthening of already present antisemitism in response to the crises of 1918 onwards, there were also moves against Jews as the *Volksgemeinschaft* ('national community') was created in the Nazi image. The Nazi project for eliminating those presented as 'community aliens' was expressed in terms of 'cleansing the national body' and thus, in Nazi eyes, strengthening the nation for its future tasks. In 1933, Jews were removed from much of professional life and banned from owning land or being journalists and the number of Jewish pupils in schools and universities was limited.

In 1934, rearmament began. Hitler ordered a trebling of the army size from the base of 100,000 men permitted under the Versailles settlement as well as the creation of an air force, illegal under that treaty. Rather than respond to the fiscal strains of the year by restraining rearmament, Hitler pressed ahead the following year, when he also banned Jews from military service (conscription was introduced that year) and passed the Nuremberg Laws, which were a clear signal to Jews to emigrate.

The laws defined Jews and also banned marriages between Jews and non-Jews. Philanthropy, furthermore, was redefined, with Jewish philanthropic foundations (many of which in practice catered also to Christians), brought under Aryan control, while Jews were no longer to receive support. This was a key erosion of the public sphere and an institutionalisation of the new discrimination. It was particularly significant in cities where the network of philanthropy had helped underpin the civic culture and had acted as an expression of it.

Hitler was a vicious antisemite who would not be satisfied with discrimination. For Hitler, there had to be persecution and it had to be a decisive and total step that would end what he saw as the Jewish challenge. To Hitler, this was a meta-historical issue, not an add-on designed to fulfil other Nazi policies, such as the redistribution of goods, the raising of funds or the rallying of popular support. The pronounced cult of personality was linked to a sense of historical mission: history to Hitler was a lived process that he embodied; his personal drama became an aspect of the historic mission of the German people. To Hitler, racial purity was a key aspect of this mission, at once both means and goal.

Propaganda was pushed hard, with Joseph Goebbels, the propaganda minister, proving particularly adroit, as when he produced the *Volksempfänger* (People's Receiver), an inexpensive radio designed to link Hitler with the people. The *New York Times* noted in 1936, 'It is the miracle of radio that it welds sixty million Germans into a single crowd, to be played upon by a single voice.'

Alongside brutal thuggery towards those considered opponents and different, the potential of a police state was increasingly focused on Jews. The pressure to make much of Germany 'Jew-free' entailed driving Jews out, especially from rural and small-town Germany, which tended to be the areas most sympathetic to the Nazis. In contrast, support in the major cities and industrial zones was more limited, notably so in Berlin. Antisemitic legislation and Jewish emigration also greatly widened the pool of those who benefitted from discrimination against Jews by providing them with jobs and property. Those who profited were opportunists or antisemites and many were both. They would inform on Jewish neighbours to the authorities in order to be allocated houses owned or occupied by Jews.

'Degenerate Art'

The Nazi critique of modernism led to the removal of works of art presented as un-German as well as bans on teaching or exhibiting art. In 1937, a 'Degenerate Art' exhibition was held in the Nazi-era, brutalist *Haus der Kunst* in Munich in order to denigrate such works. It included paintings by Max Beckmann, Marc Chagall, Otto Dix, Max Ernst, George Grosz, Wassily Kandinsky, Paul Klee, Paul Kleinschmidt, Ernst Ludwig Kirchner, Kurt Schwitters and others in a real roll call of talent. Bauhaus, cubism, dada, expressionism, impressionism and surrealism were all out. In 1939, four thousand paintings and drawings were burned in Berlin. There had also been very extensive book burning in 1933 by Nazi students, with all copies of some four thousand titles set for destruction in order to produce a 'pure' culture.

Similarly, 'degenerate music' – notably atonal and jazz works – were castigated. Instead, order and exemplary clarity were in demand, a process enforced by Joseph Goebbels through the Reich Chamber of Culture, founded in 1933. The Nazis backed their own styles, notably in literature, painting, dance, pseudo-Wagnerian music and, especially, architecture and sculpture, as with the work of Arno Breker (1900–91). He was made official state sculptor by Hitler in 1937 and produced works in a neo-classical style.

The flirtation of the Nazis with modern times, seen in their fascination with flight and by their use of radio, cinema and typography, did not extend to modernist painting. Emigration led to an enormous cultural bloodletting. Beside writers like the Mann family, there was Berthold Brecht, Lion Feuchtwanger, Sebastian Haffner, [Erich Maria] Remarque, Kurt Tucholsky, Carl Zuckmayer, Arnold Zweig and Stefan Zweig, actress Marlene Dietrich, directors Ernst Lubitsch, Fritz

Lang, Max Ophüls and Billy Wilder, composer Erich Korngold, artists like Lyonel Feininger, Walter Gropius and Max Oppenheimer, scientists like Albert Einsten, Gerhard Herzberg, Theodor Adorno, Ernst Bloch, Franz Oppenheimer and Alfred Vagts; a list that is far from complete. All these men retained their influence elsewhere, especially in the USA. They were a major loss to German cultural life, both between 1933–45 and in the post-war period.

Nazi Films

Alongside entertainment, the cinema had to serve Nazi purposes. This was seen in historical works, such as films about Frederick the Great (1942) and Bismarck (1940, 1942) and also in antisemitic films. *Der Ewige Jude* (*The Eternal Jew*, 1940) was virulent hate propaganda and a box-office failure, whereas the no less antisemitic *Jew Suss* (1940) was a popular narrative in which a fiendish Jewish money-lender covets and terrorises a virtuous Aryan maiden, only to be publicly executed. In *Friedrich Schiller* (1940), the poet was presented as a pan-German able to see beyond the atomistic politics of Germany before unification. Set in 1807, during successful resistance against French invaders, *Kolberg* (1945) was a call for continued effort in war even when it went very badly.

Thuggery, which was always part of Nazi activism, both under Weimar and thereafter, became increasingly organised, most prominently in the *Reichskristallnacht* ('Night of the broken glass'), on 9–10 November 1938. Ordered by Hitler, this assault served to

lower barriers against fresh violence, as well as to draw partici-
pants and bystanders into a web of murderous complicity. This
process was on display, for example, in Berlin, where the nation's
largest Jewish community was ravaged. Across Germany, about a
thousand synagogues were destroyed and as many as 7,500
Jewish businesses attacked and there was much looting, with the
police not intervening. In addition, Jews were 'fined' one billion
Reichsmarks.

The destruction of synagogues was designed to destroy a cohesion and a presence that was at once different and yet also integrated physically into the centre of German society. Already, in
June 1938, the main synagogue in Munich had been destroyed; to
Hitler it was an 'eyesore'. Other such centres of Jewish activity
and culture were also demolished; for example, the main synagogue in Dresden.

After the *Reichskristallnacht*, in which possibly several hundred
Jews were killed, the number of Jews held in concentration camps
sharply increased by about thirty thousand prisoners; the killing
of Jews was also stepped up. Measures to encourage emigration
were pushed forward and about 60 per cent did. This was permitted until October 1941, although not for men of military age after
the outbreak of the war. Jews were not allowed to take possessions
with them. The rate of emigration was higher among younger
Jews and lower among older Jews, especially those who hoped to
see out the crisis, believing that the Nazis would change policy or
be replaced, or those who had less confidence in a new start
abroad. Many Jews, notably veterans, also retained their German
patriotism.

While conscription contributed to social militarism and
international aggression, the Nazis sought to repurpose German
history to serve their theme of a depoliticised, nationalised
homeland and a repoliticised stance towards outside powers.
Alongside a traditional emphasis on conflict with foreign states
could be found a concentration on ethnic rivalry between

Germans and others. Conversely, the Nazi vision of the German past was to an extent depoliticised. Instead, internal divisions were largely blamed on the Jews; once they were defeated, the race would be united. Present needs were set in the context of past threats.

In *Werden und Wachsen. Ein Geschichtsatlas auf völkischer Grundlage* (1938), Bernhard Kumsteller presented Germany as the bulwark against attacks from Asia, the communists shown as being the latest in the series and Berlin, 1918–33, depicted as a site of conflict. Readers could turn to maps of the growing influence of the Nazis, their agricultural and regional policies and their autobahns: strength through straight lines. Separately, archaeology was put under the control of the SS.

Mediocrity to the Fore

Hanns Johst (1890–1978), a Saxon who spent most of his life in Bavaria was, from 1935, president of the Reich Chamber of Literature and SS *Oberführer*, a dramatist and poet of Nazi themes and language. He was close to Goebbels and Himmler, a fan of Hitler, an SS groupie who was witness to SS atrocities and one of the many acquitted when tried after the war. He remained unrepentant to the end.

Performed on Hitler's birthday in 1933, Johst's play *Schlageter* included the line 'When I hear "culture" . . . I release the safety catch on my Browning.' The hero, Albert Schlageter, had in real life been a *Freikorps* member executed by the French in 1923 for sabotaging a railway. Also referred to in *Mein Kampf*, he was commemorated in memorials. Separately, temples of honour were built in Munich for those killed in the 1923 coup attempt. They were demolished after the war.

Germany became a *mélange* of established governmental systems repurposed to Nazi goals, alongside those groups that were more directly linked with Hitler, notably the Nazi Party and the SS and other novelties including the Hitler Youth. Membership of the latter became compulsory from March 1939. As a result, there were often contradictory but also cumulative drives and pressures. The churches were exposed to criticism, cajoling and seduction and responded with a range of behaviours. Indeed, while outspoken clergy were sent to concentration camps, some bishops recast the Bible and produced a grotesquely distorted new version of the 'Sermon on the Mount'. Both Protestant and Catholic churches proved all too willing to accommodate Hitler.

In 1936, Hitler unilaterally remilitarised the Rhineland and initiated a four-year plan designed to ensure self-sufficiency and readiness for war. This remilitarisation, like rearmament, could be cast as an attempt to regain Germany's former position. But when Hitler occupied Austria on 12 March 1938, uniting it with Germany in the *Anschluss* (union) the following day, it was more a fundamental redrawing of the map of Europe than a revision of the Versailles settlement. The *Anschluss* was publicly labelled in 1938 as the *Wiedervereinigung* (Reunification), unlike the Unification with East Germany of 1990.

Later in 1938, Hitler turned on Czechoslovakia, where there was an ethnic majority of Germans in the Sudetenland. In practice, his bullying relied in part on bluster. At the time, he lacked enough trained troops, while shortages in raw materials hit armament production. Indeed, German rearmament had a 'shop window' character and was a failure in many ways. There was little appropriate long-term planning and, aside from the serious shortage of iron and steel that hit production, there was a lack of skilled workers. Moreover, Germany's dire fiscal situation greatly exacerbated the problems created by the shift to oil-based weapons systems.

Fortunately for Hitler, an isolated Czechoslovakia was under pressure from the other powers and was driven to accept the German occupation. This helped thwart both the short war Hitler had hoped for and a plot for a coup organised by Ludwig Beck, the chief of the army general staff. Beck also suffered from a lack of wider support within the military. That year, Hitler had already taken effective overall control, sacking Werner von Blomberg, the minister of war, and Werner von Fritsch, the army commander, and leaving the position of minister vacant. As supreme commander, Hitler carried out the functions of the war ministry.

In March 1939, Hitler renounced the guarantees he had made at Munich and destroyed Czechoslovakia. The following month, he renounced the 1935 Anglo–German Naval Agreement. However, he did not wish to go to war with Britain and did not expect the country to begin hostilities in the summer of 1939. Indeed, he was undecided whether or not to go to war with Poland – which presented a more formidable military challenge than Czechoslovakia, let alone Austria. A key element in his decision was the assurance by his foreign minister, Joachim von Ribbentrop, that Britain would never declare war to protect Poland. On 5 April 1939, Wilhelm Keitel, the head of the Wehrmacht High Command, told the Italian chief of staff that no war was to be expected for 'three or four years', which accorded with Ribbentrop's approach to Mussolini in late 1938, when he offered an alliance and promised no war for two or three years.

In order to facilitate action against Poland, and to offset Britain, Hitler concluded a ten-year Non-Aggression Pact with Stalin on 23–4 August 1939. The agreement is often named after the two foreign ministers, Ribbentrop and Molotov, and was celebrated by Stalin at the signing in Moscow with a toast to 'the health of this great man', the absent Hitler. The pact had secret clauses that determined spheres of influence in eastern Europe, leaving no effective independence for local states and no role for other European powers, nor for international organ-isations. To his delight, Hitler was therefore freed from the prospect of a two-front war against major powers and, thereby, apparently from risking a repetition of the stalemate of the First World War.

The pact also had great strategic importance, as Hitler was seeking to counter the effects of a possible British blockade with imports of grain, oil and other resources from the Soviet Union. That the home front could suffer, as it did in the First World War, might have been of greater concern to him and thereby to German strategic planning, than the question of a two-front war. In combination with this, the pact made the war possible – certainly in the form it took in 1939 – and thus the Soviet Union carries part of the responsibility for what happened, although this was something it was subsequently largely able to evade.

Such an agreement was not necessary to overcome Poland, which, in the face of a surprise German attack benefitting from air superiority in a number of directions, lacked the necessary strategic defence, irrespective of Russia's deep enmity. However, the 1939 pact both helped to speed up Poland's defeat and was the key strategic element in the fall of France in 1940.

Hitler to War

The German attack on Poland on 1 September 1939 led Britain and France to declare war two days later. Rapidly conquered, Poland was followed by Denmark, Norway, the Netherlands, Belgium and France the following year; Yugoslavia and Greece fell in early 1941. This left Germany the dominant power in west-ern and central Europe, with Italy its ally, Spain supportive, Portugal, Sweden and Switzerland neutral and Germany taking a role akin to Napoleon's France. Alongside a degree of fatalist reluctance, Hitler's repeated successes were widely popular in Germany and helped dampen criticism.

In 1919, a report from the British general staff had argued that 'taking the long view, it is unquestionable that what the British Empire has most reason to fear in the future is a Russo–German combination'. This was to be overturned in 1941 by the German attack on the Soviet Union. With his construction of politics in terms of race rather than states and of races supposedly engaged in an existential struggle, Hitler had no time for any limitation of German expansion on other than a short-term, tactical basis motivated by opportunism. Redressing the 1919 Versailles peace settlement was at best a tactic for Hitler, as was cooperation with Russia in 1939–41.

Indeed, the attack on the Soviet Union in June 1941, Operation Barbarossa, brought forward the millenarian strain in Nazism and encouraged Hitler to give deadly effect to his aspirations and fears, notably so against Jews. A 'new order' was planned, with an enlarged Germany central to a new European system and with the Germans at the top of the racial hierarchy. The European economy, whether allied or conquered, was to be made subservient to German interests.

The Holocaust

The reality of this plan was the mass slaughter of Jews, including that carried out by army units. The conquests of 1939–42 had fuelled the racial arrogance and sense of entitlement to rule and direct of Nazi ideology. Servicemen's letters of 1941 suggested that antisemitic propaganda had been widely internalised and become a dominant consensus. It was not until 1943 that it was felt necessary to introduce the National Socialist leadership officers in order to stiffen morale. The conversations of German prisoners-of-war (POWs), bugged and recorded by the British, revealed a widespread lack of any remorse or sense of responsibility.

Meanwhile, the mass deportation of German Jews to extermination camps in Poland led to Germany being declared '*Judenfrei*'

('Jew-free') in June 1943. In practice, possibly 10–12,000 German Jews went into hiding, of whom 3–5,000 survived the war. Known as 'U-boats' – submerged in ordinary life – they faced hazardous conditions. While some Germans provided shelter, in many cases knowing the risks they ran by harbouring Jews, others denounced the hidden, for whom the Gestapo searched with great vigour. Sheltering in dangerous circumstances, short of food and lacking medical attention, some Jews died. Some were killed by Allied bombing while, for yet others, this bombing provided an excellent opportunity to explain their loss of papers that would otherwise identify them as Jews.

It was not only the Jews who suffered in the Nazi persecution. Large numbers of Roma were killed in a separate genocide. Hitler also authorised in 1939 the slaughter of mentally ill and disabled Germans unable to work – in total about 212,000 people – which reflected his longstanding support for 'euthanasia' and his opposition to 'useless eaters'. Many were gassed or killed by lethal injection. There was no shortage of willing killers.

Separately, asocial 'misfits' among German prisoners (many were petty thieves, the work-shy, tramps and alcoholics or, rather, those categorised as such) were allocated to the SS from 1942. They were deliberately worked to death, reflecting a drive to 'purify' German society. In addition, homosexuals and Jehovah's Witnesses were sent to concentration camps where they suffered particularly brutal treatment, from which many died. From late 1942, the SS established a total of 560 work camps near existing factories, thus moving their controlled labour, rather than attracting and attaching industrial plant to the camps.

'This war is not the Second World War, this war is the great racial war,' declared Hermann Göring in October 1942. The idea of war against Jews remained crucial to Hitler's motivation until the very end. He sought what he regarded as a moral victory for his concept of the German people. Public knowledge and, separately, complicity have long been issues of discussion post-war because Hitler did not announce the 'final solution' publicly. Indoctrination has also been debated, such as that of the Hitler Youth and the League of German Girls. Those who did not join in persecution were not generally punished, which highlights individual responsibility and gives the lie to the convenient argument that the guilty were in some way passive victims of an all-powerful system and ideology. Amid false news and the rumours of a totalitarian society, knowledge of persecution varied, but was extensive. That so many Germans thought the Anglo–American air offensive was carried out in retribution for antisemitic measures indicates that they knew what was being done to Jews.

Support for Hitler

Far from limiting support for the Nazis, antisemitism provided themes for its expansion. This was not only the case for Christian antisemites, but an appeal was made to left-wing views, by presenting the unattractive side of business and finance as being Jewish.

The incoherent nature of Nazism was an aspect of its strength, as it ensured that the movement could reach out to a large number of constituencies, in part by representing itself directly – or through its intermediaries in these constituencies – in very different lights. Furthermore, in reaching out in various ways, there was an opportunity to respond to what were seen as popular drives and discontents. There were core groups and regions of support for Nazism, not least among young men, but backing was wide-ranging. Consent as well as coercion, collusion as well as coping, were all seen in the responses to a set of ideas and practices that could be emotionally gripping and cohesive, as well as frightening.

Regional and local research into Nazism became more prominent from the 1980s. The findings both provided a way to recognise the variety in Germany and to dispense with a central, national perspective in favour of one that allowed more of an understanding of the different responses to Nazism. The impact of specific political, social and ideological milieux has become more apparent. They both helped the Nazis and acted as limitations, although those who were not enthusiasts tended to become compromising bystanders.

On the part of the Nazis, compromises with particular milieux helped in the stabilisation of the system around differing manifestations of a common extreme nationalism. These compromises operated within a context of widespread obedience and consent, notably by sources of traditional authority who proved very ready to operate their structures to support the Nazi use of the state. This involved such actions as the seizure of Jewish property, helping to provide a predatory basis for the shifts and expedients by which Germany sought to operate as a people's (racist) welfare state, as with the Winter Help Charity.

Resistance to Hitler in Germany was patchy and brutally repressed, as exemplified by the non-violent White Rose group around Sophie Scholl. They printed and distributed leaflets only to be executed in 1943.

The war, as much as Nazism, brought major changes to the nation and further brutalisation, rather than resistance. This was in part the result of cumulative pressures of defeat; a failure brought home by Allied bombing that led to social dissolution. In neither peace nor war was there any equivalent to the violently suppressed demonstrations of East Germany in 1953 nor to the manifestations of 1989.

Yet, from the outset, alongside the sense of destiny that helped give force to Nazi plans and a widespread popular view of the conflict as another manifestation of the First World War, one forced on the Germans, governmental confidence in popular responses was variable. In addition to fanatical support for the regime, which continued until the very end of the war, failure and disillusionment led to a fall in morale. The firestorm in

Hamburg caused by British bombing in July 1943 created a crisis of public confidence in the regime. However, the Nazi surveillance system's brutal repression of disaffection and any sign of 'defeatism', presided over by Heinrich Himmler, the head of the SS who also became minister of the interior in August 1943, helped ensure that there was no repetition of the German collapse of 1918. Workers were very much directed by the regime through, in particular, the German Work Front, the *Gauleiters* (district political governors; a system introduced in 1933) and the Armaments Commission. Moreover, the judicial system willingly responded to Hitler in dramatically increasing the harshness of its sentences.

In the unsuccessful bomb plot of 20 July 1944, a brave group of German officers narrowly failed to assassinate Hitler and to overthrow his regime in pursuit of their plan to end the war with Britain and the USA and only to fight the Soviet Union. In contrast, the bulk of the military command rallied to Hitler. Moreover, part of the Nazi leadership continued to believe that willpower and improved weaponry – in the shape of rockets, submarines and jet aircraft – would deliver victory.

In 1945, the weakness of popular resistance on behalf of the Nazis during and after the Allied conquest was a demonstration of their eventual unpopularity. This did not mean that there had been a lack of consent and enthusiasm in earlier years, although there was also an important sceptical strand that played a part alongside the impact of social atomisation and totalitarian control.

BOMBING GERMANY

A British strategic review of August 1941 had noted the consequences of British forces being unable to compete with the Germans in continental Europe. The response of Britain, at that stage the operationally weaker power, was to seek strategic advantage from indirect attack, in the shape of bombing, blockade and subversion, each of which was designed to hit the German economy and German morale:

> 'Bombing on a vast scale is the weapon upon which we principally depend for the destruction of German economic life and morale. To achieve its object, the bombing offensive must be on the heaviest possible scale and we aim at a force limited in size only by operational difficulties in the UK. After meeting the needs of our own security we give to the heavy bomber first priority in production.
>
> 'Our policy at present is to concentrate upon targets which affect both the German transportation system and morale. As our forces increase, we intend to pass to a planned attack on civilian morale with the intensity and continuity which are essential for success. We believe that by these methods, applied on a vast scale, the whole structure on which the German forces are based can be destroyed. As a result, these forces will suffer such a decline in fighting power and mobility that direct [British] action will once more become possible.'

It was even mistakenly believed that these methods might be enough to make Germany sue for peace.

On the night of 30–31 May 1942, the British launched over 1,050 bombers at Cologne: forty were lost. The raid saw the use of the 'bomber-stream' tactic, in which bombers gathered in one stream, using mass to counteract the power of the defences. Although the attack, which killed over 460 people, did not achieve all its objectives in terms of the destruction of industry and morale, it showed that the British had the ability to mount a major attack on a German city and was seen as a way to persuade the British public that the Germans could be hit hard. As a sign of what was to come, most of the casualties in Cologne were civilian. Arthur Harris, appointed commander-in-chief of Bomber

Command that February, was determined to show the viability of RAF attacks and to terminate the talk of reallocating the bombers to help the navy and the army.

In attacking Germany, the RAF was supplemented by the Americans (flying from British bases) from July 1942. Aside from the Cologne attack, most of the raids in that year were fairly small-scale. The cities of the Ruhr industrial region, notably Essen and Dortmund, were the main targets. The raids were important to the development of an effective ground-support system to underpin a bombing offensive, as well as in the gaining of operational experience, a process necessary for the American and British armies and navies as well as for the air forces. The Germans, in turn, continued to bomb British cities, especially in the Baedecker raids devastating, for example, the city of Exeter.

Germany was under heavy air attack by 1943. Wartime factors accentuated the use of bombing, not simply the determination to employ available forces, but also the need to show domestic and international audiences that efforts were being made. A belief that the war being waged was a total one served to justify bombing and, in turn, the bombing was an instrumental demonstration that the war was indeed total.

At the Casablanca Conference that January, the Americans and British agreed on what was termed the 'combined bomber offensive', with the Americans attacking by daylight and the British by night. This was seen as a way to show Stalin that the Western Allies were doing their utmost to weaken Germany and thus to aid Soviet operations. Similarly, the commitment at Casablanca to unconditional surrender by the Axis Powers as a war goal was also designed to reassure Stalin.

At Casablanca, it was agreed that the bombing should serve to destroy the German economic system and so damage German popular morale that the capacity for armed resistance would be fatally weakened. As most German factories were in cities, these goals were linked. Until the opening of the second front, the invasion of German-held France in 1944, this was the most effective way to strike at Germany. Although challenged by the strategic depth Germany enjoyed, thanks to its conquests in 1940, strategic bombing was made more feasible by four-engined bombers – such as the British Lancaster – as well as by heavier bombs and developments in navigational aids and training.

The availability of large numbers of bombers reflected Allied industrial capacity, with American and British production of aircraft rising from over seventy thousand in 1942 to over 120,000 in 1944. The Allies considerably out-built their opponents in the air. Numbers, however, were not the sole issue. The Allies also developed the ability to organise production so that it could be retooled quickly for improved specifications and to ensure the creation of a range of aircraft with different capabilities.

There was no electronic navigation, target identification or guided bombs. Instead, concerned about the daytime vulnerability of their bombers, from March 1942, the British focused on night-time area bombing. They wished to destroy industrial targets, but the Butt report on night raids in June–July 1941 showed that they were not doing so. Accuracy was difficult in night-time free-fall bombing – as it was, despite American bomb-sights, in daytime bombing. There was a similar contrast in the bombing of Italy by the Americans and the British.

Area bombing could lead to heavy civilian casualties, especially among factory workers, and supporters of the policy – notably Harris – saw this as likely to wreck German and Italian morale, and thus their ability to continue the war. Cities were ranked on their economic importance as targets. About 34–40,000 people were killed in the British raids on Hamburg in July 1943, notably on 28 July, as the result of a firestorm created by a combination of incendiary and high-explosive bombs. The impact was horrifying: those killed were either suffocated or burnt to death. The raid, which followed the first firestorm, at Wuppertal on 29–30 May, in which over 3,500 people were killed, badly affected German morale, leading to the partial evacuation of cities, including Hamburg and Berlin. Dresden was to be very heavily bombed in 1945.

The first American raids deep into Germany occurred in February 1943, when the major rail marshalling yard at Hamm was attacked, with success coming on 2 March. The Americans focused on daytime, high-altitude, precision bombing to hit industrial targets, especially ball-bearing factories. This reflected the unsuitability of the B-17 bomber for night flying and American criticism of the value of British area bombing.

Mobilisation and Resources

The German public had been pummelled by Allied bombing, but benefitted from the looting and harshly administered, forced labour of much of Europe, as well as that of German Jews. Reluctant to conscript married women for the industrial workforce, Hitler's conservative social policies led him to see German women as wives and mothers. The mobilisation of men and women in the civilian population was relatively late, by the standards of Britain and the Soviet Union.

Nevertheless, 57 per cent of German women, nine-tenths of them single, were working in 1944. There were half a million volunteer women auxiliaries with the Wehrmacht, and many women were employed in agriculture. Demand remained high, due to Hitler's opposition to a cut in rations which remained at close to 2,000 calories. However, the Germans lacked mechanisation in agriculture, did not mobilise sufficient women and, as a consequence, drew on forced labour, which in 1944 represented 22.5 per cent of the workforce. Reliance on foreigners meant that Germany was more ethnically mixed than hitherto, although labourers' relations with Germans were firmly policed.

The army's demand for soldiers – 17.3 million men in total – was a major constraint on available workers. The number of divisions rose from 104 in 1940 to 219 in 1943 and 238 by 1945, although their size varied. An average of 17,000 men in 1939 per division had fallen to 10,000 by the end of 1944.

A wide-ranging failure to mobilise resources owed something to the mistaken expectation of a speedy victory. In 1938, Germany had a per capita GDP of $5,126, compared to $6,134 for the USA, $5,983 for Britain and $4,424 for France. Some 28.5 per cent of the active population were in agriculture, 47.3 per cent in industry and 24.2 per cent in services. The percentages for the USA and Britain were lower in the first and higher in the third. Germany, in 1938, had 22 per cent of the world's chemical production, which was second only to the USA, but electricity production – at 451 megawatts per hour in 1939 – was below that of the USA, Britain, France and Japan. Oil needs depended heavily on imports and on synthetic petrol from coal. The latter provided 40 per cent of fuel needs in 1943, only to collapse due to air attack in 1944. In September 1939, there were only 3.2 months of industrial fuel reserves and 5.2 months of motor fuel.

Göring proved incompetent in his direction of economic planning in 1936–8 and serious inefficiencies in munitions production continued, although there was considerable improvement from 1942 when Albert Speer increased central control. Yet resources still proved a major problem for Germany, notably in shortages of steel, non-ferrous metals and oil. Accentuated by poor planning and further damaged by Allied air assault, this ensured that German war production was inadequate, notably so in artillery shells and lorries. On the other hand, German production of fighter aircraft, submarines and machine guns remained high. Overall, German manufacturing techniques did not match the high output of the USA, the Soviet Union and Britain. There was a relative lack of assembly lines, notably in aircraft manufacture. The Germans failed to exploit mass-production techniques as successfully as their opponents. The Nazi state's vicious ideology – at once murderous, bombastic and rhetorical – had serious managerial flaws, as well as multiple inefficiencies.

Volkswagen

Founded in 1937 by the German Labour Front, a Nazi organisation launched in 1933 in order to direct workers, this 'people's car', pre-sold on a subscription basis, was from 1938 manufactured in Wolfsburg, east of Hanover. It eventually became the site of the world's largest car factory. The city of Wolfsburg itself had been founded in 1938 to house the workers. Hitler was a keen supporter of the project, but the economic and financial model was poor and the large amount of money already paid in was confiscated by the government in September 1939 at the outbreak of hostilities. During the war, the factory manufactured vehicles for the army, mostly by means of slave labour from concentration camps.

As a totalitarian regime, the Nazi state lacked the efficiencies of market discipline but, additionally, the duplication of competing agencies led to serious rivalry, both institutional and personal, and resulted in acute confusion in policy implementation. For example, German espionage was affected by the systemic rivalry between the Abwehr, a branch of the military, and the SD, which was the SS security service. There was no war cabinet to provide coherence.

Despite the energy transmitted by personal networks and the pressures of war, endemic rivalry and incessant confusion focused decision-making on Hitler, who was a lazy and disorganised leader. He was seriously unable to provide clear, coherent and systematised direction. His failure included a lack of understanding of economic issues and structures, as well as his confused responses to economic mobilisation and planning. Willpower was no substitute for sensible processes, and violence was part of an expedient of hasty improvisation that could not replace rational and effective crisis management.

Allied bombing helped greatly to exacerbate the problem of economic mismanagement. Despite the limited precision of bombing by high-flying aircraft dropping free-fall bombs, strategic bombing was crucial to the disruption of communications and logistics, largely because it was eventually done on such a massive scale and because the targets could not be attacked by any other means. Raids on communications hit the integration of manufacturing, while the oil industry was pummelled. Furthermore, from 1943, the Germans diverted massive resources to anti-aircraft defence forces, including much of the Luftwaffe itself.

The extent to which civilian morale was broken is controversial. The Nazi inability to stop the bombing encouraged, as in Nuremberg, a sense that defeat was likely, indeed, was already occurring. Much of the bombing happened in the hard-fought final six months of the war, including that of Dresden where, alongside heavy civilian casualties, there was also the destruction of a railway node and a major military-industrial complex. The controversies about the bombing continue, the German far right referring to 'a holocaust of bombs' in 2006, but it was the Germans who had launched a total war and it was visited on them as well. At the time of that Allied bombing, the Germans were not only firing rockets indiscriminately at London and Antwerp, but also fighting on with great vigour and determination, unlike the Italians in 1943.

Defeat

The war had turned against Germany in late 1941, when the Soviet Union could not be driven to defeat. Hitler's declaration of war on the USA in the aftermath of the attack on Pearl Harbor by his ally Japan was followed by the Americans' focus on Germany. There were some German successes in 1942 but, finally, serious defeats in the Soviet Union and North Africa.

In 1943, the Soviets regained much territory while Anglo–American forces drove the Germans from North Africa and invaded Italy, where Mussolini was overthrown by a rebellion from within the system, something that was not seen in Germany. In 1944, the Soviets advanced as far as Warsaw and into the Balkans and Anglo–American forces invaded France. The Germans were driven from France and Belgium and abandoned by Finland, Romania and Bulgaria.

The Allies were determined to maintain their coalition and not to accept a peace settlement that might leave Germany able to start a new conflict. They demanded unconditional surrender, rather than the change of governmental system sought in late 1918. Alongside occupation, re-education was seen as a necessary aspect of de-Nazification.

No system of resistance had been left in place after the bomb plot against Hitler of 20 July 1944 and, instead, there was a commitment to protect Germany against invasion, especially by Soviet forces. There was also a fatalistic resilience and fear of the Nazi regime, which used terror to ensure consent.

Hitler, for whom a stalemate peace was also unacceptable, was determined to fight on to destroy Europe's Jews, as well as to achieve what he regarded as a moral victory for his concept of the German people. As a consequence, a notion of heroic self-destruction – for himself, the military, the regime and the nation – which may always have been present, became a decisive part of the regime's ideology and therefore of its strategy. Never clear, the distinction between them had collapsed.

Always a struggle of the will in Hitler's eyes, the war was increasingly organised in those terms, notably in the extent to which political commitment was crucial to military appointment and subsequent promotion. The *Volkssturm*, a Nazi-run, compulsory, local defence militia for men aged between sixteen and sixty, was established in July 1944. It was designed to inflict casualties on the advancing allies such that their morale could not tolerate, and also to indoctrinate the German civilian population into a total struggle.

Left to the control of Himmler and Martin Bormann, the party secretary – rather than being under the jurisdiction of the army – the *Volkssturm* served a political as well as a military function in making the war a matter of morale. This strategy encouraged the appointment of officers from among those who were politically committed to Nazism. The strategy was similar to that employed by the Japanese. Thus, the politics of the war became a matter of will as, in Hitler's view, it had been throughout. This, however, was not forced on an unwilling army and public. Instead, the degree of Nazi commitment on the part of the officer corps – young and old, recent and long-established – was considerable.

Hitler was reduced to vain hopes. His sense of his destiny interacted with his ideological drive and his determination that there should be no repetition of the surrender in 1918. Indeed, the Germans fought on, their effort including killing those suspected of defeatism and/or whose political views were unwelcome. Moreover, atrocities against prisoners and the slaughter of the Jews continued until the very end of the war. This determination indicated the difficult task facing the Allies.

Indeed, Hitler hoped that the alliance against him would dissolve because of Germany's resolve and the Allies' own, inherent divisions. Goebbels was told by Hitler on 11 March 1945 that he believed Churchill was determined to exterminate Germany and would refuse to ally against the Soviets. Hitler claimed that it was Roosevelt's wish that the Europeans destroy themselves through war and that it was necessary for Germany to fight sufficiently well to lead Stalin to seek a separate peace. Hitler's views were unfounded. As prime minister in 1951–5, Churchill came to see a reconstituted German army as important in the defence of Western interests against the Soviet Union.

More specifically, Hitler relied on the death of Roosevelt on 12 April, which he saw as proof of a providential salvation that would lead to a change comparable to that following the death of Tsarina Elizabeth of Russia in 1762. Her passing had unravelled the alliance against Frederick the Great of Prussia during the Seven Years' War.

The Soviets launched their final offensive on 16 April and, with his victorious opponents having fought their way into the centre of Berlin, Hitler committed suicide on 30 April. He had not fled to an Alpine redoubt, as was thought possible by the Allies, in part because he believed (correctly) that his 'Eagle's Nest' retreat in Berchtesgaden in the Bavarian Alps was vulnerable to American air attack. Moreover, flight did not match Hitler's monomaniacal vision of his destiny and legacy.

Yet, even as the regime collapsed, no local revolutionary movements erupted. Instead, the population remained politically passive, along with some displaying a degree of continued fanaticism (not least supported by the young). Peter Downward, a British officer, noted among the German POWs the large number of very young soldiers 'dedicated to the aims of Adolf Hitler's Third Reich. They would not believe that Hitler was already dead. The older men accepted the news with almost grateful resignation . . .' The fear of the SS and the Gestapo was to remain deeprooted, even in captivity. US assessments of German prisoners also noted Nazi loyalties, including among Catholic and workingclass soldiers. After the war, and well into the 1980s, many Germans regretted only that they had lost the war.

Based at Flensburg, Hitler's designated successor as chancellor, head of the armed forces and Nazi Party leader, Admiral Karl Dönitz, wanted to continue resisting the Soviets while negotiating surrender terms with the Americans and the British. Dönitz hoped that this strategy would enable more Germans to escape Soviet occupation. However, the Western Allies insisted on unconditional surrender to all the Allies and Dönitz complied on 7 May. It was only the Allied conquest and Hitler's suicide that overcame the German will to resist.

Defeat was total. Hitler had completely failed, as was made clear by the final fighting amid the ruins of the grand buildings of his imperial capital. The Third Reich's military deaths (which included those of Austria) numbered 5.3 million, including 30.9 per cent of the army, with 16.8 per cent of those born between 1900 and 1928 dying in the conflict – and over 40 per cent of those born in 1919 and 1920. The years 1944–5 were the deadliest of the war. In total, 11.1 million German prisoners were taken, with many of those captured by the Soviets subsequently dying, essentially because of the horrible conditions of Soviet POW camps. There are major differences between German and Soviet statistics of deaths, the former reporting closer to a third and the latter 12 per cent. The last prisoners were released in 1956.

About 20 per cent of German housing was totally destroyed, 20 per cent damaged and 30 per cent of the population left homeless. Money was worthless, gas and electricity supplies broken and the transport system was bomb-wrecked, meaning that surviving factories could not operate and there was no work other than that which could be found on the land. Yet, recovery began rapidly. Although coal and iron ore production remained lower by 1948 than in 1938, industrial production had returned to 1938 levels by 1948 and equipment was updated. Peace had come. However, not only were there very few signs amid the wasteland of Hitler's empire of the genesis of any Fourth Reich, but also few signs of the remarkable developments and growth of the following decades.

Confronting the War

In the 2000s, an emphasis on the Germans as victims re-emerged; suffering at the hands of Anglo–American bombers and advancing Soviet troops. The complete lack of proportionality these comments generally reveal is notable. If they testify to a determination to express and make sense of personal experience, there is also a bleak moral emptiness in much of the self-serving blame-shifting. An example is the misleading claim that, in attacking the Soviet Union, Hitler had pre-empted a planned Soviet assault on Germany – an argument that went back to Goebbels. Moreover, in response to the correct stress from the 1990s on the brutal conduct of the Wehrmacht, came attempts to argue that the Soviet army was as bad – attempts that ignored the extent to which the Soviet presence in Germany in 1945 was a direct consequence of the German invasion of the Soviet Union.

This holds true with the critique of Allied bombing, as in Hermann Knell's 2003 account of the devastating British bombing of Würzburg in 1945, which inaccurately presented German policies in the 1930s and the attack on the Soviet Union as defensive and preventive. In October 2004, the tabloid press, notably *Bild*, stoked up pressure on the British to apologise for the bombing prior to a visit by Queen Elizabeth II of Britain. Victimhood was also a continuing theme in the response to the issue of post-war German refugees from eastern Europe, as in 2007 when the Czechs and Poles again firmly rejected the idea that these refugees were victims.

The popular television series *Unsere Mütter, Unsere Väter* (*Our Mothers, Our Fathers*, 2013) excused the willingness of German soldiers to commit atrocities, blaming it on compulsion. This led to complaints. It can then be said that, on the one hand, Germany is confronting the past, which deserves praise – as in its recognition of the Holocaust, not least with a major museum on the subject in Berlin. On the other hand, the terms and content of this confrontation are inevitably contentious.

Opened in 2015, Munich's *NS-Dokumentationszentrum* (Documentation Centre for the History of National Socialism) emphasises the radicalisation of many because of the short-lived Communist takeover of the city in 1919. This is cited as the reason why Munich was the birthplace of the Nazi movement. This could be seen as downplaying antisemitism, although the exhibits include posters and photographs of antisemitic activism.

10

Germany Divided, 1945–90

The Second World War destroyed both the Nazi regime of 1933 and the German state created in 1919 from the ruins of that founded in 1866 and 1871. Territorial changes were accompanied by demographic ones, as Germany's eastern frontier was moved westwards with the loss of Silesia and eastern Pomerania to Poland and of East Prussia to Poland and the Soviet Union. Millions of people of Germanic origin fled prior to the end of the war, the great majority moving westwards to escape the Soviets, who were frequently harsh towards civilians, although generally far less so than the Germans had been to the population of the Soviet Union.

After the war ended, in what was the largest human migration in modern Europe, more people were displaced, including 2.8 million from Czechoslovakia and 2.5 million from what is now Poland. Alongside large numbers of refugees, others had been made homeless by bombing and many were unemployed. Many faced pressures from food and coal shortages, high rates of crime and the psychological impact of defeat, family loss, dislocation and occupation that included curfews and travel restrictions. There were also the trials of Nazi leaders, notably through the International Military Tribunal at Nuremberg in 1945–6.

Unlike the situation of 1918–19, the Allies had conquered Germany and definitively so. This ensured that Germany would be occupied. Henry Morgenthau, secretary of the US Treasury, had suggested in 1944 that Germany be divided in two and deindustrialised, indeed essentially turned into an agricultural economy. This would prevent an apparently immutable pattern of national interest, but the idea was not pursued. The French had plans for undoing the German unification of 1866–71, transforming

Germany into autonomous states. This was a bolder version of the interest shown in 1919 in an independent Rhineland, but it was one that didn't gain traction among the major powers. The schemes were rejected in favour of a joint occupation by the victorious powers of a still unified Germany. The Soviets occupied what was to become East Germany, the Americans a southern and central zone including Bavaria and Hesse, the French a southwestern zone, including Baden and the Palatinate, and the British a north-west region, including Lower Saxony, North-Rhine Westphalia and Schleswig-Holstein.

These zones were to be the basis for new *Länder*, the states that comprised the Federal Republic of Germany founded in 1949, a process that still involved much politics. This was especially so with the unification of Baden, Württemberg-Baden and Württemberg-Hohenzollern in 1951 after a referendum the previous year. Opposition in Baden led to another referendum in 1970 with 82 per cent support that settled the matter. The occupied powers were determined that Prussia should no longer be dominant. As a result, it was divided into new provinces, notably – in West Germany – Rhineland-Palatinate, North Rhine-Westphalia, Lower Saxony and Schleswig-Holstein.

The French supported a different status for the Saarland. Initially part of the French zone of occupation, it was placed from 1947 under a high commissioner, separate from Germany and, indeed, in an economic and currency union with France. This was intended as a prelude to French-linked independence. In 1954, a European status for the Saarland as an independent state appeared likely, but it was heavily rejected in 1955 in a referendum. French control had become clearly self-interested as well as rather oppressive, while West Germany seemed more attractive. Saarland became West German in 1957 and West Germany then comprised ten states.

The agreement for joint administration of Germany, not least by means of the Allied Control Council, could not be sustained, not least due to French obstruction and Stalin's pressure for control both in the Soviet zone and more generally, as well as his anger about the unification of the western zones. Reparations also proved a key element, with the Soviets demanding payments from the occupation zones of the Western powers, as well as a four-power supervision of the Ruhr, which was in the British zone. Such demands challenged Western plans for the regenera- tion of the German economy and the management of their zones, as well as crystallising a growing desire to limit the westward penetration of Soviet power and influence. The Soviets were keen to use German resources to help cope with their war-damaged economy as well as to further damage Germany itself, but the latter aim became less significant as they understood that East Germany would become an area they had to stabilise.

The Soviets sought to foster the Communist Party in Germany and, to that end, forcibly merged the Social Democrats (SPD) – the alternative left-wing party in their zone – with the Communists, creating in 1946 the Socialist Unity Party (*Sozialistische Einheitspartei Deutschlands*; SED). It remained the governing party until East Germany collapsed and served as cover for communist domination. This policy was rejected by the SPD in the western zones and hit communist popularity.

The SED leadership at first pursued the goal of communism with German unity but adapted to circumstances, benefitting from Soviet dominance of East Germany, which indeed ensured that the strength of other parties in the elections there in late 1946 could be ignored. Soviet occupation policies alienated public and political opinion in the western zones, which influenced the authorities of the occupation there as they sought to develop a democratic political system. As a result, the Soviets lost their opportunity to influence developments in West Germany, just as in 1990 they were to do in East Germany.

The traditional right was discredited by its association with the Nazi regime in the aftermath of total defeat, with all major parties looking to the future. It was reborn in the rather different form of Christian Democracy, which was more corporatist and more ostentatiously concerned with social welfare, its roots in Catholic political activism. The nuclear family became a key theme in West German social assumptions, with the CDU Party (Christian Democratic Union) being especially active in portraying this social construct as a way to avoid, at the social level, the state-driven extremism that the new Germany was designed to thwart at the national level. A view of a benign, pre-modernist society was part of the idea. Yet, as with the pension reform of 1957, this looked to state support and sought to avoid reliance on pensions. This new scheme was generous (not least in comparison to East Germany) and indexed to economic growth.

Christian Democracy was consistently stronger in Catholic than Protestant areas; in the Rhineland and the Palatinate, rather than Bremen, Hamburg, Lower Saxony and North Rhine-Westphalia. Anti-Prussianism was part of its thinking, with Prussia, socialism and authoritarianism all linked, the alleged alternative to federal democracy and liberalism. The CDU was conceived as a deliberate attempt to unite both Christian denominations in the political middle. It was intended to rectify a weak aspect of the politics of Weimar Germany and took over the mantle of the Centre Party (dissolved in 1933) as the representative of Catholic political interests. Refounded after the war but affected by the widespread weakening of established political links in the Nazi era, the Centre Party rapidly sank into insignificance and, due to very limited electoral support, dropped out of the Bundestag totally in 1957. Many former Centre politicians, notably Konrad Adenauer and many leading Catholic clerics, such as Archbishop Josef Frings of Cologne (r. 1942–69), endorsed the new CDU, which Adenauer co-founded. Catholicism was proportionately far more important in West Germany than in the Weimar Republic (as was the female vote) and the Catholic church was suspicious of the SPD.

Meanwhile, the Soviet rejection of American aid from the Marshall Plan created a new dividing line between the parts of Germany that received such support and the part that did not. This boundary line meant that much of the old Prussia was excluded from West Germany, which had important electoral consequences. This also pertained to the legacy of the war, not least the failure of the July 1944 bomb plot and the largely conservative Protestant elite linked to it. This created a particular basis for the new state and its political society.

Isolated within the Soviet occupation zone, Berlin was divided between the four occupying zones. This appeared to challenge the Soviet position, not least as it was possible for people to move within the city between the zones and thus 'leave' East Germany. Berlin also provided an apparently vulnerable target for Soviet attack. They did indeed blockade West Berlin (the American, British and French zones) in 1948-9, in an attempt to force a unification of the city. This blockade was met by an impressive and successful Anglo-American airlift of supplies into the city, with nearly 200,000 flights supplying 1.5 million tons of supplies. The Soviets had to abandon their blockade.

No desire existed in West Germany for a return to the factious Weimar politics of 1919-33, with its stark divisions and large number of parties. It was appreciated that the bitter rivalry between the Communists and Social Democrats had played a major role in enabling Hitler to rise to power. An inspiration, or even model – notably for the SPD – was the coming to power of the Labour Party in Britain in 1945, but the SPD were weakened by the extent to which so much of their core support was in the Soviet zone.

The SPD's two major policy outlines, the 1951 Frankfurt Declaration and, more significantly, the 1959 Godesberg Programme, removed Leninist thinking and Marxist class warfare from SPD doctrine. Thus, the late 1940s and 1950s proved a formative era for the later evolution of the SPD, which proved to be a major force for stability in West Germany, not least as a result of support leeching from the Communist Party, which initially had enjoyed considerable popularity. The West German concept of the social market contrasted with the nationalisation and state control seen in Britain, France and Italy, as well as with East German communism and American economic liberalism. The SPD was a moderate force and this made it a viable alternative to the CDU, encouraging the latter to compete for the moderate vote.

Konrad Adenauer (1876–1967), a Cologne-born politician and devout Catholic, had been a member of the Centre Party, serving as mayor of Cologne in 1917–33. An opponent of Prussianisation, he had backed a Rhineland *Land* (province) separate from Prussia in 1919, but found no support at federal level. Adenauer was considered for chancellor in 1926, but would not work with Stresemann. Willing to accept a political role for the Nazis on the basis of their electoral strength, although not willing to shake Hitler's hand, Adenauer, in turn, was dismissed and imprisoned for a short while. After the war, he backed the CDU, whose independent sister party in Bavaria, the more right-wing CSU (Christian Social Union), was based on the solid support of the Catholic bulk of the population. It also benefitted from its strength in the Protestant areas of Franconia, notably round Ansbach and Bayreuth.

Chairman of the parliamentary council of 1948 that drafted a new constitution for West Germany, Adenauer – the father figure of the new republic – became chancellor in 1949, in the aftermath of the elections of that year. The CDU (including, unless otherwise mentioned, its Bavarian CSU allies) won 31 per cent of the vote, the SPD – which wanted a united, socialist Germany – 29.2 per cent, the centrist, economically liberal Free Democrats (FDP) 11.9 per cent and the Communist Party took 5.7 per cent. Adenauer's coalition partners were the FDP, which was affected by neo-Nazi entryism, and the conservative German Party (DP), which took 4 per cent. As chancellor, Adenauer backed Bonn for 'provisional capital', as opposed to Frankfurt and Heidelberg, and took obdurate lines against recognising the Oder-Neisse line as the new boundary with Poland, over the rights of German refugees and in opposing de-Nazification.

An adroit politician, good at repeatedly outmanoeuvring both colleagues and opponents – a skill later seen also in Helmut Kohl and Angela Merkel – Adenauer was re-elected in 1953, 1957 and 1961. In 1953, the CDU vote went up to 45.2 per cent, the SPD dropped to 28.8 per cent, the FDP went down to 4.5 per cent, DP to 3.3 per cent and the Communists to 2.2 per cent. A new party, the All-German Bloc/League of Expellees (GB/BHE), won 5.9 per cent.

In the 1957 elections, the CDU was helped by the success of achieving rearmament and by its warnings about the risks of endangering prosperity. On a turnout of 87.8 per cent, the CDU won 50.2 per cent, the SPD 31.8 per cent, the FDP 7.7 per cent, the DP 3.4 per cent and the GB/BHE 4.6 per cent. Prosperity had helped enormously – as it would also for Harold Macmillan in Britain in the election of 1959.

The 1961 election saw the CDU share of the vote fall to 45.3 per cent, the SPD – under Willy Brandt, the mayor of West Berlin – rise to 36.2 and the FDP hit 12.8 per cent. The merged DP and GB/BHE only won 2.7 per cent: The expellees, who had been influential as a cause and chorus in the 1950s, were becoming less so in the 1960s, notably as a different analysis and narrative of past and present interests came to the fore. In the late 1960s, the Holocaust and *Ostpolitik* played a larger role. In 1961, Adenauer had to build a coalition with the FDP, accepting that he would not see out his fourth term.

Adenauer helped ground the new democracy (although the Communist Party was banned in 1956 and the SPD was spied on), assisted by a doubling of real wages between 1950 and 1963 and the integration of the expellees and refugees, who by late 1960 made up about a quarter of the population. An effective social welfare system was created. Less attractively, Adenauer proved far more sympathetic to active former Nazis, such as Theodor Oberländer, the minister of refugees in 1953–60, than now looks acceptable. Hans Globke, the chief of staff of the chancellery from 1953 to 1960 and a key ally of Adenauer, had been an active bureaucrat under the Third Reich, not least in drafting antisemitic measures. Moreover, his amnesties for former Nazis, notably of 1949 and 1954 and the 1951 law on the civil service, chimed with a widespread refusal to accept individual and collective responsibility for the actions of the Third Reich, as well as opposition to what was termed 'victors' justice' which, in practice, was very limited.

This represented an aspect of achieving a consensus in the new state, but in a distinctly unpleasant fashion. Those given a green light to return to public life included former active SA, SS and Gestapo members. The Nuremberg verdicts on Nazi war criminals were repeatedly publicly denigrated, not least by church leaders, underlining the failure of Catholic clerics to speak out about Nazi crimes, a point noted by Adenauer in 1946.

However, conspiracy theorists who saw neo-Nazis as still widely active and a threat were proved wrong. This theme was very much one taken up in the 1950s and led to concern about German rearmament, but it proved totally unfounded. Indeed, the lack of revanchism, notably compared to the 1920s and 1930s, was more apparent. Adenauer urged 'allowing the past to be the past', a silence designed to bring stability, and was not personally sympathetic to Nazis. Presenting the Germans as victims of the Nazis served to help create distance. Although this process could result in an acceptance of deceitful self-presentation, some Nazis were punished. Yet, a 'model democracy' in which many were not called to account for vile crimes, was apparent and the latter was not necessary to the former part of the equation. The destruction of some wartime records was another aspect of the situation. The American focus on confronting the Soviet Union encouraged the overlooking of Nazi activity.

Football

As in Britain and France, football as a popular mass specta-
tor sport was in part a product of large-scale urban industrialisation, but amateurism long remained important.

In 1900, the *Deutscher Fussball-Bund* (DFB), a federation
of regional associations, was founded. Whereas the English
professional league was established in 1888, its West German
counterpart, the *Bundesliga*, was not founded until 1963. Until
then players were still amateurs, while the Third Reich period
continued to cast a baleful shadow. The league was followed
by a major change in football as it became increasingly
commercialised as part of its professionalisation.

Costs rose rapidly – notably salaries – which put a major
burden on club finances and led to the introduction of a
measure of local government support. Linked to this role
came a change in football supporters. They went from being
drawn from the local working class to coming from a more
socially mixed support base.

Bayern Munich, a team founded in 1900, won the champi-
onship in 1968–9 and were to be the dominant club thereafter, although with challenges from Borussia Mönchengladbach,
founded in 1900, in the mid-1970s and Borussia Dortmund,
founded in 1909, in the mid-1990s and early 2010s.

The first World Cup win came in 1954 – the 'miracle of
Berne', a psychologically incredibly important moment that
showed that military prowess was not necessary to a sense of
pride and that also helped ground West Germany as Germany.

Football, while also popular and important in East Germany,
continued – at least officially – to be an amateur sport. From
1949, clubs were organised in the Oberliga. State influence was
significant. The rivalry between Dynamo Berlin and Dynamo
Dresden represented the traditional Prusso–Saxon rivalry, with
spectators shouting 'Prussia' and 'Saxony' during the game,
even though the states had been abolished.

The German Cold War in Sport

Designed to be a clear political contrast to the 1936 Berlin Olympics, the 1972 Munich Olympic Games was a demonstration of a modern, democratic Germany, not least in its designs of open-style buildings of glass and steel. But it was to be most noted for a Palestinian terrorist attack on the Israeli team.

The Cold War was very differently presented in the competition between East and West Germany – coming third and fourth in the medal table. These were the first games in which the East German team appeared in fully independent form. East German success in sport owed much to illegal, performance-enhancing drugs and to widespread success in concealing their use. There were also suggestions of state-subsidised doping in West Germany, which it appears may have continued after unification, although the East German practice was more systematised and prevalent. National football teams also seemingly used drugs. Over six hundred sportsmen and women fled East Germany, in part due to its autocratic direction. Their families remaining behind were treated harshly by the East German authorities.

The 1950s did not see the grand coalition and unification that had taken place in Austria; there the occupying powers departed in 1955 having established a united country. Rather, the two Germanies moved further apart. West Germany emerged into new forums, notably NATO, which it joined in 1955, and the European Economic Community of which it was one of the six founding members in 1958. West Germany also benefitted greatly from the international post-war boom that lasted until 1973. It became the leading European economy and profited from the cutting in tariffs after the General Agreement on Tariffs and Trade was signed in 1947.

Returning West Germany to pre-war living standards by 1955, economic growth owed much to the country's skilled labour force and the application of new technology in manufacturing and agriculture, which resulted in important productivity gains. Agricultural mechanisation led to a movement of workers from the land. In manufacturing, the use of mass production in new, purpose-built plants permitted an effective introduction of technological and organisational methods.

American investment and the catch-up factor of applying advanced – also mostly American – technological and production methods were significant. American state aid was also helpful and was largely spent on industry, but growing global demand was at least as important as this in causing economic expansion.

The Student Prince (1954) and Other Films

Based on Wilhelm Meyer-Förster's novel *Karl Heinrich* (1898), via his successful play *Alt Heidelberg* (1901), silent films of 1915 and 1923 and the 1924 operetta *The Student Prince*, the anachronism of the 1954 film version was a great success and provided an account of Germany that worked well for American audiences with their troops then in West Germany. The extent to which Heidelberg was earlier a centre of Nazi sympathy was, of course, ignored.

The Americanisation of West German culture in this period was much more profound and insistent, with the 1950s dominated entirely by light, and lightheaded, '*Heimatfilme*' ('Homeland films'). These were Technicolor romances set in idyllic villages and oblivious to the just-lost war, the ruins or the direness of social conditions, much less confronting the moral responsibilities of the previous two decades.

Immediately after the war, however, there had been a number of '*Trümmerfilm*' ('Rubble film') that focused on post-war suffering. The first and best, Wolfgang Staudte's *Die Mörder sind unter (The Murderers Are Among Us*, 1946), had echoes of Weimar expressionism.

Germany's political economy remained the focus during the 'chancellor democracies' of Adenauer and Ludwig Erhard. These years were centred on economic activity, especially at the expense of politics and, to a degree, of social liberalisation. Erhard, who directed economic policy from 1948 to 1963, pushed economic liberalisation, especially in trade, as did other leaders. The policy marked a major break from the cartels characteristic of earlier German history and was important to growth. In pursuit of a general societal goal of security, some liberalising moves were cancelled – not least the liberalisation of rent and prices – but competition was fostered alongside currency stability in an economic system that contrasted with the nationalisations and state control seen in France and Britain.

West Germany at its inception faced major limits in currency, capital, liquidity and autonomy, but the removal of exchange controls and import restrictions contributed to it becoming the economic centre of western Europe, a pivotal place of advanced manufacturing and a beneficiary of growth elsewhere. Export surpluses rose rapidly. The European Payments Union helped enable this system.

West Germany also benefitted from the longstanding skill of its engineering industry and from more harmonious labour relations than those seen in Britain. This reflected a West German corporatism that encompassed government, business, banks and trade unions and rested on the social cohesion that the exclusion of the far left and far right from politics helped encourage. Prosperity and consumerism lessened tensions and helped make modernisation more acceptable. Both were to lead to criticism from the radical young in the 1960s, but, in the meantime, living standards and property ownership rose and the middle class expanded considerably. Affluence helped bring individualism. Moreover, the more prosperous working class did not join the radical young in 1968.

The Beatles on the Elbe, 1960-2

Frequently performing in Hamburg, the Beatles developed their style and image, with Astrid Kirchherr (1938–2020) playing a major role in creating their distinctive 'moptop' haircut. The nightclubs, notably the Indra and the Kaiserkeller, proved very rough and ready but, with time, the venues got better. The Beatles recorded two of their singles in German – '*Komm gib mir deine Hand*' ('I Want to Hold Your Hand') and '*Sie liebt dich*' ('She Loves You'), which reached No. 5 and No. 7 in the charts. Constructed in 2007, Beatles-Platz contains statues of the band members. British beat music was popular in East Germany but disapproved of by the authorities. This led to the banning of beat music, resulting in protests in Leipzig: the 'beat rebellion'.

There was very much a regional dimension to economic growth. In a continuance of earlier patterns, North Rhine-Westphalia was the centre of activity, with a focus on heavy industry that reflected the governmental economic priorities of the period, as also seen in East Germany. By 1957, the *Land* was responsible for close to a third of West Germany's domestic product. However, this focus on heavy industry created problems for the region in the successive economic crises that followed the end, in the 1970s, of the 'long boom'. Instead, much industrial growth then focused on Bavaria and Baden-Württemburg.

Economic growth meant jobs when the male labour force had been hit by heavy war losses. Unemployment fell to 0.4 per cent in 1965. Prior to 1961, when the Berlin Wall was built, completely sealing the frontier, over three million East Germans went west in a fundamental rejection of the communist system. They went in search of jobs and economic liberty and what they could produce in terms of living standards as much as for political freedom. The socialist planned economy with the 'new economic system' in East Germany did not provide the same standard of living and prosperity as the 'social market economy' closely associated with the 'economic miracle' in West Germany. In turn, that failure helped stabilise West Germany.

Rioting workers killed by troops was not part of the East German prospectus, but there was large-scale unrest in June 1953. Over one million people demonstrated, notably in East Berlin but also elsewhere, especially in Halle, Jena, and Magdeburg. It was a reflection of the failure to address living standards. In unrest that was very varied in its objectives, there was criticism of the government and its incarceration of political prisoners and demands for the refoundation of the SPD and for price cuts. The unrest, blamed by the regime on the West German government, was suppressed by Soviet tanks and East German security forces, with a large number of people arrested and many executed. The episode ended up strengthening the position of Walter Ulbricht, the East German leader, as first secretary of the Socialist Unity Party (i.e. Communists) until 1971, while also making him more concerned about worker attitudes, in part with the aim of discouraging emigration.

To meet labour needs, particularly as a result of the building of the Berlin Wall, there was also large-scale migration into West Germany from Mediterranean countries, notably Italy and Turkey. The latter in particular affected the range, in terms of composition, of West German society and culture, as well as its demographic structure.

There was a general willingness in West Germany to join the European Coal and Steel Community (ECSC), first agreed in 1951, and its sequel, the European Economic Community (EEC). Some critics – wrongly – saw this as a continuance of the economic integration of Nazi-dominated Europe. While drawing on ideas of the Christian West, which linked Adenauer with Charles de Gaulle, West German willingness to accept the ECSC and the EEC was designed to affirm its legitimacy and help its exports.

France accepted constraints to aid in its modernisation, but also to control West Germany, a goal that was worth some loss of sovereignty and that matched the subordination of the 'German problem' by means of accepting German rearmament. West Germany was part of NATO and lacked the nuclear weaponry France was to gain. Fear of American disengagement from Europe was part of the equation, as were more positive Franco–German relations and assumptions. In the initial years of the EEC, in the 1960s, West Germany had an average annual growth rate of 5 per cent. While unwilling to back West German plans to gain nuclear capability, the American government keenly encouraged Franco–German reconciliation as an aspect of a necessary European self-reliance.

The Cold War Beat

The fiction of the Cold War focused on Germany and especially on Berlin, not least because 'the Wall' (no other epithet was ever really necessary) provided symbolism and site, as with the killing of the protagonist in John Le Carré's *The Spy Who Came in from the Cold* (1963), a novel about division and betrayal in East Germany, with the sinister ex-Nazi winning over the idealist. Len Deighton's *Funeral in Berlin* (1964), about smuggling out a defector, also involved betrayal. The film adaptation of the latter in 1966 added even more betrayals. Post-Cold War novels continue the genre as in the American author Joseph Kanon's focus on the CIA and a grim East Berlin, notably in *Leaving Berlin* (2014).

In return for the political weight West Germany gained from French support, the government was willing to make economic concessions to France, notably in agriculture, and to accept the French verdict on excluding Britain from the EEC. This prefigured the closeness between the two powers during the Mitterrand–Kohl and Chirac–Schröder partnerships in opposition to Britain, once it was a member, from 1973, of what became the European Union.

West Germany's politics changed in 1969 when the Social Democrats under Willy Brandt came to power. Brandt, leader of the SPD from 1964, had fled Germany in 1933, becoming a Norwegian citizen from 1940 to 1948 and going on to make his name as mayor of West Berlin. The SPD share of the vote rose from 39 per cent in 1965 to 43 per cent in 1969, while the CDU dropped from 48 to 46 per cent, and the FDP from 9.5 to 6 per cent.

Brandt left the grand coalition with the CDU that had been formed in 1966 under their leader, Kurt Georg Kiesinger, creating a coalition instead with the FDP and was elected chancellor. He was the first Social Democratic chancellor since 1930. In contrast with the politics of the early and late Weimar periods, this was a transition handled without a crisis of parliamentarianism and without disruption. Indeed, this outcome ensured that the late 1960s, despite the events of 1968, largely in the form of significant student demonstrations, were less disruptive for West Germany than for many other states.

Brandt promised 'continuity and renewal', with both stability and 'the rule of social law'. The new government wished to transform the inherited hostility to East Germany and eastern Europe into a more benign relationship that would bring stability and also enable West Germany to take a more central role in Europe. The previous, CDU-dominated governments, which were politically linked to the refugees from eastern Europe, had refused to recognise East Germany and to accept the latter's border with

Poland and therefore massive losses of territory. The anniversary of the 1953 popular rising in East Germany was celebrated in West Germany as the 'day of German unity'. This policy, however, had not delivered results, a failure driven home by the building of the Berlin Wall.

Ostpolitik also reflected a degree of assertion based on West German economic recovery and political stability, as well as a rejection of the nostrums of a previous generation. Brandt wanted a German solution for a German problem. In 1970, West Germany signed treaties with the Soviet Union and Poland recognising the existing borders. In place of the Hallstein Doctrine of 1955, under which West Germany claimed to represent all Germans, there was now to be one German nation and two German states, the East German principle. This was enshrined in the Basic Treaty with East Germany, signed in 1972 and ratified in 1973. Brandt's victory in the 1972 elections made this certain. The SPD vote rose to 46 per cent and the FDP to 8 per cent, while the CDU fell to 45 per cent. The SPD–FDP coalition was resumed.

This 'normalisation' of relations with East Germany meant, however, recognising the legality of a totalitarian state that treated its citizens harshly and now put more of an effort into the Stasi (secret police). Much of the left, both in West and East Germany, wanted a permanent division of Germany to thwart the legacy of past nationalism and create a new order. Another unpleasant aspect of the process were secret payments made by the West German government in return for people being allowed to leave East Germany, many for family reunification. Moreover, the killing of refugees by East German border guards continued.

More positively, little would have been achieved by upholding the Hallstein Doctrine and continuing to refuse dialogue with East Germany. The change in policy brought real relief in the form of visiting rights and family reunifications. The era of Helmut Schmidt, SPD chancellor from 1974 to 1982 and of his East German counterpart, Erich Honecker, general secretary of the Socialist Unity Party from 1971 to 1989 and chairman of the state council from 1976 to 1989, led to a sober, measured rapprochement and a resolution of relations between the two states. A communist activist, Honecker had been imprisoned from 1935 to 1945. The member of the politburo responsible for security, from 1958 he was the organiser of the building of the Berlin Wall. He gained power from Ulbricht with Soviet backing. The 1970s were seen as a period in which a German–German community of responsibility was set against the background of a reduction in international tension.

As part of this community spirit, concern within West Germany about the plight of East Germans, let alone reunification, markedly declined. No real West German support for the citizens' rights movements of East Germany existed. Instead, stabilisation was a more significant goal. Recognised for the first time as a state by much of the world in 1973, East Germany was admitted to the United Nations and other international bodies. Indeed, *Ostpolitik* stabilised the communist regimes of eastern Europe without bringing much liberalisation.

Nor, despite fears of some sort of recurrence of the fall of Weimar, was the political system in West Germany threatened by the very different challenge of the terrorism of the left-wing *Rote Armee Fraktion* (Red Army Faction, or the Baader–Meinhof gang). Murders of such leading personalities as Hanns-Martin Schleyer, the president of the Employers' Association and Siegfried Buback, the federal chief prosecutor, indicated the destructiveness of the terrorists but they were captured and their imprisoned key leaders died, allegedly by suicide, in 1976–7.

More generally, West Germany waived the challenge of the extremes, as – in far more difficult circumstances and with far more powerful extremes – Germany had been unable to do in the early 1930s. In part, this reflected greater prosperity and social welfare, as well as the generally good relationship between capital and labour as part of a broader economic and social

Cinema

Adapting to circumstances is the theme of Rainer Werner Fassbinder's film *The Marriage of Maria Braun* (1978), a powerful account of the recent weight of history through the means of sexuality, as superbly presented by Hanna Schygulla in the title role. The film is at once a witty take on the betrayal of ideals and a searching capture of empty expediency.

The Bavarian Fassbinder (1945–82) brilliantly pushed bounds, as in the all-female *The Bitter Tears of Petra von Kant* (1972), in part a portrayal of lesbian narcissism. He was a key figure in the New German cinema movement of 1962–82, which included creative figures such as Werner Herzog and Wim Wenders. His subsidised art-house works enjoyed international attention.

As a student in the 1970s, I can remember watching Herzog's *Aquirre, the Wrath of God* (1970), a first-rate depiction of a manic quest and Volker Schlöndorff and Margarethe von Trotta's *The Lost Honour of Katharina Blum* (1975), a strong critique of policing and the popular press and I later saw Herzog's *Fitzcarraldo* (1982), another manic quest on film.

High culture scarcely exhausted the range. Genre directors were also very successful. Active from 1958 to 1984, Alfred Vohrer turned out a large number of mystery films based on the novels of Edgar Wallace, such as *Der Hexer* (*The Warlock*, 1964). There were also the films of Karl May novels and – both set in New York – the Jerry Cotton and Kommissar X series. The new-wave directors attacked these films as '*Opas Kino*' ('Grandpa's cinema'), but most of the new-wave cinema had limited commercial success or artistic legacy. East German films included many Westerns.

partnership. The role of international bodies, notably NATO, and influences, were also significant. The West German engagement across the political spectrum with learning from the weaknesses of the pre-1933 years played a part in emphasising a quest for compromise and stability (this was seen very differently in East Germany). These latter elements were linked and grounded in the social market economy. This democratic transformation was helped by Americanisation but not dependent on it.

Precipitated by the recession as a result of the massive rise in the price of oil in 1973, the 1970s saw declining growth rates, unemployment, inflation and terrorism, with fears of a recurrence of Weimar. However, in large part due to strong economic fundamentals, there was no major crisis. Instead, the economy remained strong, as did consumerism. Car purchases remained buoyant, alongside foreign tourism.

Replacing Brandt in 1974, Schmidt put the emphasis on stability and continuity, rather than reform. The challenge of terrorism led to legal changes, notably in terms of preventing radicals from working for the civil service. Internal security became a major theme in government policy and public discussion. This broadened out in the late 1970s as concern about the nuclear balance of power increased, notably with the deployment of Soviet SS-20 missiles and NATO's response. Germany was in the front line of anxiety.

Policy towards East Germany did not change in 1982 when Helmut Kohl's Christian Democrats gained power, with the Free Democrats switching to support them. Economic growth resumed in western Europe as a whole, which greatly helped West German exports. Indeed, there was a boom over much of the 1980s. In 1983, this helped the CDU increase its share of the vote in the election to 48.8 per cent, that of the SPD falling to 38.2 per cent and the FDP to 6.9 per cent. The SPD was hit by the rise of the Greens, established in 1980, to 5.6 per cent. In the 1980 election, the respective percentages had been 44.5, 42.9, 10.6 and 1.5.

These results showed the significance of the establishment in 1953 of the 5 per cent hurdle, which required a party to gain at least that share of the vote to enter the Bundestag. In part this stipulation was a legacy of the early 1930s, when the Nazis in part won power by bringing the small parties into line and in part it was an attempt – which worked – to keep the far-right and far-left parties out of the Bundestag while West German democracy was established.

The Greens' entry into the Bundestag in 1983 marked a major change in political practice, one that was welcome to the Soviet Union. In the 1987 election, the percentages were 44.2, 37, 9.1 and 8.3. The CDU benefitted from divisions in the opposing parties, especially the FDP in 1983 and the SPD in 1987 and also from having strong bases in a number of *Länder* and being identified as defenders of regions and traditional values. Kohl, who very much saw himself in terms of the Catholic provincialism of a *Heimat* in the Palatinate, presented himself as Adenauer's political 'grandson'.

EAST GERMANY

The situation was very different in East Germany, which had a poorly functioning economy and was unable to improve its situation. Despite the presence of plentiful lignite ('brown coal'), which itself was used with no concern for humans or the natural environment, the East German economy suffered from a lack of natural resources. Like most of eastern Europe, it was dependent on Soviet assistance, not least in the form of cheap oil, but declining assistance in the 1970s, combined with *Ostpolitik*, helped ensure the build-up of very large external debts to the west.

Such debts and deficits did not permit the capital accumulation necessary for the industrial modernisation that was required in the 1980s if the communist economies were to compete – if only to service their heavy debts – by means of earning export income and by import substitution. Many West German firms, such as Madeleine Schickedanz's Quelle AG mail-order empire, became very successful in part by using cheap East German manufacturing labour. Thus, West Germany benefitted through the supply of inexpensive manufactured goods, while also supplying the financial fuel to keep East Germany going, a system that was reset from 1990. Arcandor AG, into which Quelle merged in 1999, went bankrupt in the different circumstances of 2009.

Economic rationality was not possible due to the political structure and ideology of East Germany, notably the ideological commitment to heavy industry, especially steel production, and to the political, social and gender narratives bound up in this commitment. Moreover, machinery was run into the ground before being replaced, whereas Western economies depreciated their machine tools and other capital machinery after several years, being aided to that end by tax deductions, and could thereby introduce innovations and productivity gains. Over time, the gap in factory technology widened and this was a major contribution to East Germany's economic stagnation.

It was not possible to provide productivity increases that could sustain the relatively high wages that workers received, especially those in industry. Indeed, the state was not able to produce the goods to deliver Honecker's promise of 'consumer socialism'. He was influenced by a fear of the recurrence of the 1953 demonstrations. Most basic consumer goods, such as bread, were sold at subsidised prices, as were travel tickets – especially for the tram – and the focus on living standards and social welfare from the early 1970s hit the overall economy. Cheap, but sometimes innovative, housing was widely built, including new settlements such as Dresden-Gorbitz. Whereas many nineteenth-century buildings only had toilets outside apartments on staircases, the newer flats had central heating systems and inside bathrooms. The possibilities for decorating flats, however, were very limited because a lack of acceptance of individuality existed.

One clear sign of economic failure was that workers had a high saving ratio because they could not find sufficient things to buy. A more profound sign was the inability of the state to support the aspirations for social welfare expressed in rhetoric and policy.

Visiting East Germany for archival research in 1980, I was repeatedly struck not so much by the limited nature of goods available for personal consumption, which I had expected, as by the poor state of public provision in terms of street lighting and pavements and the frequency of postal collections and rail services. Little money was spent on saving existing infrastructure. Moreover, poor air quality – due to the use of lignite – was readily noticeable, while rivers were badly polluted.

Pollution also affected health, underlining the social failure of the economy and challenging the legitimacy that the communist government claimed on the basis of social progress, including good universal health provision. Moreover, political failure was seen in widespread instances of corruption, not only carried out for personal profit but also simply to get economic processes to work. Unreported and illegal production and trades became necessary for the economy to function, not least through a large-scale barter system that encompassed industry, agriculture, the bureaucracy, services and individuals; it was very different to the cartels seen earlier in German history. Middlemen traded goods between factories to meet planned goals. To a degree tolerated by the Stasi – led to the development of a parallel world of personal gain regulated by bribery. *Bückware* (meaning goods that you had to bend or stoop over to get, in other words, going 'under the counter') was the term for things sold to special friends and customers.

The practices made a mockery of the rhetoric of communism, not least as this parallel world included public institutions. The ability of party officials to gain special privileges, notably in housing, the purchase of goods, travel and education, and preference for relatives, further helped to discredit the East German system and made it unpopular.

Favouritism interacted with ideology: children of workers and peasants were preferred in school, being marked as such in the class registers, while the offspring of intellectuals – such as teachers – and Christians came second. Although many appreciated the benefits of the social system, it registered only limited general identification and the government and media were widely regarded as corrupt cheaters. Election results were doubted. People also knew that citizens in West Germany had more consumer goods and were free to travel. The legal position of women, however, was better than in West Germany: they were integrated into the workforce and received support during pregnancy and the first year of motherhood, subsequently being guaranteed re-entry into the workforce with kindergarten places for children.

Between 1961 and 1988, nearly 400,000 East Germans formally applied to leave. There was no equivalent in West Germany, but the unpopularity of the state was curtailed by surveillance. It was not enough to act only against those judged to be dissidents – in itself a very arbitrary process. Instead, the entire East German population was under surveillance, with informers in every workplace and apartment block, and family members and lovers encouraged to spy and report on each other. In the 1980s, pursuing 'class enemies', the ubiquitous Ministry for State Security, the Stasi, read 90,000 letters and 2,810 telegrams daily and tapped telephones on a large scale, activities that required huge numbers of workers.

A tradition of scholarship on East Germany argues that most citizens accepted the legitimacy of the regime and that it drew on German ideologies in the shape of socialism and communism and was thereby not a Soviet puppet regime. That is an optimistic view of a malign system. The idea of a 'people's state' ensured that human rights were treated as a bourgeois illusion and conceit. Yet, communist ideology – not least the practice of Soviet pseudo-internationalism and 'socialist citizenship' – engaged relatively few people. Anti-fascism was an important part of East German ideology and created a way to link past, present and future. Schools were named after anti-fascist heroes and memorials were deployed accordingly. Legitimation, institutionalisation and narrative interacted, but the popular response was somewhat weary.

Hitchcock in East Germany

Have you ever been so irritated that you have felt like putting someone headfirst into a kitchen oven? Well, Cold War films may be for you, notably Albert Hitchcock's *Torn Curtain* (1966), in which an American nuclear physicist appears to defect, in order to discover information about Warsaw Pact anti-missile systems. His long fight to the death with a Stasi agent is gripping.

Inertia was also a potent force. A fatalist sense persisted among the public that there was no alternative to communist rule. This encouraged not only grumbling conformity but also widespread despair and high rates of drunkenness, in turn affecting health and life expectancy. Alongside this sense of lethargy and the state's use of coercion, its ability to seem to offer improvement or benefits was also useful in creating particular constituencies of support, notably in the bureaucracy and the military. Enthusiasm, however, was limited and the Communist Party, which did not succeed in inspiring many people, was pushed into the background by the deadening state bureaucracy.

In addition to rejecting the political, a sense of commitment was widely privatised at the individual and household level; the focus was on getting by and on the shifts and expedients of life under communism. This involved bartering, persuasive corruption and often shoddy compromises. Personal integrity and self-worth were repeatedly bargained away, both to obtain benefits and in reporting on others. Suicide rates among the young were particularly high.

GERMANY

 This situation did not lead to significant active opposition, but it left government and the Communist Party in a vacuum, with party members largely cut off from the working class they were supposed to represent. A disconnect from the peasantry and intelligentsia also existed, although much of the latter traded compliance for position. As a consequence, political opposition could hope to win a measure of public acceptance, possibly support, even if it was denied the means of expression employed in the West. In a perceptive 2019 interview with *Süddeutsche Zeitung*, Chancellor Angela Merkel noted the role of compromise in East Germany and the difference between individuals and the state, saying, 'Life was sometimes almost comfortable in a certain way, because there were some things one simply couldn't influence.'

 At the same time, alongside the common experience of life in East Germany, there were (as in West Germany) major contrasts in place, occupation, ideology, connections, luck, age and much else. The age factor was a matter of the generations of citizens but also the circumstances of particular periods. Thus, the early 1970s, with the 'normalisation' of relations with West Germany, was an easier period than the last years of Ulbricht's dominance.

East German Culture

The link of culture with politics was demonstrated in the Palace of the Republic, opened in East Berlin in 1976. It housed the East German parliament, leisure facilities and works of art commissioned under the rubric 'Are communists allowed to dream?' notably Hans Vent's painting *People on the Beach*. In the event, the use of asbestos in the palace led to its being condemned shortly before the fall of East Germany. Functionality was a key goal, as in the influential Office of Industrial Design, but this functionality could not be defined simply in terms of consumer appeal.

Meanwhile, West German television and radio were popular in East Germany, making East Germans well aware of better conditions elsewhere. East German television countered this by producing popular entertainment. There was also a resistant underground culture, for example the punks in East Berlin and Dresden.

East German Historical Highs

East Germany was presented by the regime as a product of a true German political culture in the shape of popular radicalism. Non-Marxist historians faced increasing pressure, which led many to flee to the west, and publications were expected to reach appropriate conclusions. Thus, Alexander Abusch's *Der Irrweg der Nation* (1947), which searched for Nazi origins not in capitalism but across German history back to Luther, was condemned in 1951. The purging of historians was matched by the destruction of sites that marked an undesirable public memory. The country houses of *Junkers* (Prussian aristocrats) were demolished, as were the city palaces in Berlin and Potsdam.

The content, organisation and presentation of history reflected communist perspectives through a German prism. There was a focus on past radicalism, for example on the Peasants' War of 1524–5, which was depicted as having been widespread. In January 1989, East Germany held a conference attended by Erich Honecker to celebrate the five-hundredth anniversary of Thomas Müntzer's birth, a radical cleric celebrated in Engels' 1850 book on the Peasants' War. Müntzer was presented as a social revolutionary who offered an alternative to Martin Luther (seen as part of a bourgeois revolution) and therefore a precursor to East Germany. He was said to prefigure the historical mission of the working class. Müntzer appeared on the five-mark bill and many things were named after him, including factories and streets. A biographic film about Müntzer was released in 1956.

The year 1989 also saw the opening in Bad Frankenhausen of the Panorama Museum, housing the *Bauernkriegs-panorama* (*Peasants' War Panorama*), a massive painting by Werner Tübke of the battle of Frankenhausen in 1525 at which the peasants were defeated. Müntzer was captured and killed soon after in the town. The museum is still open. Another curiosity of Frankenhausen is that it has a church tower which is more slanted than that of Pisa.

The Mainz Republic of March–July 1793, an untypical episode of German radicalism based on the model of revolutionary France, also attracted attention. East German scholars argued that the Social Democrats of 1918–19 were 'class traitors' who allied with the military against the workers. There was an annual commemoration of the murder in 1919 of the revolutionaries Rosa Luxemburg and Karl Liebknecht although, in 1988, there were protests then by those seeking to leave the country.

The 20 July 1944 bomb plotters were criticised as reactionaries and the Second World War itself was presented by the communists as an imposition by the Nazi regime on German worker-soldiers. There was an effort thereby to create an anti-fascist unity, or at least friendship, with the Soviet Union. It was hoped that this would bring legitimacy to the East German system which, in practice, rested on Soviet conquest and support.

Historians played a role in the system. In 1980 Gerhard Schilfert, of the Humboldt University, complained to me about the difficulty of getting English language books and about the funding focus on the sciences. Yet he also displayed his loyalty to the state and commented on how he was very proud of his secretary having secured him a Cuban orange in the market. As an ironic comment on communist priorities, Carlrichard Brühl – a West German medievalist – had told me that summer that he would say to his colleagues that, if the East Germans took over, they, as socialists (and thereby rivals) would be shot, while he – as a conservative – would be put in charge of the archives.

East German accounts tended to neglect the Holocaust or to mention it either as a product of capitalism – specifically the need for labour and capital – or of an attempt to divert attention from the failings of capitalism and the Nazi system. Compensation was not paid to Jews because East Germany did not see itself as being in the lineage of previous German states, whereas West Germany saw itself explicitly as the legal successor of the German Reich and accordingly paid compensation to Israel. In East Germany, the victims of Nazi killing were presented as opponents of fascism and not as Jews.

The East German View of Saxony

Under East Germany, the argument that the Polish connection of 1697–1763 was unhelpful to Saxony was strongly made. This thesis served to demonstrate an opposition of ruler and population that accorded with communist views and offered an ahistorical reading of Saxon statehood

> separable from sovereignty. It was also part of the denial of
> the validity of a distinctive Saxon political identity separate
> to that of the future East Germany. In contrast, past
> episodes of worker radicalism in Saxony attracted state
> historical attention. Set in the era of the Saxo–Polish Union,
> a certain Saxon identity was presented late in East Germany
> with the popular television series *Sachsens Glanz und
> Preussens Gloria*.

By the autumn of 1989, East Germany was on the edge of bank-
ruptcy. Apparently the most successful communist regime, its
economy had been wrecked by ideologically driven mismanagement. It had only been able to continue as long as it did thanks to
large loans from the west, notably West Germany. As a sign of good
relations, Erich Honecker in 1987 paid an official visit to West
Germany, the first by an East German head of state. Many of the
past predictions of East German continuity should underline for
today the roles of contingency and the unforeseen in German
history.

THE FALL OF EAST GERMANY

With the shortcomings, if not failure, of its centrally planned
economy, the East German government could no longer finance
its social programmes. Mikhail Gorbachev's *glasnost* and *pere-
stroika*, to which Honecker reacted critically, intensified the
regime's loss of legitimacy. In 1989, the East German government failed to rise to the challenge. Promises of reform proved to
be too little, too late, as did the change in government.

By September 1989, East German society was dissolving, as its
citizens – especially the younger generation – left in large numbers.
Hungary's opening of its Austrian border had permitted

substantial numbers of citizens to leave for West Germany via Hungary and Austria from August. They abandoned not only economic failure but also the lack of modern civilisation in the shape of free expression, tolerance, opportunity and cultural vitality. Hungary refused to heed pressure from East Germany to stem the tide of departures and Gorbachev, whose renunciation of interference in other communist states was crucial, was unwilling to help. In the first nine months of the year, 110,000 East Germans resettled in West Germany. Others took part in mass demonstrations, notably in the major city of Leipzig. From 4 September, steadily larger numbers bravely and peacefully demonstrated in the Autumn Revolution, one in which the Protestant church played a major role. The call for German unity was strong.

A sense of failure and emptiness demoralised supporters of the regime, while West German consumerist democracy – epitomising what had been pejoratively termed the fetishism of 'things' – proved far more attractive to the bulk of the population. The repressive state, moreover, no longer terrified. Indeed, it had suffered a massive failure of intelligence, with a serious inability to understand developments, let alone to anticipate them. All those intercepted letters and spying availed the Stasi naught. In addition, the situation was different to that faced by East Germany in the disturbances of 1953 and 1961: unwilling to compromise its domestic and international reputation, the regime no longer wished to rely on force. The old ruthlessness was no longer there: the Leninist instinct for survival had been lost. The East German army, anyway, was unwilling to act. Moreover, the nature of the demonstrations – both peaceful and lacking central leadership – lessened the opportunity for repression (although a similar domestic scenario had not prevented the Chinese authorities cracking down earlier in the year).

Even though Honecker was deposed by his colleagues on 16 October 1989, they remained under pressure from popular action and could not gain control of the situation, nor even – more significantly – create an impression of control. The entire government and politburo resigned on 7–8 November and, on 9 November, the Berlin Wall was opened. An occasion and symbol of freedom, the fall of the Wall became a totemic event, like that of the storming of the Bastille in Paris in 1789 at the French revolution's outset. However, whereas as a result of that earlier act only a few insignificant prisoners were freed from prison, large numbers of East Berliners poured over the now open border. The significance of this popular action was picked out in 2014 when President Park Geun-hye of South Korea spoke in Dresden setting out proposals to ease reunification with North Korea.

Developments in East Germany invite counterfactuals including, 'What if the Hungarians had not opened their Austrian border, permitting a mass exodus of East Germans that destabilised the state?', as well as the question of whether or not the East German system could have been stabilised by removing Honecker earlier and giving reform communism a greater chance. Alternatively, had Gorbachev been replaced, could Chinese-style repression have worked in East Germany? Confidence that such action could not have been attempted is misplaced. Hans Modrow, the Communist Party's first secretary in Dresden from 1973, and a critic of Honecker, suppressed a demonstration in Dresden on 4–5 October, arresting 1,300 people.

UNIFICATION

After the fall of the Wall, pressure for reform in East Germany was increasingly supplemented by further demands for German unity, although a significant portion of the citizens' movement preferred a liberal East Germany to unification. Meanwhile, with Gorbachev unwilling to pursue the repression that Khrushchev employed against Hungary in 1956, governmental authority in East Germany collapsed.

Honecker's successors, Egon Krenz – Honecker's deputy

from 1984 and general secretary of the party and chairman of the state council from October to December 1989 – and Gregor Gysi – who became party chairman in December and sought to democratise the Communist Party – failed to provide the reform from above that they sought to ensure stability. Modrow, chairman of the Council of Ministers from November 1989 to April 1990, attempted to delay reform and unification. However, the pace of events was against him. The Stasi headquarters in Berlin was occupied by demonstrators in January 1990. Communist, one-party rule was followed by multi-party politics while constitutional change gathered pace. On 1 February, Modrow unveiled a plan for a German–German confederation as part of a 'united fatherland'. Gorbachev responded to Modrow that a unified Germany was acceptable only if it was demilitarised and neutral, but the Americans were unwilling to accept the Soviet proposal for the mutual withdrawal of troops from Germany.

Free elections, held in East Germany on 18 March, demonstrated the lack of support for communism. Helped greatly by the initially cautious Kohl's campaigning and also by the fiscal inducements offered by unification, the East German CDU won 40.8 per cent of the vote as part of an Alliance for Germany that won 48.0 per cent. The newly relaunched SPD won 21.9 per cent, while the SED – renamed the Party of Democratic Socialism – won only 16.4 per cent. These figures in part reflected the extent to which not all who wanted to bring the Wall down sought to dismantle East Germany.

Lothar de Maizière, the leader of the East German CDU, was elected prime minister on 12 April by 265–108 votes with nine abstentions. He backed rapid unification. Once democratised, communism had, therefore, become redundant as a governing medium and the Communist Party itself was now irrelevant as a major political party. The same process affected the very state of East Germany. Currency union with West Germany was a priority for the new government, which was well aware of the precarious economic situation. It took effect on 1 July but undermined the viability of East German companies.

East Germany stopped being a separate state on 3 October and all-German elections followed on 2 December 1990. This was a unification very different from that achieved by Bismarck; 3 October, thereafter, was celebrated as a new national day of commemoration.

The economic crisis of East Germany, with the pressures of competition and the collapse of its markets in the communist bloc, helped drive unification in 1990, not least by leading more East Germans to migrate westwards. This also depended on international acceptance – notably by Gorbachev – of the US demand that a unified Germany be part of NATO rather than becoming the neutralised state long sought by the Soviet Union. Margaret Thatcher, the British prime minister, was unhappy about unification while President François Mitterrand of France, although concerned about the implications of unification for French national interests, proved more accommodating. His view was formed not least because of a promise from Kohl that French companies would be allowed to acquire East German state-owned companies in the rapid privatisation that was pushed through. Kohl traded subsequently on his role in securing unification, and this helped him win re-election as chancellor of the now united Germany in 1994.

Although some opposition to unification existed in West Germany, notably from the Greens, Kohl was determined to carry through with the process, following the West German model. This plan entailed the end of any prospect not only for an independent East Germany (in the form, say, of a distinctive German state like Austria), but also of a different former East Germany within a united Germany. The citizens' movements that had spawned the mass demonstrations of late 1989, such as New Forum, were thus not to serve as the genesis for a new vision of German society. This reflected more than simply the external pressure and financial prospects deployed by the anti-communist

Kohl. The citizen movements, which did not compare to Solidarity in Poland, lacked unity, and the pressures of practicality – not least of responding to economic failure – undermined any mass enthusiasm for taking a different path to that of West Germany.

Unification arose from more than just the political and financial strength of West Germany, but the latter was a key element in ensuring that no other options appeared to be viable. This unification was then to help define legitimacy as well as power in post-communist Europe. Krenz was sentenced to six years' imprisonment in 1997 for the manslaughter of East Germans who had tried to flee East Germany. An equally unrepentant Modrow was convicted of electoral fraud in the Dresden municipal elections in 1989.

Nordsee

If, like me, you like your fast food in the shape of inexpensive seafood, rather than burgers, then one of the pleasures of travelling in Germany is Nordsee, a food empire founded in Bremen in 1896 and expanded in 1964 with Nordsee Quick takeaways. Dependable food at reasonable prices is on offer.

DEBATING RECENT HISTORY

History was politics or, at least, political. Academic controversies were extensively reported in the press. A key work was Fritz Fischer's *Griff nach der Weltmacht: die Kriegszielpolitik des kaiserlichen Deutschlands, 1914–1918* (1961), a book translated into English as *Germany's Aims in the First World War*. Fischer focused on the primacy of domestic policy, particularly the response by the conservative elite to rising socialism. Condemning conservatism and capitalism, Fischer sought to undermine the attempt to present Wilhelmine Germany as a model for post-1945 West Germany and the Nazis as an aberration. Fischer, instead, argued that there was an essential continuity from Wilhelmine Germany through to the Hitlerian regime, not least in seeking to control territory. Historical examples have to be used with care. Naming battleships *Bismarck* and *Tirpitz*, the latter after Alfred von Tirpitz, the ambitious head of the navy from 1897 until 1916, was indicative of more than simply claiming a legacy, although Bismarck proved a difficult example for Hitler, not least because he did not favour union with Austria or war with Russia.

The Fischer controversy was linked to the challenge to the dominant conservative (and gerontocratic) character of post-war West German historical scholarship, as well as to the extent to which a misleading and self-interested account of German scholarly impartiality during the Nazi years was propagated. The reality was far bleaker. Numerous academics had profited personally and knowingly from the removal of Jewish colleagues, while many were involved in work that contributed directly to the regime's propaganda and planning. These academics went on to profit in the post-war order. So it was with Hermann Aubin (1885–1969), who had been a key figure in work on the 'German East' and was to become chairman of the Association of German Historians and president of the Historical Commission of the Bavarian Academy of Sciences. He referred in 1957 to Germany as the 'sentinel of the west' against the 'Slavic east'.

Politics played a major and continuing role; senior academic appointments were very much under the control of the government and academic debates were seen as playing a role in the validation of competing voices in West Germany. Aubin was given the title of adviser by Franz-Josef Strauss, the conservative head of the CSU. In contrast, in what was called the '*Kniefall*', Brandt fell to his knees in 1970 before the monument at the Warsaw ghetto. His act shocked many Germans far more than Beate Klarsfeld slapping Chancellor Kurt Kiesinger in 1968, shouting 'Nazi.'

Subsequently, the '*Historikerstreit*' (controversy among German historians) of 1986–7 – which linked discussion of the

Holocaust to the question of how best to present national history
– was played out in a very public fashion, with many articles
appearing in prominent newspapers. In part, this controversy
was a product of the attempt by historians close to Chancellor
Helmut Kohl, the leader of the CDU, which gained power in 1982,
to 'normalise' German history. This was taken to mean to make
the history more acceptable; both to ground national identity and
to reject the criticisms made by the 1968 generation. Kohl saw
this process as a necessary basis for patriotism, national pride and
spiritual renewal, a theme taken up more generally on the
German right. The controversy was also closely related to the
attempt to create a favourable climate of opinion as a background
to the federal elections of 1987, elections won by Kohl.

In the controversy, the degree to which the Holocaust arose
from specific German characteristics was debated, as was the
extent to which the German state had a historical mission to resist
advances from the east – the Soviet Union. However, justifying
the German generals in the final stage of the war as if they were
in some way defending civilisation was self-serving and, indeed,
ignored the extent to which they mounted a fierce resistance to
Anglo–American forces as well as the Soviets. Fighting on, of
course, also provided more time for the Holocaust.

As a related instance of the concern with historical appear-
ances, German officials in the 1980s perceived the establishment
of the Holocaust Memorial Museum in Washington, USA, as
being 'anti-German' and, unsuccessfully, attempted to alter what it
would contain. They suggested the inclusion of references to the
anti-Nazi resistance and to post-war German history. However,
from the 1980s, the West German government also became more
willing to acknowledge wartime crimes. Moreover, on 8 May 1985,
President Richard von Weizsäcker felt able to declare the date of
surrender as being a day of liberation for Germany from Nazi rule.

By the 2000s, the issue of surviving Nazis ebbed as they died
out, but they had been much discussed. The career of Hans

Filbinger (1913–2007) was symptomatic: minister-president of Baden-Württemberg from 1966 to 1978 and a critic of the left, Filbinger was correctly named in newspaper articles as a wartime military judge who sentenced deserters to death. Filbinger responded with a denial, suing for libel, claiming, 'What was lawful then cannot be unlawful now.' In the face of public criticism he was, nevertheless, forced to resign, and his rehabilitation in the 2000s was controversial. At his funeral, an eulogy was read by Günther Oettinger, minister-president in 2005–2010, leading to successful pressure for an apology from him. This was not simply a dispute about the past, but also part of the struggle over the character of the CDU. Angela Merkel, who was among those demanding an apology, was a centrist whose views on the CDU were very different to those of Filbinger and Oëttinger.

It wasn't only figures on the right who were involved in such controversies, but they tended to be more prominent. As a separate issue, but one drawn into the debate, there was also the extent to which former Stasi operatives were integrated into society after the fall of East Germany.

At present, within most, but by no means all, parts of German society, government and academe, war guilt is accepted. There is a willingness to see Germans as victims of the bombing war but – apart from on the far right – this is not used to downplay German guilt for the Holocaust.

On the contrary, many Germans reject everything to do with the Nazis. Thus, there was significant opposition to the rebuilding from the late 2010s of the Garrison church in Potsdam, due to its role in Hitler's staging of politics in 1933. Damaged in British bombing, it was demolished by the East German government in 1968. The difficulties of presenting and contextualising German history continue to engage many Germans.

11

Unification and
Pressures, 1990–

Germany devoted much of the 1990s to the consequences of unification. Some issues were not hard to resolve, as in 1990, when West Germany's flag and anthem became those of the new state. Key topics included the choice of the capital (Berlin), the reconstitution of the *Länder*, land ownership, the restitution of property in former East Germany, abortion and the consequences of currency union – which included cutting the value of East German savings, a cause of anger in the former state. Huge West German transfers of funds to the former East Germany greatly affected German public finances, although East German society also contributed greatly to unification.

Unification led to administrative problems and reorganisation, but also provided opportunities for refinancing and reform. Thus, in 1994, the railway systems united to form the German Railway Corporation (DB). This provided the context for the extension of high-speed lines, which had begun in 1991 with the Hamburg–Mannheim and Stuttgart–Munich services. Among others, Bremen to Munich via Nuremberg followed in 1992 and Hanover-Berlin in 1998, the latter a key link across former East Germany. The corporation moved its headquarters from Frankfurt to Berlin in 1996, part of the process by which the capital became significant in a way that Bonn had never been. By the mid-2010s, some of the rail services could reach speeds of 300 k.m.h. (190 m.p.h.). Frankfurt, however, remained the location of the European Central Bank.

A Unified Football Team

In 1990 West Germany won the World Cup and, later, the members of the East German association joined with their West German colleagues. In Euro 1992 (when there was also a united Olympic team), Germany got to the final, losing to Denmark. They did far worse, however, in the 1994 World Cup, when they were beaten by lower-ranked Bulgaria in the quarter-finals. Success continued to be variable, but Germany was generally a key player.

In Euro 1996, Germany won the final against the Czech Republic, only to be knocked out by Croatia in the quarter-finals of the 1998 World Cup. A poor performance in Euro 2000 led to demands for change in German football and although, unexpectedly, they reached the World Cup final in 2002, to be beaten by Brazil, Germany were knocked out in the first round of Euro 2004.

Germany was the host nation for the 2006 World Cup and did well, only narrowly losing a semi-final match to Italy. Young talent helped Germany reach the final in Euro 2008, losing to Spain, and the semi-final of the 2010 World Cup, again losing to Spain. In 2014, Germany won the World Cup, beating Argentina in the final, only to be knocked out in the Euro 2016 semi-finals by France and to be beaten in the group stage of the 2018 World Cup. They lost against England in the Euro 2020 semi-finals, the games themselves delayed to 2021 due to the coronavirus pandemic.

Narrowly re-elected in 1994, Kohl ran out of steam after unification, facing rising unemployment (9.4 per cent in 1998), and lost the chancellorship to the SPD candidate, Gerhard Schröder, in 1998. The SPD saw its percentage rise from 36.4 to 40.9 and the CDU (including CSU) share fell from 41.4 to 35.1 while the

Greens won 6.7 per cent, the FDP 6.2 per cent and the Party of Democratic Socialism (PDS, the successor to the East German Socialist Unity Party) 5.1 per cent. The constituency results saw the CDU dominant in the South, Saxony and the Catholic north-west, and the SPD take most of the rest of the country. An SPD–Greens coalition was founded, the first solely centre-left government of the united Germany. Kohl resigned as CDU leader.

There was no question of Schröder rejecting the policy of the previous government and going for one-nation reflation, as Mitterrand had sought to do in France in 1981. Schröder stood as a pragmatist, keen on labour and welfare reforms which, however, helped lose him left-wing support. By 2002, he was an unpopular chancellor, yet surprisingly won re-election, if very narrowly. Each party stood on 38.5 per cent with the Greens on 8.6 per cent, the FDP on 7.4 per cent, and the Communists on 4 per cent.

In large part, this re-election was due to two unexpected events. Schröder's opposition to Anglo–American policy over Iraq won him support, particularly in the former East Germany, as did a prompt response with substantial financial assistance to serious floods in the region. Moreover, Schröder's opponent, Edmund Stoiber, was a Bavarian Catholic; regional and religious issues and identities continued to be of major consequence. In 1980, when the CDU had also backed a CSU candidate for chancellor, Franz Josef Strauss, against an SPD incumbent, Strauss had been defeated. The CDU was also hit in 2002 by a funding scandal over illegal practices that broke in 1999–2000 and led to the disgracing of Kohl.

In 2002, the Social Democrat and Greens coalition was re-elected in Germany as the less radical choice, but this government then found political division and unpopularity greeting the attempts made to reform the economy, not least in order to provide the growth necessary to help the 4.7 million unemployed. The government's 'Agenda 2010' economic reform programme was rejected by left-wing critics within the government, as well as

by the large number of often poorly skilled, elderly, manual workers who felt challenged. Moreover, the Social Democrats lost
control of North-Rhine Westphalia, its key electoral stronghold
and Germany's most populous province.

In July 2005, Schröder deliberately triggered a parliamentary
vote of no confidence in order to prepare the way for a general
election a year early. His speech in the Bundestag spoke more
generally to the political problems: 'The steady confidence that I
need to carry out my reforms is no longer present even within my
own coalition government. Dissent and criticism of my policies
are on the increase. This is a high price to pay for reform.'

Both electorate and politicians found it difficult to face up to
the need to keep the economy competitive and to look at the costs
of social welfare. Cutting taxes, notably on business, Schröder
attempted to change course, but lost approval, step by step. Under
Kohl, the electorate had become used to a major reform bottle-
neck and substantial structural deficits.

The Social Democrats were rejected by the electorate after this
government crisis. The CDU became the foremost party in the
elections held on 18 September 2005, although with a smaller
lead than they had hoped: the CDU (including the CSU, as usual)
won 35.2 per cent of the vote compared to 34.2 per cent for the
SPD. This result led to a grand coalition with the Social Democrats
and CDU leader Angela Merkel was elected chancellor on 22
November 2005.

In part, the grand coalition was a response to the growing
strength of the far left, which caused an earthquake in the German
political system. Winning seats in the national election because of
the unpopularity of Schröder's 'Agenda 2010', the Party of
Democratic Socialism (PDS) – the heir to the Socialist Unity Party
of East Germany (the Communist Party) – had made it impossi-
ble to establish a more natural coalition, of either the SPD and the
Greens or the CDU/CSU and FDP Liberals. In 2007, Die Linke
(the 'Left Party') was formed by an alliance of the PDS with the

Electoral Alternative for Labour and Social Justice, the West German left-wing party. The strength of the party in eastern Germany became an indication of the disaffection of former East Germans with developments since unification. Die Linke also established itself in four western German state parliaments. Germany, therefore, acquired a five-party political system, with all the headaches this brings.

Better public finances stemming from economic growth enabled the grand coalition to avoid the consequences of its limited ability to introduce structural economic reforms. Looked at less benignly, the opportunity for reform in Europe's most powerful economy presented by the creation of this coalition was thrown away. The government seemed only able to find new solutions on a limited basis. The population/labour force was an instance of this. Supporters saw immigration as helping address the challenges created by an ageing population and a potentially declining labour force. This situation led the government in 2007 to raise the retirement age to sixty-seven. Yet, this was done only slowly, reflecting the caution arising from the consensual tone of government and society and the consequential constraints placed upon reform. When a more radical solution – welcoming large numbers of immigrants – was proposed in 2015, however, it proved highly contentious.

More generally, Germany's federal system created far too many important state elections, voting in which was inevitably in part influenced by current national politics, although there was no equivalent to the strains created by devolved assemblies in the UK and no equivalent to Catalan or Scottish separatism. German politicians on the national level were in danger of spending too much time campaigning and watching the opinion polls, and not enough on long-term policy-planning.

This reflected a failure of leadership seen in other aspects of German policy, notably that of their unwillingness to maintain defence preparedness, let alone use force in NATO and EU missions.

Thus, there was a curious contradictory response from other European states, particularly Italy, Greece and Poland; a fear at once of German hegemony – notably within the EU – but also a concern that the Germans did not make appropriate use of their power and position. This took a number of forms: the Germans proved reluctant to limit Russian influence in Ukraine just as, in the early 1990s, there was a lack of commitment to NATO expansion into eastern Europe. This concern was repeatedly expressed by American politicians, while their German counterparts also showed considerable independence in ignoring American priorities.

Very differently, Germany put a lot of effort into developing the EU, not least encouraging the application of federalism as practised in Germany, as well as drawing on its experience of integrating East Germany. A different form of integration has been shown in the increased knowledge of the English language, very much the second language, and the importing of English words and phrases.

Discontent in the former East Germany became more pronounced from the 2000s, along with a notable rise not only in far-left politics, but also in far-right political identity and activism, particularly – but not only – in Saxony-Anhalt. On one level, this was ironic, as East Germans had benefitted considerably from unification, but that did not assuage a sense of discontent.

Environmentalism

The longstanding German engagement with the natural landscape, one seen in the Romantic movement, led some after the Second World War in West Germany to a Green ethos. From the 1970s and, in part, drawing on the role of the '1968 generation', *Bürgerinitiativen* ('citizens' initiatives') focused on the idea of the city as a liveable community and this led to numerous pedestrian zones and bike lanes. From 1983, Greens were represented in the Bundestag. Greens also became more significant in state governments, while other political parties had to embrace some of their ideas. The separation and recycling of waste became important with the 'green dot' programme that began in 1990. The abandonment of nuclear power in the 2010s very much reflected the Greens' consciousness. It had provided 22 per cent of electricity in 2010 but by 2017 that had dropped to 12 per cent, and the entire industry is due for closure in 2022.

By contrast, East Germany had very high per capita carbon dioxide emissions and very bad river pollution. In Wolfen, north of Leipzig, a centre of the chemical industry near which there were open-cast lignite mines, the pH level was 0.9, an acidity between battery acid and vinegar. After unification, many factories closed and were demolished, and people moved away.

A continuing contrast, still apparent when I visited in 2019, was that in parts of East Germany there still appeared to be relatively few flowers in gardens, possibly a continuing consequence of the economics and values of the communist years.

Across Germany, there were not only important regional variations, albeit lessened by the mass movement of people – notably in 1944–8 – but also significant social variations at all levels. Thus, the *Gymnasien* (grammar schools), the better secondary schools, were disproportionately used by the middle class. Gender conventions changed, not least as the Catholic church became less powerful. From 1972 to 1976, Anemarie Renger was speaker of the Bundestag and, from 2005 to 2021, Angela Merkel was chancellor, very much dominating both national politics and her party.

Some East German women benefitted from the changes offered by unification, but others suffered from the weaknesses in family, work and neighbourhood support systems. These issues owed much to large-scale migration to West Germany and to a different attitude on the part of post-communist employers. Moreover, industrial transformation hit the economic prospects of many women who did not migrate, with numerous factories closing in a widespread deindustrialisation, although the service sector provided other opportunities.

Homosexuality was legalised in East Germany, where it had been presented as bourgeois decadence, in 1968 and in West Germany in 1969. The age of consent was equalised with that for heterosexuals, in East Germany in 1988 and in unified Germany in 1994. As a reflection of its Catholic links and conservatism, the CDU had been opposed to gay rights. Homosexuality was also increasingly a subject in the arts, as in Fassbinder's film *The Bitter Tears of Petra von Kant* (1972).

The established churches continued to support a national tax for church support. Under Merkel – the daughter of a Protestant cleric brought up in East Germany – the CDU increasingly dissociated itself from its Catholic tradition, although church membership in general, but especially for Catholics, is growing in some parts of eastern Germany, notably Saxony and Thuringia. Many CDU members are Catholics.

Benedict XVI, pope from 2005 to 2013, the Bavarian Joseph Ratzinger, the first German Pope since Leo IX (1049–54), was more conservative. A priest teaching theology at the University of Tübingen, he had opposed the student activism of 1968 which he saw as a challenge to the Church. In 1981, he was appointed by John Paul II to head the Congregation for the Defence of the Faith, the body charged with maintaining Catholic orthodoxy. In this role, he was regarded as John Paul II's 'enforcer' but, although his election to the papal office was widely noted in Germany with a form of national pride (newspapers claimed, 'We are pope'), he had little traction in Germany. Nevertheless, he and Merkel were the most prominent Germans of the period, each very different paternalists. Other prominent Germans included sports figures, notably Boris Becker, and those in popular culture, especially Heidi Klum and Claudia Schiffer.

Variety in German culture and aspirations was readily apparent, as in the still powerful capacity of ruralism for offering both identity and heritage. More than four hundred books with '*Heimat*' ('Homeland') in their title were published between 1995 and 2001 and polls indicate that the word has very positive connotations for Germans. The '*Heimat*' film genre, which had been popular in the 1950s, notably in Bavaria − offering a sense of security and restoration − revived in the 1980s, in some cases providing a link to '*Problemfilm*', cinema concerned with social issues.

Unification in 1990 strengthened the emphasis on *Heimat*, although several films incorporated areas that Germany had lost because of the Second World War. It was unclear how far this should be seen as a depoliticised sense of loss and how far as a more significant declaration of irredentism; pressure for the return of lost territories. Leaving aside this loss, Edgar Reitz produced three effective television series that were actually called *Heimat* about the sense of belonging. They were located in a discussion of German history from 1918 until 2005, made from the perspective of a village community in the hills of the Hunsrück, a conservative and somewhat rural district that had been part of West Germany.

Yet, there was also a marked interest in the city as a longstanding cultural entity, notably in the rebuilding of bombed urban centres − such as Nüremberg − on the basis of the old city. This stress on cultural identity had not been a theme for most bustling West German centres in the 1950s and 1960s; it became more important from the mid-1970s. The process was encouraged in 1975, the European Year of Historic Preservation.

In the 1990s, the urban theme was conspicuously extended to include former East Germany, with the large-scale reconstruction of the former centre of Dresden. This was successful at one level, although it proved difficult to recapture the atmosphere of corners as well as the splendour of vistas. Much of East Germany's architectural heritage was removed, notably in Berlin. The city as place also emerged in television crime series, such as the popular *Tatort* (*Scene of the Crime*) programmes produced from 1970, where episodes take viewers to cities such as Leipzig, Munich and Münster.

Contrasts: Magdeburg

Any visitor today is struck anew by the contrasts. A city on which history rests heavy, in the shape of its brutal sacking by the Catholic League in 1631 and its bombing in 1945, Magdeburg has the oldest German Gothic cathedral, a truly massive structure that contains the grave of Otto I, as well as providing arresting views from above the nave.

Within a pleasant and easy walk, there is also Die Grüne Zitadelle ('The Green Citadel', 2005), a housing development designed by Friedensreich Hundertwasser. It is a work at once on a human scale, variable in its format, arresting in its shapes and endlessly fascinating, as well as a very different but still pleasant place for a coffee.

My guide to the city in 2019 had recognisably been trained under the East Germans, being keen to boast of social amenities, such as the number of rubbish collection lorries in the city.

National pride has revived considerably in Germany in recent years, with the football World Cup competition of 2006 of particular importance and marked by scenes of large numbers of fans clad in national colours and singing the national anthem in public places. The earlier post-war period lacked that national rhetoric or even thought, in public discourse. This was a consequence in part of the heritage of American re-education after the Nazi era and it has been replaced by a growing re-evaluation of national pride, although not to the level of French or British nationalism.

The starting point was German unification and, later, the Schröder government of 1998–2005 with its public commitment to a 'German' foreign policy with renewed self-confidence. This re-emerging sense of nation, however, clashed with post-war conceptions of national identity and problems emerged as a result. Thus, over the NATO mission in Afghanistan, Germans confronted the question of whether foreign policy entailed the commitment to fund and dispatch a robust army into conflict that would likely result in casualties.

In East Germany, a degree of public nostalgia for the communist past (*Ostalgie*), for example, for its material culture, was accentuated by the extent to which unification was seen by many in terms of a conquest made by West Germany. Nevertheless, this nostalgia was limited.

A degree of far-right support exists in former East Germany, as in the Pegida (Patriotic Europeans Against the Islamisation of the Occident), founded in Dresden in 2014. Although concern about immigration is the key driver, the extremism and the type of negative nationalism it spawns, draw on wider anger and prejudice. To a degree, this is a comment on the failure of East German political culture and indoctrination, although many neo-Nazis grew up after East Germany ceased to be a separate state. High rates of unemployment are part of the equation, which readily manifests itself in anger and opposition, as in the response to coronavirus pandemic regulations in 2020–1. Concern about the ideological, political and public order consequences encouraged a growing governmental response, as in 2009 when the Interior Ministry banned the group Homeland-Faithful German Youth on the grounds that it organised apparently harmless activities in order to promote racist and Nazi views among the young.

Unification brought access to more consumer goods. Thus, there was a major increase in the vehicle stock in East Germany and the number in Germany as a whole rose to 48 million by 2001. Yet, exposed to competition, the industrial base in East Germany shrank and many of the young moved to take advantage of the opportunities offered by the former West Germany. This became an aspect of what to some seemed to be a malaise of despair, anger and lower birth rates, with consequences for an ageing population, an issue that had attracted attention since the 1930s. There was a massive drop in the birth rate in East Germany from 200,000 in 1989 to 115,000 in 1991 and this continued into the 1990s. In order to provide sufficient labour, East Germany by the late 1980s had close to 60,000 Vietnamese contract workers.

In Germany as a whole, birth rates per thousand people fell from 9.9 in 1997 to 8.2 in 2006, a year in which the population fell by 130,000. In response, in 2007, the CDU government increased the payments for new parents if they stayed at home, and did not make such payments income dependent. Childcare facilities were improved. Birth rates rose and hit 9.4 in 2019, when there was a record 83.2 million in the population, compared to 80.2 million in 2011. The fertility rate among those of Turkish descent was higher soon after migration, while more educated immigrants had a birth rate similar to those of women born in Germany.

On average, German women have their first child soon after turning thirty (the average age being highest in Hamburg), but many have no children, notably in cities. By 2019, only 16 per cent of German families had three children or more. These families were principally Muslim or Catholic and lived in rural and suburban areas. Of the states, Berlin had the lowest birth rate and Bremen and Lower Saxony the highest. In 2019, it was estimated by the UN that by 2050 Germany would have fifty-eight people over the age of sixty-five for every hundred people aged twenty to sixty-four. The workforce – 51.8 million people in 2018 – is predicted to be 45.8 million to 47.4 million strong by 2035 and the total population likely to rise at least until the year 2024 and to decline from 2040 at the latest.

The falling population made the issue of immigration even more significant. By 2019, it would have been declining by about 160,000 annually without new arrivals. Germany was a particularly important destination for migrants, especially because the 1949 constitution of West Germany allowed citizenship to all ethnic Germans who relocated. This migration had ceased due to the establishment of the iron curtain, as indeed did other migrant flows within Europe. Numbers shot up anew in 1989–90: nearly 800,000 ethnic Germans from eastern Europe migrated to West Germany. On top of that, economic opportunity led 538,000 East Germans to move into West Germany in 1989–90. Both flows continued thereafter, especially the latter, which was encouraged by the markedly contrasting economic fortunes of the two areas. Neither the inflationary and unrealistic valuation of the East German mark as being equal to its West German counterpart nor massive government aid could prevent an outflow of people from the state. Without these measures, it would have been far greater. This stream can be seen to have had an even larger impact if broken down by age, as it was particularly the young who left run-down parts of what had been East Germany, while pensioners were disproportionately ready to stay.

Moreover, the movement to what had been West Germany was not uniform. Migrants focused on areas with economic growth, just as the Poles had gone to the Ruhr in the nineteenth century. The newly arrived could create a marked sense of change. In Meersburg on Lake Constance in 1992, I was told that the town had been spoilt by an influx from former East Germany, a view that owed much to a snobbish disdain both for a new type of tourist and for an increase in tourism.

It was, therefore, not simply an issue of non-European migrants, but the extent of this migration of Germans increased tension about those individuals from Africa and Asia (it had already led to a hostile response in the 1970s) by raising sensitivity to total numbers. Moreover, an emphasis on an ethnic definition of nationhood left non-European migrants in a secondary legal and social position, as well as facing competition at the workplace from migrants from former East Germany. In practice, Germany became more multicultural as well as more European in this period.

Troubled by the rapid rise of the Alternative for Germany movement, established in 2013 and becoming the third largest party in the 2017 federal election, the German government sought to rebut far-right agitation and to integrate the large immigrant community by aiding naturalisation, while also limiting the constitutional right to asylum. This was a departure from the earlier situation in which the right of asylum for Germans had been the focus, rather than a right to migration by ethnic non-Germans. In 1990, in contrast, second- and third-generation ethnic non-German residents were allowed to begin the process of naturalisation, which, in 1999, was automatically granted to third-generation residents. The children of foreign national parents resident in Germany for at least eight years received dual citizenship, until, at eighteen, they were allowed to choose German citizenship or take the citizenship of their parents.

This engagement with the substantial German community of non-German ethnic origins has not yet, however, greatly affected popular perceptions of Germanness. Nevertheless, the privileged position of foreign ethnic Germans in the nationalisation process was eroded in the 1990s, in what was a major political reconceptualisation of nationality, one pushed through by the SPD–Greens coalition that came to power in 1998.

By 1993, children born to legally resident 'aliens' made up 14 per cent of births in Germany. This reflected both the low German birth rate and the extent to which those who arrived under the '*Gastarbeiter*' ('guest worker') schemes settled permanently, rather than temporarily, as had been the intention. The scheme ran until 1974. The offer of money in 1983 to migrants who returned home found few takers.

By 2007, there were nearly three million Turks in Germany, the largest ethnic minority, and by the 2010s estimates were raised still further. As they increasingly claimed citizenship and the right to vote, this population became more politically significant, while also largely successfully integrating. On the whole, mainstream German culture has devoted scant attention to this migration, although the politically committed filmmaker Rainer Werner Fassbinder produced *Ali: Fear Eats the Soul* (1974) about foreign workers.

It is unclear where the future will lead, but Germany has been more successful than France in integrating immigrants. By 1995, there were nearly 350,000 Bosnian refugees in Germany but in 2015 the response to Syrian immigration was highly contentious. Immigration led to the population rising that year by 717,000 and, by 2020, 12.6 per cent of the population were foreigners.

More generally, unification and the end of the Cold War greatly changed Germany's geographical and political positions within Europe. This worried some. Thatcher saw German policy in terms of a menacing historical continuum, rather than the new start in 1945 prefiguring another new start in 1990. There was talk of Germany being in the centre of Europe, not part of the West, and there was a consideration of what this would mean for its history.

At the same time, new issues were thrown into prominence, notably the treatment of the communist years and sites of memory regarding that period. There were disputes over whether the memorialisation of victims of the Third Reich should take precedence over those of the communist years in locations where both held meaning, such as the concentration camp at Sachsenhausen and the former military prison in Torgau. Within the CDU, there was pressure for equivalent treatment, as from Bernd Neumann, the cultural representative of the federal government. Born in Elbing, now in Poland, in 1942, he had fled to Bremen as a child. The Central Board of German Jews rejected such equivalence, correctly arguing that it diminishes the Holocaust. Furthermore, it was necessary to rely on invading Soviet forces to end the Holocaust.

In former East Germany, the language of the communist years was discarded and its critics validated. However, the preservation or destruction of the physical remains of oppression were sometimes controversial, as with local opposition in 2000 to the demolition of the last of the watchtowers of the Berlin Wall. Personal experiences presented an alternative source of tension, although not only for former communists. Thus, the revelation in 2006 that the Nobel prize-winning novelist Günter Grass had been a member of the Waffen-SS caused controversy.

The communist years were debated, as well as depicted fictionally, as in Florian Henckel von Donnersmarch's film *The Lives of Others* (2007) about the Stasi, and, humorously, in *Good Bye, Lenin!* (2003). Birgit Vanderbecke's novella *Das Muschelessen* (*The Mussel Feast*, 1990), presented, in a family, the tyrannical nature of the East German state, and ably revealed the psychological nature of its rule and fall. The German government sought to address the broader public culture. There were two commissions of inquiry set up by the Bundestag in the 1990s, followed in 2005–6 by the Sabrow Commission.

It wasn't only East Germany that experienced a change of image. In West Germany during the Cold War, a historical picture had emerged of its being an heir of the Germany that had been replaced in the nineteenth century, first by French conquest and subsequently by Prussian nationalism. The earlier Empire, replaced in 1806, was seen as a prelude to the federalism of West

Germany and the 'Third Germany' of the other parts of Germany – much of which had become West Germany – as a positive alternative to Austria and Prussia. Indeed, in 2000, Jean-Pierre Chevenement, the somewhat aggressive French minister of the interior, accused the German government of holding up the political system of the Empire as a model for Europe so as to favour German interests at the expense of national powers. The German defence of federalism aligned with the idea of the European Union as a union of the regions, an idea that appeared to give force to Thomas Mann's call in 1953 for a European Germany, not a German Europe.

In 2007, when Germany held the presidency of the European Union, Merkel proposed, without success, a standardised history textbook, while also passing laws against race hate. This was seen as an historic legislation and an opportunity for leadership, only for the issue to become complicated by the differing historical legacies of Europe, notably the experience of Soviet rule.

A New Landscape of Memorialisation

Capital of very different regimes in the past, Berlin left legacies that had to be confronted. The intention in Berlin, once it again became Germany's capital, differed from that of previous regimes, as did its stylistic language and its degree of self-critical appraisal. If there was also a common element of conviction in this memorialisation, the context was very different, not least with the opening of the restored Reichstag in 1999.

In Berlin, the Jewish Museum, opened in 2001 – with its deliberately disorientating layout and exterior – was followed in 2005 by the opening of the Memorial to the Murdered Jews of Europe, which was designed to represent

---

a Jewish cemetery. A large work, the size of two football fields, built close to the Brandenburg Gate and the site of Hitler's bunker, the memorial was presented not simply as a response to the past, but also as a warning. In 2004, Wolfgang Thierse, the speaker of the Bundestag, praised the memorial for being also 'about the future: a reminder that we should resist antisemitism at its roots'. Resistance to Hitler was memorialised at the Plötzensee prison and in the Bendlerblock, the army headquarters where bomb plot conspirators were shot in July 1944.

There was also a Berlin Wall Memorial and a documentation centre in place of the communist depiction of the Berlin Wall as a defensive barrier and the communist-era memorialisation of border guards, after whom streets, schools and youth clubs were named. In 2020, the Humboldt Forum was opened in Berlin, much of it a replica of the royal palace wrecked by allied bombing and then demolished as part of East Germany. This museum included much accumulated during the period of colonial activity.

The energy and independence of the city remains the clearest instance of change. So also with the freedom of travel, by means of the new railway station opened in 2006.

The Former Stasi

In former East Germany, despite concern about its activities and scandals about its alleged informants – as in 2018 over Eduard Geyer, one of the honorary captains of Dynamo Dresden – the role of the Stasi did not become a political issue comparable to that of the secret police in Poland.

Thus, despite the large-scale oppressiveness of its policies and attitudes, the Stasi was never declared a criminal organisation, unlike the Gestapo. Many senior Stasi operatives received relatively light sentences, while numerous Stasi members were re-employed in the police. They benefitted from an effective support network. Public debates were challenged by ex-Stasi demonstrators, while there were also attempts to alter Wikipedia entries on East Germany.

Yet, there have been attempts to highlight the nature of Stasi activity. The Stasi Records Law was passed by the Bundestag in 1991 and, in 1992–2003, over five million applications were received from people who wanted to inspect their own personal files.

The Stasi Records Office carried out its own research. In 2007, a written order of 1973 was discovered in Stasi files, disproving claims by East German officials that there was no shoot-to-kill policy against those trying to flee. There have been exhibitions about the Stasi and it was possible to visit Stasi prisons, such as that in Rostock. In 1992, the prison complex at Berlin-Hohenschönhausen was listed as a historical monument and, by the mid-2000s, over 120,000 people were visiting the site annually. Its director, Hubertus Knabe, emphasised the extent to which the communists persecuted the Social Democrats and pressed for more of a focus on the crimes of the East German regime. The Association for the Victims of Stalinism also sought to focus attention.

Property, as both instance and power, was at issue, both with the resolution of property disputes and with the role of the Treuhandanstalt, the agency with executive competence established to dispose of state-owned concerns.

THE AGE OF MERKEL

The length of Chancellor Merkel's period in office underlines her own political qualities, notably as a survivor fending off potential challengers within the CDU, but also the deficiencies of her opponents. In part, Germany has moved from a two-party state to a more diverse political pattern, but it has done so without confronting the atomising chaos seen in Italy nor the repurposing of politics in France or the separatism in Britain.

Born in Hamburg in 1954, but moving to East Germany because her father received a clerical appointment, Merkel was a research scientist until entering politics after the 1989 revolution, becoming a Bundestag member in 1990 and then minister for women and youth in 1991. CDU general secretary in 1998–2000, she became leader of the opposition in 2002 and chancellor in 2005 after the CDU (including CSU) won 35.2 per cent and the allied FDP 9.8 per cent. The SPD took 34.2 per cent, a fall of 4.3 per cent.

In the 2009 election, the CDU won 239 seats on 33.8 per cent of the vote. The FDP won 93 seats on 14.6 per cent, a big increase over the 2005 election. The SPD won 146 on 23.0 per cent. In the 2013 election, the CDU went up to 311 seats on 41.5 per cent, but the FDP received no seats as it only took 4.8 per cent. As a result, the CDU formed an alliance with the SPD, which had won 193 seats on 25.7 per cent.

In the 2017 election, in which there were more seats, both the CDU and the SPD lost votes, down to 32.9 per cent and 20.5 per cent respectively. In contrast, in a trend that had been gathering pace, the other parties all won representation, the AfD on 12.6 per cent, the FDP on 10.7 per cent, the Left on 9.2 per cent and the Greens on 8.9 per cent. Politically damaged by membership of the coalition, the SPD was unwilling to renew the arrangement. As a result, the CDU tried to enter a coalition with the FDP and Greens, but the FDP were unwilling to accept

Green terms. Finally, the CDU and SPD resumed their grand coalition, and a new government took office in March 2018 after a majority of SPD members agreed the deal. The elections showed the continued role of regional difference, with the SPD strong in the Ruhr, Bremen, Hamburg, Hanover and Hesse, the Left in East Berlin, the AfD in eastern Saxony and the CDU elsewhere.

Widely referred to as 'Mutti', and sometimes also 'Königin', Merkel faced a whole series of challenges, notably the global financial crisis and European debt crisis of 2008, the subsequent Eurozone crises, the European migrant crisis of 2015 and the Covid-19 pandemic of 2020–1. There is much to be said in favour of Merkel's sound stewardship of Germany, her support for '*markt-konforme Demokratie*' ('democracy conforming to the market'), her crucial leadership role in the European Union – not least in climate change, political conciliation and fiscal stability – the management of transfer payments, and her influence on the world stage. However, criticisms can be made. In part, they exaggerate what any chancellor could have been expected to achieve, not least given the role of other players such as the Federal Constitutional Court. But then there are issues that have arisen during her period in office, ranging from failures to reform the EU, to the rise of political extremism in Germany (although, by Merkel's standard, much of European politics is extremist) and the difficulty of achieving a defence sufficient to confront Russian aggression. Delaying decisions is also not always the best way to move forward. The EU, notably its Mediterranean states, has suffered from German fiscal policies via the euro that help make German exports more competitive, and protectionism, but there is no German interest in mutualising the debt. Moreover, Merkel's response to China, with which – as with Russia – Germany has close economic interests, begs questions about the country's compliance with dictatorship.

There has also been a failure to manage Merkel's succession, in part because she has looked for politicians completely in line with herself and in part because several potential successors weakened themselves or made themselves ineligible. Setbacks in state elections in Bavaria and Hesse in October 2018 led Merkel to resign as party leader that December and to decide to stand down as chancellor with the 2021 federal election.

Her protégé, Annegret Kramp-Karrenbauer, succeeded her as CDU head, but, in 2019, she proved a weak leader, lacking Merkel's dexterity. In 2020, Kramp-Karrenbauer was unable to master the political crisis caused by politics in Thuringia, where the votes from the far-right AfD helped lead to the election of a minister president otherwise backed by the FDP and CDU. This was followed by a governmental impasse in Thuringia, amid misleading talk of parallels with the rise of Hitler to power in 1933. In the event, the Left-SPD-Greens candidate became minister president of Thuringia again.

This crisis led Kramp-Karrenbauer to announce her resignation, only for that to be delayed by the Covid pandemic. The latter has brought out tensions, not least between federal and state governments, but Germany handled the pandemic relatively well, by European standards.

In January 2021, the CDU, long regarded as a wide-ranging *Volkspartei* and a 'chancellor machine', chose Armin Laschet, the premier of North Rhine-Westphalia, as head of the party. He emphasised the need not to 'polarise. We must be able to integrate, hold society together.' However, he failed to enthuse the electorate and, although the polls at the beginning of 2021 gave the CDU/CSU 36 per cent, the Greens 18 per cent, the SPD 16 per cent, AfD 9 per cent, the Left 8 per cent, and the FDP 7 per cent, the CDU/CSU then declined. The election of 2021 saw the CDU/CSU alliance fall to its lowest share of the vote, providing the SPD, which had done better than earlier anticipated with an opportunity to form a coalition. Fortunately for Germans, their economy easily outperformed the politicians.

The response to the Covid pandemic highlighted drawbacks in the federal system, with clashes between federal government and the state governments that had responsibility for health regulations. Indeed, the quasi-nationalism of many German regions emerged anew, underlining the saying about many feeling Bavarian, Saxon etc. first, Europeans second and Germans third – although I would juxtapose the last two for most Germans. Regional identity and autonomy have been important to the constitution and political practice since the middle ages and have been present in several different versions of federalism. There were attempts to destroy regional identity by dismantling the German states – notably the Nazis and East Germany – but also, to a far lesser extent, by successive re-organisations, particularly in the Napoleonic period and in 1866.

However, the resilience of federalism in Germany's deep history is readily apparent and was clearly seen in the Covid crisis, with many states developing their pandemic strategy and challenging Merkel's responses. This regionalism is readily present in strong local accents and is also seen with geographical links to the outside world, as with Schleswig-Holstein, Mecklenburg and Western Pomerania looking to the Baltic and Scandinavia, while the Rhineland looks to France and Benelux, Hamburg to the Atlantic world and Bavaria to an Alpine one.

The interaction during the Wilhelmine period of rapid modernisation, economic dynamism, establishing a welfare state, increasing democratisation and a federal system, is still, albeit very differently, present and with the welcome absence of Wilhelmine militarism, authoritarianism and sabre-rattling. What this interaction will bring, however, is unclear.

Size and Strength

Dominating the European Union with France, Germany is its economic and financial powerhouse, as well as the leading western economy after the United States. This has all been achieved without the focus on size seen until 1945. West Germany comprised 95,976 square miles and Germany has 137,988. This contrasts with France (213,011), Spain (192,476), Sweden (173,860) and the UK (93,628). The situation by population, however, is very different, with Germany at 83.8 million in 2020, larger than the UK (67.9), France (65.3), Italy (60.5) and Spain (46.8).

Moreover, the impression of size for Germany is accentuated by it bordering nine countries and by its length: stretching from the Baltic to the Alps. With its cities and *Länder*, it also is a more truly multi-centred country than France or the UK.

Conclusions

....

'The particulars of that dismal scene have been transmitted from father to son and are still spoke of with horror by the peasantry of that country, among whom the French nation is held in detestation to this day.'

John Moore, 1779, of the French
pillaging of the Palatinate in 1689.

In the aftermath of the horrors of 1914–45 – notably, but not only those horrors of 1933–45 – that owed all too much to Germany, it was all too easy to suggest that German history was somehow a better and easier process for Germans and others when the state was weak. This was meant in the sense that size, population and economic strength then did not translate into political power.

The 'German question' or 'problem' appeared easy to solve in this light and this remains the case. There is a view that the independence and/or role of the 'Third Germany', rather than a strong Prussia, or indeed Austria, and the limited and limiting power of the imperial constitution, were necessary safeguards. This very much accords with current suppositions or requirements, not least the role of regions in the European Union, as well as in the political culture and constitution of modern Germany.

The more cautious suggestion here, however, is that the analytical process of a ready transferability of past to present and vice versa is not particularly helpful and certainly does not necessarily establish a case. Thus, it is readily possible to advocate a political situation for Germany today without implying that a similar one was appropriate in 1500, 1700, 1900 or any other date. This is important due to the tendency to present German history both in judgemental terms and with reference to some supposed pattern not only of narrative but also of analysis. Readers might have wondered at the space dedicated in this book to the power politics of the seventeenth and eighteenth centuries; yet this repeatedly demonstrates a lack of patterns – let alone certainty – and, in a way, that is easier to demonstrate and understand in those periods than it is, say, for the ninth or tenth centuries. It was a scenario that reoccurred until the French defeat at the battle of Leipzig in 1813: a territory that did well and seemed in a strong position could also be cast down. This happened not only to Bavaria, Hanover and Saxony, but also to Prussia and Austria between 1618 and 1813 – and repeatedly so.

To a degree, the transitions of 1866, 1918–19, 1945 and 1990 were different stages of the same process. After 1918, the dynastic presence, which had been both a complication and a clarification, was absent. The list above would suggest caution about readily referring to 1990 as a 're-unification' rather than a unification. To do so implies a degree of natural and necessary progression. This may be pertinent from one perspective, as an undoing of the Cold War partition established in the late 1940s, but possibly not in another. Indeed, there was no natural and necessary progression. Thus, to imagine that West and East Germany had to unite is problematic, given the wariness about similar arguments in 1938 for the union of Germany and Austria or, indeed, for the breakup of that relationship in 1866.

The common issue of international context linked the dynastic period with the democratic or participatory politics that followed from the late nineteenth century, but more importantly from 1918. This linkage was not simply a matter of the absence of natural frontiers but also of the degree to which the process of intervening in the politics of neighbouring areas, to win allies or harm opponents, was accentuated by the Reformation and its consequence, the Counter-Reformation. The wars of religion not only led to a contested 'home front' character in conflict and intervention, but also to a more insistent pattern of external intervention. This was clearly seen by the Spanish troops in Charles V's victorious army at

Mühlberg in 1547. It also related to relations between and within territories and, indeed, between and within families, both ruling and otherwise. And so it was with the pattern of revolutionary and counter-revolutionary sympathy and support during the 1790s and afterwards, with the Napoleonic recasting of that pattern.

As with France and its bitter internal struggles from the fourteenth century, so also with Germany (but not Poland), it is understandable that a situation of internal division and external intervention led to a stronger state, not simply through the happenstance of conflict, but also due to a desire for order, stability and strength. In the case of Germany, as with France, several different versions existed across the centuries but, in the German case far more than in that of its French counterpart, it was also the geographical centring and indeed, identity, that was uncertain. The challenge to order came not only from territorial expansionism and even the rival values of potential internal contestants for nationalist centring. It also came from external threats, making the situation more complex. In addition, the interplay between the internal and external helped to provide the narrative.

The Idea of a 'Sonderweg' ('Special Path')

The notion of national uniqueness is scarcely a prerogative of the present and, indeed, lies deep within all religious and national historical accounts. Thus, the *translatio imperii*, a thesis that dominated German imperial ideology from the tenth century, was one of a 'Sonderweg', and the Empire that was its context and product was dissolved in 1806, and then only due to the chance of it being defeated.

The term 'Sonderweg' was used from the late nineteenth century by conservatives praising a middle path between autocratic Russia and liberal, republican France; the idea took on a different historical mission with twentieth-century accounts of 'specialness', both from the reference point of Wilhelmine and, more particularly, Nazi systems and with hostile discussion of German aggression, as in consideration of the *Junker* and/or Prussian background to German and militarist aggression.

Historians, notably from the 1960s, sought to describe long-term factors that they held responsible for the Third Reich, usually advancing a political–cultural interpretation of German history. There was particular interest in the idea of a misconceived modernisation, one of economic change without its necessary political counterpart, that was widely related to the failure of the Frankfurt Assembly of 1848–9 and the subsequent conservative elite that dominated the Second German Empire. The fate of Weimar was then presented as another iteration of the same contrast.

The debate has been valuable, but risks a misleading degree of simplification and reification, as well as underplaying the extent of middle-class influence in the Second Reich and the role of contingency. War and politics are key examples of the latter, as are the events of 1918, 1945 and 1989–90, which produced, rather than reflected, a *Sonderweg*.

To move from abstractions, the Prussian narrative of protecting Germany from outsiders, one that embraced a language of German nationalism during the Seven Years' War (1756–63) and again in 1813–14, was compromised, certainly for many contemporaries, by Prussian power-politics within Germany. This was also true of the earlier, Austrian-dominated imperial model, which was imbued as well with Counter-Reformation purposes. The idea of a somewhat benign 'Third Germany' and imperial system, moreover, underplays the extent to which they were unable to provide security against external expansionism, notably from France, but also from the Netherlands, Denmark and Sweden, as well as against internal ambitions and the combination of the two. It was the very experience of these problems that helped provide a dynamic for German history and the knowledge of them that complicated debates over political structures and related cultural idioms.

Thus, the rollercoaster ride of the last 160 years was not some add-on to an earlier age that was somehow more settled, even attractive. Despite the medieval massacres of Jews, there were certainly no horrors to prefigure those of the Third Reich, but the Thirty Years' War (1618–48) was no walk in the park and nor was the chaos of 1792–1813. The rollercoaster was in part made up of a jostling for solutions, with force, or its failure, the context, causes, conjunctures, course and consequences. Ultimately, external forces did determine the outcome, both in 1945 – when they brought down the Third Reich – and in 1989–90 when, by not intervening, they permitted a unification and, moreover, one that was disruptive but peaceful.

Since then, Germany has – by global standards and those of its past – known prosperity and peace. It is the key state in a European Union that, despite its directing partnership with France, it does not dominate in an old-fashioned power system. The centres of world instability are at a distance and Germany plays a very modest role in the resulting confrontations. Within Germany, this helps the attempt to define an acceptable, coherent and attractive civic nationalism that can regard Nazism as a surmountable aberration.

And what about the future? History suggests the unpredictability of developments and events. The past does not set a pattern for the future, but nor should it be swept aside. Most Germans are well aware of this quandary and most respond with maturity to the weight of the past and the hope of the future.

As in other societies, the experience – indeed, management – of diversity has been a key experience over the last half-millennium, with the Reformation and the resulting solutions and compromises opening up differences over fundamental issues within communities, including the issue of Germanness. In part, the ideological challenges of the last century can be seen as following the same pattern.

Bremen: Forgotten State

The smallest and least populous of Germany's sixteen *Länder* consists of two enclaves, Bremen and Bremerhaven, both within the state of Lower Saxony. Part of the North German Confederation of 1867, Bremen was re-established as a state in 1947. The site of the future Bremerhaven was bought by Bremen in 1827 from Hanover, while what became the nearby naval base of Wilhelmshaven was purchased by Prussia from Oldenburg in 1853, although it did not go on to become part of the state.

The eleventh largest city in Germany, Bremen is the country's second port after Hamburg. Traditionally working class and left wing, the city has a historical core in the *Altstadt* (old town), which includes a Renaissance-façade town hall, a thirteenth-century cathedral, the old harbour and fishermen's quarter and the ugly, equestrian Bismarck monument. A more attractive statue, *Town Musicians of Bremen* by Gerhard Marcks, based on *Grimms' Fairy Tales*, offers a story of resolve and justice that testifies to Bremen's reputation for liberty. Marcks (1889–1981), a Berliner, was a teaching member at the Bauhaus, dismissed by the Nazis and, as a producer of 'degenerate art', forbidden from exhibiting. The interesting museum of his work is in Bremen.

There are also differences of locality, life, experience and assumptions. The German 'condition' or 'path' has very varied contents and meanings and it is best to end on this mature understanding rather than on the immaturity of trying to find clear patterns, obvious lessons and apparent *Zeitgeists*.

Postscript: Travelling German History

Intensely personal, travel in German history is a matter of individual preference and offering advice can be unwelcome. Those who make trips out from Munich tend to go to Neuschwanstein to see Ludwig II's exuberant castle – a trip readily doable by rail and bus or directly by bus – rather than to closer Dachau. Both, however, are part of German history, as are a posse of more conventional historic sites, such as nearby Freising, where the richly decorated Baroque interior of the cathedral is like the inside of a jewel box of chocolates. The same goes for other cities and areas. There should be no set itinerary for what to see in Berlin or Cologne. If time presses in the latter, most will go to the cathedral, but the Roman remains are also amazing.

If time is no problem, try visiting areas where relatively few foreign tourists go: the *Bayerischer Wald* (Bavarian Forest), which I found dominated by the presence of conifers rather than settlements. The past includes the memorial chapel at the Flossenbürg concentration camp.

A very different Germany that also attracts relatively few tourists includes Bremen and Hamburg. Each have historic areas that survived very heavy bombing, but it is the more recent juxtaposition of waterways with rebuilding that is of interest, as well as their energy. Indeed, travellers have the choice once offered to those coming to Britain in the eighteenth and nineteenth centuries: the fascination of the present is important, alongside the extent to which there is so much of the distant past. This would encourage you to go to Frankfurt-on-Main with its skyscrapers, as

well as the far more historic nearby Mainz; the motor car museums in Stuttgart as well as the artistic treasures in the recently
built art gallery; the cafés of Berlin as well as its museums; the
beer halls and gardens of Munich as well as the Residenz which,
to do properly, takes several hours.

There are also itineraries to arrange. Many years ago, I managed
to follow one of Goslar, with its half-timbered houses and walks
into the Harz Mountains, as well as Wolfenbüttel, part of classic
small-town, historic Germany, and Brunswick (or Braunschweig),
a once bomb-shattered, now rebuilt, city which includes a superb
art gallery. If you are in the Harz, Quedlinburg is as impressive as
Goslar, while Wernigerode and Stolberg are worth visiting.

For landscapes, there are the classics. These include walks
between lavish cakes in the Black Forest, or the Rhine Gorge above
Bingen – although most of the Rhine is, elsewhere, more canal-
ised. The Moselle valley is more natural than the Rhine, offers
impressive castles, small towns, excellent wine and the impressive
Roman heritage of Trier. If, like me, you are keen on rivers, you
can go from the fortress at Königstein to Dresden on the Elbe by
paddle steamer, although of late water levels have affected tourism
on the river. The *Partnachklamm* (Partnach Gorge), south of
Garmisch-Partenkirchen, is a gorgeous hike for the fit.

Yet, there are other – less visited – areas that are worthy of
attention, such as the regions near the coastlines. Moreover, such
a tour can take you to neighbouring places, such as Groningen in
the Netherlands and Ribe in Denmark, each of which is
attractive.

With its limited woodland, broad skyscapes, wetness and sense
of being on the edge, East Friesland is reminiscent (but more so) of
East Anglia, although there are also the East Frisian Islands, just as
there are the North Frisian Islands of Schleswig-Holstein. The
character of the islands varies, including their accessibility. The
East Frisian Islands are more for birdwatchers, while Sylt island in
the North Frisians is far busier and easier to access.

This is also true of the Baltic coastlands where, at Rostock, you can visit the Stasi prison and see the Blücher monument. The traditional Hansa cities on the Baltic coast – Lübeck, Wismar, Greifswald, Stralsund and Rostock – have impressive and well-preserved old towns, while the island of Usedom offers the V2 museum.

The Rhineland and the Black Forest dominated the tourism of the nineteenth century but, of course, there have been changes in priority over the centuries. Later, there was a greater focus on Bavaria although what, to many foreigners, was/is a Germany of *Oktoberfest*, lederhosen and Neuschwanstein, is really a misleading image of the region.

Heligoland at War

Acquired by Britain in the post-Napoleonic settlement but transferred to Germany in 1890 in exchange for Zanzibar, Heligoland became a major fixture in German naval defence plans.

However, the Germans did not have time for *Projekt Hummerschere*, a plan unveiled in 1938 for the transformation of the island, designed to make it big enough to house nearly the entire High Seas Fleet. The land mass of Heligoland was to be more than tripled and a harbour built with a circumference of over ten kilometres. In May 1939, with the works well under way, the navy calculated that they would take ten years to complete. A subterranean labyrinth provided cover and supplies to enable the island to hold out even if cut off. This was not only a project of dubious strategic sense but also a symbolic resurrection of the Wilhelmine dream of sea power, one underlined when Hitler visited in 1938. It was certainly the counterpoint to the ambitious ship-building intentions of Plan Z, approved by Hitler in January 1939.

The project was halted with the outbreak of Operation Barbarossa in 1941 and, although the U-boat pens were already completed, they were scarcely used. Submarines tended to operate from France and Norway and, instead, Heligoland became a radar station against Allied air attacks. In part, these were directed against the submarine base, but the island was devastated by bombing and the Germans evacuated the civilians.

Having occupied Heligoland, the British blew up the military facilities in 1947. Operation Big Bang is generally regarded as the largest non-nuclear explosion in history. There were many German complaints. The RAF then used the uninhabited island as a bombing range until it was handed back to Germany in 1952.

So, we only have two weeks. I suggest flying to Berlin and spending a couple of days in the city, including a visit to Sanssouci palace in Potsdam, and a trip out – it's better to go to Meissen than to busier Dresden, where much of the Zwinger art gallery is closed for long-term maintenance at the time of writing in 2021. In Meissen, be sure to climb to the top of the compact historic town and, from there, walk on to the porcelain factory. Impressive German long-distance trains will then take you, via stops at Weimar and Würzburg, to Munich. Spend several days there, with trips to Dachau and (very different) Regensburg. In your last section, do less travelling, more landscape, in the Swabian Alps. End at Stuttgart with a walk in the historic centre, seeing the art gallery and having an open-air lunch.

You still have masses to do on subsequent trips, which is the right way to leave a country.

Selected Further Reading

....

Adler, Jeremy, *Johann Wolfgang von Goethe* (London, 2020)

Arnold, Benjamin, *Power and Property in Medieval Germany: Economic and Social Change c. 900–1300* (Oxford, 2004)

Asch, Ronald, *The Thirty Years War: The Holy Roman Empire and Europe 1618–1648* (Basingstoke, 1997)

Ashton, Brodie, *The Kingdom of Württemberg and the Making of Germany, 1815–1871* (London, 2017)

Attfield, Nicholas, *Challenging the Modern: Conservative Revolution in German Music, 1918–33* (Oxford, 2017)

Bachrach, David, *Warfare in Tenth-Century Germany* (Woodbridge, 2012)

Baranowski, Shelley; Nolzen, Armin and Szejnmann, Claus-Christian (eds), *A Companion to Nazi Germany* (Oxford, 2018)

Betts, Paul, *Within Walls: Private Life in the German Democratic Republic* (Oxford, 2010)

Black, Jeremy, *The Holocaust and Memory* (Bloomington, Ind., 2016)

Black, Jeremy, *Rethinking World War Two: The Conflict and Its Legacy* (London, 2015)

Blackbourn, David, *The Conquest of Nature: Water, Landscape and the Making of Modern Germany* (London, 2006)

Clark, Christopher, *Iron Kingdom: The Rise and Downfall of Prussia, 1600–1947* (London, 2006)

Confino, Alon, *The Nation as a Local Metaphor: Württemberg, Imperial Germany and National Memory, 1871–1918* (Chapel Hill, NC, 1997)

Croxton, Derek, *Westphalia: The Last Christian Peace* (New York, 2013)

Davis, Belinda, *Home Fires Burning: Food, Politics and Everyday Life in World War I Berlin* (Chapel Hill, North Carolina, 2003)

Evans, Richard, *The Coming of the Third Reich* (London, 2003)

Evans, Richard, *Re-reading German History: From Unification to Reunification, 1800–1996* (London, 1997)

Frei, Norbert, *Adenauer's Germany and the Nazi Past: The Politics of Amnesty and Integration* (New York, 2002)

Fritzsche, Peter, *Germans into Nazis* (Cambridge, Massachusetts, 1998)

Fulbrook, Mary, *Anatomy of a Dictatorship: Inside the GDR 1949–89* (Oxford, 1995)

Gagliardo, John, *Reich and Nation: The Holy Roman Empire as Idea and Reality, 1763–1806* (Bloomington, Indiana, 1980)

Gellately, Robert, *Backing Hitler: Consent and Coercion in Nazi Germany* (Oxford, 2001)

Gerwarth, Robert, *The Bismarck Myth: Weimar Germany and the Legacy of the Iron Chancellor* (Oxford, 2005)

Green, Abigail, *Fatherlands: State Building and Nationhood in Nineteenth-Century Germany* (Cambridge, 2001)

Heinzen, Jasper, *Making Prussians, Raising Germans: A Cultural History of Prussian State-Building after Civil War, 1866–1935* (Oxford, 2017)

Hellmuth, Eckhart (ed.), *The Transformation of Political Culture: England and Germany in the Late Eighteenth Century* (Oxford, 1990)

Hendrix, Scott, *Martin Luther: Visionary Reformer* (New Haven, Connecticut, 2015)

Hewitson, Mark, *Absolute War: Violence and Mass Warfare in the German Lands, 1792–1820* (Oxford, 2017)

Hewitson, Mark, *The People's Wars: Histories of Violence in the German Lands, 1820–1888* (Oxford, 2017)

Hoyer, Katja, *Blood and Iron: The Rise and Fall of the German Empire 1871–1918* (Cheltenham, 2021)

Jefferies, Matthew (ed.), *The Ashgate Research Companion to Imperial Germany* (Farnham, 2015)

Koonz, Claudia, *Mothers in the Fatherland: Women, The Family and Nazi Politics* (New York, 1987)

Loberg, Molly, *The Struggle for the Streets of Berlin: Politics, Consumption and Urban Space, 1914–1945* (Cambridge, 2018)

McAdams, James, *Judging the Past in Unified Germany* (Cambridge, 2001)

Marcuse, Harold, *Legacies of Dachau: The Uses and Abuses of a Concentration Camp, 1933–2001* (Cambridge, 2001)

Moeller, Robert, *War Stories: The Search for a Usable Past in the Federal Republic of Germany* (Berkeley, California, 2001)

Mushaben, Joyce, *Becoming Madam Chancellor: Angela Merkel and the Berlin Republic* (Cambridge, 2017)

Mustafa, Sam, *The Long Ride of Major von Schill: A Journey Through German History and Memory* (Lanham, Maryland, 2008)

Nicholls, Anthony, *The Bonn Republic: West German Democracy 1945–1990* (London, 1997)

Nipperday, Thomas, *Germany from Napoleon to Bismarck, 1800–1866* (Dublin, 1996)

Rosenfeld, Gavriel, *Hi Hitler! How the Nazi Past Is Being Normalised in Contemporary Culture* (Cambridge, 2015)

Rosenfeld, Gavriel, *Munich and Memory: Architecture, Monuments and the Legacy of the Third Reich* (Berkeley, California, 2000)

Rowe, Michael, *From Reich to State: The Rhineland in the Revolutionary Age, 1780–1830* (Cambridge, 2003)

Scales, Len, *In a German Mirror: Authority, Crisis and German Identity, 1245–1414* (Cambridge, 2012)

Schilling, Britta, *Post-colonial Germany: Memories of Empire in a Decolonised Nation* (Oxford, 2014)

Schoeps, Karl-Heinz, *Literature and Film in the Third Reich* (Rochester, New York, 2004)

Scholz, Luca, *Borders and Freedom of Movement in the Holy Roman Empire* (Oxford, 2020)

Scott, Tom, *Freiburg and the Breisgau: Town–Country Relations in the Age of Reformation and Peasants' War* (Oxford, 1986)

Sheehan, James, *German History, 1770–1866* (Oxford, 1989)

Showalter, Dennis, *The Wars of German Unification* (second ed., 2015)

Smith, Helmut Walser, *The Continuities of German History: Nation, Religion and Race Across the Long Nineteenth Century* (Cambridge, 2008)

Smith, Helmut Walser (ed.), *The Oxford Handbook of Modern German History* (Oxford, 2011)

Stargardt, Nicholas, *The German War: A Nation Under Arms, 1939–1945; Citizens and Soldiers* (London, 2015)

Stibbe, Matthew, *Germany, 1914–1933: Politics, Society and Culture* (Harlow, 2010)

Tomlinson, Alan and Young, Christopher (eds.), *German Football: History, Culture, Society* (London, 2006)

Vick, Brian, *Defining Germany: The 1848 Frankfurt Parliamentarians and National Identity* (Cambridge, Massachusetts, 2002)

Ward, Janet, *Post-Wall Berlin: Borders, Space and Identity* (Basingstoke, 2011)

Wawro, Geoffrey, *The Franco-Prussian War: The German Conquest of France 1870–1871* (Cambridge 2003)

Weinreb, Alice, *Modern Hungers: Food and Power in Twentieth-Century Germany* (Oxford, 2017)

Wende, Peter, *A History of Germany* (Basingstoke, 2006)

Wicke, Christian, *Helmut Kohl's Quest for Normality: His Representation of the German Nation and Himself* (Oxford, 2015)

Wilson, Peter, *The Holy Roman Empire: A Thousand Years of Europe's History* (London, 2016)

Zimmer, Oliver, *Remaking the Rhythms of Life: German Communities in the Age of the Nation State* (Oxford, 2013)

Index